Alan Roger's

Campsite Accommodation Guide

(Mobile Homes, Chalets and Bungalows for Rent on Campsites in Europe)

Compiled by Alan Roger's Guides Ltd

Cover design: Haynes/Sutton Publishing, Design Section, Frome

Maps created by Customised Mapping (01985 844092)
Contain background data provided by Gis Data Ltd. 2001
Maps are © Alan Rogers' Guides Ltd and Gis Data Ltd. 2000
Clive, Lois and Clare Edwards have asserted their rights to be identified as
the authors of this work

First published in this format 2001

British Library Cataloguing-in Publication Data:
A catalogue record for this book is available from the British Library

ISBN: 0 901586 87 0

Printed in Great Britain by Sherrens, Weymouth, Dorset
Distributed in the UK by Haynes Publishing, Sparkford, Somerset

Contents

Foreword

The Alan Rogers Good Camps Guides for Britain & Ireland, France and Europe have enjoyed a hugely favourable following among British campers and caravanners for over thirty years, mainly as a result of their full length objective campsite reviews, based on an extremely rigorous inspection process.

For 2002 in this new guide The Alan Rogers team are delighted to be able to provide the same kind of information to holidaymakers who do not own their own caravan, motorhome or tent but who are interested in staying in a chalet, mobile home or apartment on one of the high quality Alan Rogers Inspected and Selected campsites in the UK or Europe which provide this type of accommodation.

Our new Campsite Accommodation Guide includes an objective review of each of the campsites featured (based on our own Inspectors' Reports) , along with brief details of the type(s) of accommodation available to rent on the campsite, including an indication of the rental charges, plus a photograph or photographs.

The information provided for each campsite also includes directions, opening dates and, most importantly, details on how to go about making a booking. For many of the sites featured in this guide bookings can be made through our own Alan Rogers Travel Service, either by telephone or via our www.alanrogers.com website. Not only do we provide a booking service for the accommodation itself, we can also take care of your ferry and travel or breakdown insurance requirements too, at outstandingly attractive rates!

In fact if you have been used to booking your campsite accommodation through one of the major camping tour operators we're confident you'll be very pleasantly surprised by how much you can save either by booking your accommodation direct with the campsite, or, even more surprisingly how much you can save by booking a "package" thorough our own Travel Service!

ALAN ROGERS'
Good Camps Guides

Britain & Ireland France Europe

The campsites featured in this guide are only a selection of the selected, inspected sites featured in our three Good Camps Guides for independent campers and caravanners.

**Available from all good bookshops
or call Haynes Publishing, tel. 01963 442 030**

Introduction

How to get the best from this Guide

Campsite Reports: The most important, and unique, feature of all our Guides is the objective "campsite review" which is based on our own regular, and very rigorous, Site Inspection process – these reviews should enable you to choose your preferred campsite with confidence, rather than having to rely on the marketing-based "brochure speak" favoured by tour operators.

Facilities: The "facilities" section seeks to provide a summary of all the most important features of the campsite and its amenities, including brief details about the catering facilities, bars, swimming pools, entertainments, sports facilities etc., all in plain English without any need for the reader to de-cypher little symbols or icons!

The accommodation section: Campsites tend to provide one or two main types of accommodation, mobile-homes and chalets. Mobile-homes (sometimes described as Park Homes in Britain, or Mobilhomes in France) are generally more numerous than chalets, although the latter are becoming more popular, particularly in France and Spain. Modern mobile homes are built to a high standard, and recent innovations often include pitched roofs (as opposed to flat roofs) which improve the appearance. In almost every case the design of a mobile home includes the clever use of space and fittings/furniture to provide the ideal convenience for holiday use – usually light and airy, with big windows and patio-style doors, fully equipped kitchen areas, a shower room with shower, washbasin and WC, and cleverly designed bedrooms and comfortable lounge/dining area.

Generally speaking modern campsite chalets incorporate all the best features of mobile homes in a rather more visually attractive structure, sometimes with the advantage of an upper "mezzanine" floor for one or more of the bedrooms.

Given the large range of different types of mobile home and chalet currently available, and in use on European campsites, we are not able to inspect every single one of these individually when we make our campsite inspections (often many of them are occupied by holidaymakers who don't appreciate having their holiday home inspected!)

Our selection criteria are therefore mainly concerned with the standard of the campsite itself, the service provided to their customers (particularly to our readers!) and their record in terms of care and maintenance since we first featured them in our guides; the age and general appearance and maintenance of their accommodation to rent, and of course their adherence to the prevailing Health and Safety requirements applying to the area and country in which the campsite is situated.

For each campsite we have included details of the type, or types, of accommodation available to rent, but these details are necessarily quite brief, particularly where a campsite has a wide range of different types of accommodation, many with layouts which differ, particularly in terms of sleeping arrangements where these include a flexible provision for "extra persons" on sofa-beds, bed-settees, situated in the "living area". These arrangements may vary from chalet to chalet or mobile-home to mobile home, and if you're planning a holiday which includes more people than are catered for by the main bedrooms you should check exactly how the extra sleeping arrangements are to be provided!

Charges: An indication of the tariff for each type of accommodation featured is also included, but given that many campsites have a large range of pricing options, special deals and other discounts etc the charges we quote are necessarily just an indication and should be used only as a rough guide to the price of any particular type of accommodation. It is vital therefore that you confirm the actual cost when you make a booking, rather than simply relying on the price indications given in the guide – they are there as an aide to choosing your preferred campsite, not as a definitive or complete tariff!

BRITISH ISLES

The British Isles (England, Scotland, Wales, Northern Ireland and the Channel Islands) offer the holidaymaker a choice of just about everything you could imagine in terms of scenery, campsites and weather! Whether you choose to visit the Highlands of Scotland, the English Lake District, Snowdonia in Wales, the Norfolk Broads, England's West Country, the unspoiled beauty of Northern Ireland or the Channel Islands, you are sure to find attractive countryside and/ or much of historic interest. Visitors to the British Isles should not encounter any significant problems, other than driving on the left, and the fact that few Britons are proficient in any language other than English.

Population
57,970,200 (93), density 239 per sq.km.

Capitals
London, Edinburgh, Cardiff and Belfast.

Language
Predominantly English, although Welsh also is spoken in many parts of Wales and Gaelic in parts of Scotland and Ireland.

Climate
Changeable and unpredictable - temperatures are generally a little higher in the south and southwest, and rather cooler and wetter in the mountainous regions of Scotland, Wales and the Lake District.

Currency
The Pound Sterling (£) divided into 100 pence.

Banks
Open at least Mon-Fri 09.30-15.30 hrs, except on Public Holidays.

Time
Late October -late March is Greenwich Mean Time (GMT); during the summer (late March - late Oct) clocks are put forward one hour to British Summer Time (BST). British time is normally I hour behind the time in other EC countries.

Post Offices
Mainly open Mon-Fri at least 09.30-16.30.

Public Telephones
Two main types of public telephone boxes, coin-operated and 'phone card operated. Cards can be purchased from Post Offices, newsagents, etc.

Public Holidays
New Year; Good Fri, Easter Mon; lst Mon in May; last Mon in May; last Mon in Aug; Christmas, 25,26 Dec;

Shops
Most shops open at least 09.00-17.30 Monday - Saturday, but some still operate a half day (known as early closing day).

Motoring
In Britain one drives on the left-hand side of the road, and you go round roundabouts clockwise. The overall maximum speed limits are 70 rnph (112 kph) on motorways, and 60 rnph (96 kph) on other roads, except where a lower limit is indicated by signs. Overall limits are reduced to 60 rnph and 50 rnph respectively for vehicles towing trailers or caravans. Parking restrictions apply in most towns, and many villages, indicated by yellow lines on the roadside.

Useful Addresses
Tourist information:
English Tourism Council
Thames Tower, Blacks Road, Harnmersmith, London W6 9EL.
Tel: 0208 563 3000
e-mail: comments@englishtourism.org.uk
England is further subdivided into ten geographical regions, each with its own Regional Tourist Board, details of which can be obtained from the ETC.

Scottish Tourist Board
Scotland is subdivided into no less than 33 Area Tourist Boards -details from the STB.

Scottish Tourist Board
www.visitscotland.com
A comprehensive network of over 900 Tourist Infonnation Centres (TIC) covers the British Isles, although their opening hours vary - they are easily identified by the international "i" symbol.

049 Mullion Holiday Park
Nr Helston, Cornwall TR12 7LJ

For those who enjoy plenty of entertainment, both social and active in a holiday environment, Mullion would be a good choice. The site is situated on the Lizard peninsula with its sandy beaches and coves. This park has all the trimmings – indoor and outdoor pools; children's play areas, clubs, bars, and a wide range of nightly entertainment. There is also much to see in the area including Goonhilly Satellite Station, Flambards Village theme park, Lizard Point and Lands End.

Facilities: Large launderette in main complex. Freezer pack service. Large supermarket with off licence. Pub with family room, restaurant and takeaway (half board or breakfast options). Moonshine Club with live shows and cabarets, big screen satellite TV. Excellent outdoor children's play areas (fenced). Toddlers' soft play area. Amusement arcade, bowling alley. Heated outdoor swimming pool and paddling pool (26/5-8/9). Heated indoor fun pool with slide, both supervised. Sauna and solarium. Crazy golf, pitch and putt. Mountain bike hire. Barbecue.

Tel: (01326) 240000. **Fax:** (01326) 241141. **Reservations:** Contact site direct, as above.

Open: 12 May - 15 September.

Directions: From Helston take A3083 for The Lizard and continue for 7 miles. Site on left immediately after the right turning for Mullion. O.S.GR: SW698185.

CAMPSITE NAME Mullion	Type of Accommodation Mobile homes	Type of Accommodation Mobile homes	Type of Accommodation Bungalows
Number of Persons	Kittiwake ★★★: 2-4 persons Guillemot ★★★★: 2-4 persons	Cormorant ★★★★: 4-6 persons Fulmar ★★★★: 6-8 persons Fulmar ★★★★★: 6-8 persons	Curlew ★★★★: 4 person Kingfisher ★★★★: 4-6 persons
Bedrooms	1 bedroom: 1 x double, additional sleeping in living area	Cormorant: 2 bedrooms: 1 x double, 1 x twin Fulmar: 3 bedrooms: 1 x double, 2 x twin Fulmar Grand: 3 bedrooms: 1 x double, 2 x twin All have additional sleeping in living area	Curlew: 2 bedrooms: 1 x double, 1 x twin Kingfisher: 2 bedrooms: 1 x double, 1 x twin, additional sleeping in living area
Lounge/Dining Area	Fully furnished including colour T.V	Fully furnished including colour T.V	Fully furnished including colour T.V
Kitchen Area	Fully equipped including full sized cooker, oven and grill	Fully equipped including full size cooker, oven and grill	Fully equipped including full size cooker, oven and grill, microwave, toaster and fridge/freezer
Bath/Shower/WC	Washbasin, shower, WC	Washbasin, shower, WC	Curlew: Shower, WC Kingfisher: Shower, bath WC
Other Facilities	Heating, free gas, free electricity	Heating, free gas, free electricity	Heating, metered electricity, vehicle parking bay
Bedding	Duvets and bed linen provided	Duvets and bed linen provided	Duvets and bed linen provided
Pets	Not accepted in Guillemot	Not accepted	Not accepted in Kingfisher
Charges **From** (Low Season, per week) **To** (High Season, per week)	Kittiwake: £129 - £389 Guillemot: £139 - £425	Cormorant: £169-£519 Fulmar: £195-£ 595 Fulmar Grand: £195- £659	Curlew: £175 - £525 Kingfisher: £199 - £599

065 Looe Bay Holiday Park
Looe, Cornwall

In a rural situation a few miles back from Looe with views of the surrounding countryside, this well equipped holiday park has all the facilities that go to make a good holiday. There is a large indoor heated swimming pool with lifeguard and many other provisions for children. A half board option provides an alternative basis for booking a complete holiday "package". The accommodation is formally arranged below and to one side of the main facilities, which are based at the entrance and connected by tarmac roads. Some uphill walking from the furthest areas may be necessary. The Eden project, Dobwalls Theme Park, Newquay Zoo and many other attractions are all within easy distance for days out.

Facilities: Supermarket. Launderette. Large bar, big screen satellite TV, videos and films. Restaurant, takeaway and patio barbecue. Swimming pool and solarium. Adventure play ground, fun factory with ball pool. Multi-sports hard court, five-a-side pitch, tennis court, crazy

golf, table tennis and mountain bike hire. Some activities charged for. Range of evening entertainment, children's clubs and sports activities arranged.

Tel: 01392 447 447 **Fax:** 01392 445 202
Reservations: Contact Weststar Holiday Parks, as above.
Open: 24th March – 27th October.
Directions: Situated north of Looe on the B3265. Follow directions for the monkey sanctuary but continue past in direction of Plymouth, site is on right.

CAMPSITE NAME Looe Bay	Type of Accommodation Mobile Homes	Type of Accommodation Mobile Homes	Type of Accommodation Lodges
Number of Persons	Cawsand ★★★★: 2-4 persons Polperro ★★★★: 4-6 persons	Pensilva ★★★★: 4-6 persons Henwood ★★★★: 6-8 persons Mevagissey ★★★★★: 6-8 persons Mevagissey Grand ★★★★★: 6-8 persons	St Cleer ★★★★: 4-6 persons St Martin ★★★: 6-8 persons
Bedrooms	Caswand: 1 double bedroom Polperro: 2 bedrooms: 1x double, 1x twin, cotside available Both have additional sleeping in living area	Pensilva: 2 bedrooms: 1x double, 1x twin Henwood: 3 bedrooms: 1x double, 2x twin, Mevagissey: 3 bedrooms: 1x double, 2x twin Mevagissey grand: 3 bedrooms: 1x double, 2x twin All with additional sleeping in living area	St Cleer: 2 bedrooms: 1x double, 1x twin St Martin: 3 bedrooms: 1x double, 1x twin, 1x bunk beds both have double bed settee in living area
Lounge/Dining Area	Fully furnished, including colour T.V	Fully furnished including colour T.V	Fully furnished including colour T.V
Kitchen Area	Fully equipped including full sized cooker with oven and grill, fridge	Fully equipped including full sized cooker with oven and grill. Mevagissey and Mevagissey Grand also include microwave	Fully equipped St Cleer includes microwave
Bath/Shower/WC	Washbasin, shower, WC	Washbasin, shower, WC	Washbasin, bath with shower, WC
Other Facilities	Gas or electric heating, free gas and electricity	Gas or electric heating, free gas and electricity	Gas or electric heating, free gas and electric St Martin has double glazing
Bedding	Duvets and bed linen provided	Duvets and bed linen provided	Duvets and bed linen provided
Pets	Not accepted in Cawsand	Not accepted	Not accepted at St Martin
Charges **From** (Low Season, per week) **To** (High Season, per week)	Cawsand: £135- £395 Polperro: £145- £419	Pensilva: £169- £499 Henwood: £ 175- £499 Mevagissey: £189- £559 Mevagissey Grand: £199- £615	St Cleer Lodge: £189- £549 St Martin Lodge: £199-585

181 Newlands Caravan Park
Charmouth, Dorset DT6 6RB

This family owned park, run with care, occupies a prominent position beside the road into Charmouth village with marvellous views southwards to the hills across the valley and towards Lyme Regis. By the nature of the terrain there is some up and down walking.

Accommodation on the park includes smart pine lodges, apartments and motel rooms (double and family). All the park's facilities are located in a modern building to one side of the wide tarmac entrance. Membership of the club is automatic and the bar is open every evening and lunch times to suit. A range of family entertainment includes a children's club during school holidays with Dino Dan (the dinosaur). Out of the main season opening hours of the various facilities may vary. The smaller indoor pool and jacuzzi is open all year (limited hours Nov - March). The adjacent outdoor pool and paddling pool is walled, paved and sheltered and the outside entrance is key coded. Neither pool is supervised, both are heated, the indoor one is charged for. A super large children's play area in the field below the tenting field is open dawn to dusk - be tempted to try the maypole swing and bobsleigh ride! This is a comfortable site for families with the beach and village within easy walking distance and for those who enjoy some evening and family activity. Charmouth is also known for its fossil finds and its connection with Jane Austen.

Facilities: Well stocked shop (March-Nov). Licensed club bar (limited hours Nov - March). Restaurant (open evenings 6-9 pm. March - Nov) including takeaway. Indoor and outdoor pools. Nine-pin bowling alley for hire at £5 per half hour. Children's play area.
Off site: Fishing 1 mile, riding 3 miles, golf 2 miles.

Open: All year.
Tel: (01297) 560259. **Fax:** (01297) 560787.
E-mail: enq@newlandsholidays.co.uk
Reservations: Contact the park direct, or The Alan Rogers Travel Service on 01892 55 98 98
Directions: Approaching from Bridport leave the A35 at first sign for Charmouth at start of the bypass and site almost directly on your left. O.S.GR: SY373935.

CAMPSITE NAME Newlands	Type of Accommodation Mobile Homes	Type of Accommodation Pine Lodges	Type of Accommodation Poolside Apartments
Number of Persons	6 persons	8 persons	4 persons
Bedrooms	2 bedrooms: 1 x double, 1 x twin, 1 x bed settee in living area	3 bedrooms: 1 x double, 1 x twin, 1 x bunk beds, 1 x bed settee in living area	2 bedrooms: 1 x double, 1 x twin
Lounge/Dining Area	Fully furnished, including TV	Fully furnished, including TV	Fully furnished, including TV
Kitchen Area	Fully equipped, including cooker with oven, microwave and fridge	Fully equipped, including cooker with oven, microwave and fridge/freezer	Fully equipped, including cooker with oven and fridge
Bath/Shower/WC	Washbasin, shower, WC	Washbasin, shower, bath, WC	Washbasin, shower, WC
Other Facilities	Gas central heating, double glazing	Gas central heating, double glazing	Electric central heating, double glazing
Bedding	Pillows, duvets, sheets and pillowcases provided	Pillows, duvets, sheets and pillowcases provided	Bed linen provided
Pets	By arrangement in specified units	Not accepted	Not accepted
Charges From (Low Season, per week)	2002 £150	2002 £185	2002 £120
To (High Season, per week)	£490	£580	£420

202 Ulwell Cottage Caravan Park
Ulwell, Swanage, Dorset BH19 3DG

Nestling under the Purbeck Hills in this unique corner of Dorset on the edge of Swanage, Ulwell Cottage is a family run holiday park with indoor pool and wide range of facilities. The area occupied by the caravan holiday homes is interspersed with trees and shrubs, making it quite pretty.

The colourful entrance area is home to the Village Inn with a courtyard adjoining the heated, supervised indoor pool complex (both open all year and to the public) and the modern reception. The hill above the touring area, Nine Barrow Down, is a Site of Special Scientific Interest for butterflies overlooking Round Down. It is possible to walk to Corfe Castle this way. With Brownsea Island, Studland Bay, Corfe village and the Swanage Railway, Ulwell Cottage makes a marvellous centre for holidays.

Facilities: Well stocked shop (Easter - mid Sept). Bar snacks and restaurant meals with a family room. Takeaway (June-Sept). Indoor pool. Amusement arcade with video games. Playing field and play areas with a long slide and boat. Off site: Bicycle hire or riding 2 miles, fishing 1 mile, golf 1 mile.

Tel: (01929) 422823. **Fax:** (01929) 421500.
E-mail: enq@ulwellcottagepark.co.uk
Reservations: Contact Park direct, as above.
Open: All year except 8 Jan - 28 Feb.

Directions: From A351 Wareham - Swanage road, turn on B3351 Studland road just before Corfe Castle, follow signs to right for Swanage and drop down to Ulwell. O.S.GR: SZ019809.

Durdle Door

CAMPSITE NAME Ulwell Cottage	Type of Accommodation 12' Mobile Home	Type of Accommodation Standard Size Mobile Home	Type of Accommodation 10' Mobile Home
Number of Persons	Band 1: 6-7 persons Band 2: 4-5 persons Band 3: 4-5 persons	Band 4: 6-7 persons	Band 6: 4-5 persons
Bedrooms	Band 1: 3 bedrooms: 1 x double, 2 x twin, 1 x bed settee in living area Band 2: 2 bedrooms: 1 x double, 1x twin and over bunk or bed settee in living area Band 3: as per band 2	As Band 1	As Band 2
Lounge/Dining Area	Bands 1 & 2: Fully furnished including colour TV, video and gas fire Band 3: standard furnishings including colour TV, video and gas fire	Standard furnishings including colour TV, video and gas fire	Standard furnishings including colour TV, video and gas fire
Kitchen Area	Fully equipped, including gas cooker, fridge and microwave	Fully equipped including gas cooker, fridge and microwave	Fully equipped including gas cooker and fridge
Bath/Shower/WC	Washbasin, shower, WC	Washbasin, shower, WC	Washbasin, shower, WC
Bedding	Duvets/ blankets and pillows provided	Duvets/ blankets and pillows provided	Duvets/ blankets and pillows provided
Pets	Not accepted in Band 1 or 2 Accepted in some Band 3	Not accepted	Not accepted
Charges **From** (Low Season, per week) **To** (High Season, per week)	Band 1: £265 Band 2: £240 Band 3: £220 Band 1: £525 Band 2: £495 Band 3: £430	£240 £495	£185 £380

210 Sandford Holiday Park
Holton Heath, nr Poole, Dorset BH16 6JZ

Sandford Park is a pleasant, well run park with many first-class amenities near the popular coastal areas of Dorset. It has a large permanent section with 248 static holiday homes and lodges. Early booking is advisable. Sandford is a large, very busy holiday park with a wide range of entertainment. The clubhouse (free membership) is spacious with a dance floor, bar and seating area, and caters for different tastes and age groups. There is also a large air-conditioned ballroom for entertainment and dancing. Both are open over a long season, also a variety of bars, restaurants (book in busy periods) and simple hot meals, breakfasts and takeaway in peak season. The heated outdoor swimming pool and a very large play pool with a sandy beach, ideal for children, are attractively situated with a snack bar, terraced area and go-kart track. There is also an impressive, heated and supervised indoor pool which is a nice addition.

Facilities: Large launderette. Ladies' hairdresser. Bars, restaurants. TV lounges. Outdoor swimming pool (May-Sept) and indoor pool. Large supermarket and other shops, including well stocked camping accessory shop (all open peak season only). Soft indoor play area for children (April - Oct and Christmas, supervised). Children's playground, two tennis courts, mountain bike hire, table tennis, two short mat bowling greens (outdoor) and a large crazy golf course. Riding lessons available at stables on site.

Open: February - January.
Tel: (01202) 631600.
E-mail: bookings@weststarholidays.co.uk
Reservations: Contact Park direct. Early booking advisable .

Directions: Park is just west off A351 (Wareham - Poole) road at Holton Heath. O.S.GR: SY940913.

CAMPSITE NAME Sandford Park	Type of Accommodation Mobile Homes	Type of Accommodation Mobile Homes	Type of Accommodation Lodges
Number of Persons	Rosebud ★★★★: 2-4 persons	Orchid ★★★★: 4-6 persons Jasmine ★★★★: 6-8 persons	Hibiscus ★★★★: 4-6 persons Wisteria Lodge ★★★★: 6-8 persons Wisteria Gold ★★★★★: 6-8 persons
Bedrooms	Rosebud: 1 bedroom: 1 x double All have additional sleeping in living area	Orchid: 2 bedrooms: 1 x double, 1 x twin Jasmine: 3 bedrooms: 1 x double, 2 x twin All have additional sleeping in living area	Hibiscus: 2 bedrooms: 1 x double, 1 x twin Wisteria: 3 bedrooms: 1 x double, 1 x twin, 1 x bunk beds All have additional sleeping in living area
Lounge/Dining Area	Fully furnished including colour TV	Fully furnished including colour TV	Fully furnished including colour TV
Kitchen Area	Fully equipped including full sized cooker with oven, grill, fridge	Fully equipped including full sized cooker with oven and grill, fridge	Fully equipped including full sized cooker with oven and grill, fridge
Bath/Shower/WC	Washbasin, shower, WC	Washbasin, shower, WC	Hibiscus: shower, bath, WC Wisteria: shower, WC Wisteria Gold: en-suite shower, WC
Other Facilities	Free gas and electricity	Free gas and electricity	Free Gas, metered electricity
Bedding	Duvets and bed linen provided	Duvets and bed linen provided	Duvets and bed linen provided
Pets	Not accepted	Not accepted	Not accepted at Hibiscus & Wisteria gold
Charges From (Low Season, per week) **To** (High Season, per week)	2002 £125 - £449	Orchid: £169- £559 Jasmine: £199- £699	Hibiscus Lodge: £ 169- £615 Wisteria Lodge: £ 229- £739 Wisteria Gold Lodge: £ 249- £799 Fern Lodge: £ 229- 799
Comments	For disabled guests there is a purpose built Swiss style chalet for 6 persons " Fern Lodge". Contact park for details		

452 Flower of May Holiday Park

Lebberston Cliff, Scarborough, North Yorkshire YO11 3NU

Flower of May is a large, family owned park, situated on the cliff tops, 4¹/₂ miles from Scarborough and 2¹/₂ miles from Filey. There is a cliff walk to the beach but it is only suitable for the reasonably active - there is an easier walk down from a car park one mile away. The entrance to the park is very colourful and the reception office is light and airy. The range of leisure facilities grouped around reception, includes an indoor pool with areas for both adults and children, a water flume and a jacuzzi. In the same building are two squash courts, 10-pin bowling, table tennis and amusement machines. The leisure centre is also open to the public (concessionary rates for residents) but during high season is only available to local regulars and the holidaymakers on the park.

Facilities: Well stocked and licensed shop (closes end Sept) near the leisure centre, as is the laundry room. Two modern bar lounges, one for families and one for adults only, with discos in season, a games room with TV, large adventure playground with safety base and a café plus takeaway fish and chips. The Plough Inn near the park entrance offers a good bar meal. Pay and play golf course (£5 a round). Indoor swimming pool.

Off site: Fishing, boat slipway or riding 2 miles, bicycle hire 4 miles.

Tel: (01723) 584311.
Reservations: Contact Park direct, as above.
Open: Easter - 31 October.

Directions: Park is signed from roundabout at junction of A165 and B1261 from where it is 600 yds. O.S.GR: TA088836.

CAMPSITE NAME Flower of May	Type of Accommodation Mobile Homes	Type of Accommodation Mobile Homes
Number of Persons	6 persons	4 persons
Bedrooms	2 bedrooms: 1 x double, 1 x twin, 1 x double sofa bed in lounge	2 bedrooms: 1 x double, 1 x twin
Lounge/Dining Area	Fully furnished, including colour TV and satellite connection	Fully furnished, including colour TV and satellite connection
Kitchen Area	Fully equipped, including cooker with oven, microwave and fridge	Fully equipped, including cooker with oven, microwave and fridge
Bath/Shower/WC	Washbasin, shower, WC	Washbasin, shower, WC
Other Facilities	Gas heating	Gas heating
Bedding	Duvets and pillows provided	Duvets and pillows provided
Pets	Not accepted	Not accepted
Charges **From** (Low Season, per week) **To** (High Season, per week)	(2001) £200 £450	(2001) £180 £400

499 Fir Tree Park

Sewerby, Near Bridlington, Yorks YO16 6YG

An attractive holiday park ideally situated for walking on the impressive Flamborough Head coast, this park is situated in a rural setting in an area with a wealth of places to visit such as Bempton Cliffs, with its bird reserve, Burton Constable Hall, the Yorkshire Wolds or Bridlington itself.

With well-tended flower beds, lawn-like grass and trees around the perimeter the park has a neat and tidy and well-maintained appearance, and the reception staff are helpful and friendly.

Facilities: Indoor heated swimming pool. Games room. Family bar and lounge bar. Shop. Children's play area. Laundry.
Off-site: Golf Course (1 mile).

Tel: 01262 676442
Reservations: Contact Site Sales Information Hotline 01262 676442.

Open: Easter – 31st October.

Directions: One mile from Sewerby village, on the B1255 Bridlington to Flamborough road.

CAMPSITE NAME Fir Tree Park	Type of Accommodation Mobile Homes
Number of Persons	6 persons
Bedrooms	2 bedrooms: 1x double, 1x twin, 1x double sofa bed in living area
Lounge/Dining Area	Fully furnished, including TV
Kitchen Area	Fully equipped including cooker with oven, microwave and fridge
Bath/Shower/WC	Washbasin, shower, WC
Other Facilities	Gas heating
Bedding	Duvets and pillows provided
Pets	Not accepted
Charges **From** (Low Season, per week) **To** (High Season, per week)	(2001) £245 £445

351 Liffens Holiday Park

Burgh Castle, Great Yarmouth, Norfolk NR31 9QB

This popular well established family holiday park is in a semi-rural location, but within easy reach of Great Yarmouth.

On the park there is a large restaurant/bar that overlooks a heated outdoor swimming pool, providing club style entertainment in season, and a takeaway service (noon-7 pm). Holidaymakers can also use the indoor pool and other facilities at Liffens Welcome Holiday Centre close by. Excellent children's playground and a fenced, hard-surfaced multi-court for ball games, far enough away from the pitches to preserve peace and quiet. The park also operates a post office/shop, which is adjacent to the site, and a regular bus service runs from here to Great Yarmouth. The remains of a Roman fortress border the site.

Facilities: Laundry. Restaurant, bar and takeaway. Swimming pool (60 x 30 ft; open 29/5-10/9) with new water slide. Children's playground. Crazy golf. Bicycle hire planned. Multi-court. Torches advised.
Off site: Golf 2 miles, fishing + mile.

Tel: (01493) 780357. **Fax:** (01493) 782383.
Reservations: Contact Park direct, as above.
Open: 2 April - 30 October.

Directions: From junction of A12 and A143 at roundabout south of Great Yarmouth take Burgh Road westwards, straight over at next roundabout, then second left into Butt lane. Site is on right. Avoid width restricted road closer to Great Yarmouth. O.S.GR: TM490050.

CAMPSITE NAME Liffens	Type of Accommodation Mobile homes: Resort 10'	Type of Accommodation Mobile homes: Carlton Supreme 12'
Number of Persons	6 persons	6 persons
Bedrooms	3 bedrooms: 1x double, 2 x twin	3 bedrooms: 1 x double, 2 x twin
Lounge/Dining Area	Fully furnished	Fully furnished
Kitchen Area	Fully equipped including cooker with oven and fridge	Fully equipped including cooker with oven, microwave and fridge
Bath/Shower/WC	Washbasin, shower, WC	Washbasin, shower, WC, heated towel rail
Other Facilities	Gas/electric heating	Gas/electric heating
Bedding	Bed linen provided	Bed linen provided
Pets	Accepted only in grade 2	Not accepted
Charges **From** (Low Season, per week) **To** (High Season, per week)	(2001) Grade 1: £145 Grade 2: £105 Grade 1: £345 Grade 2: £295	(2001) £195 £395

730 Blair Castle Caravan Park
Blair Atholl, Pitlochry, Perthshire
PH18 5SR

This attractive, well-kept park is set in the grounds of Blair Castle, the traditional home of the Dukes of Atholl. The castle is open to the public, its 32 fully furnished rooms showing a picture of Scottish life from the 16th century to the present day, while the beautiful grounds and gardens are free to those staying on site. The park has a wonderful feeling of spaciousness with a large central area left free for children's play or for general use. The castle grounds provide many walking trails and the village is within walking distance with hotels, shops, a water mill craft centre and folk museum. A quality park, quiet at night and well managed. For 2002, a new central development will incorporate reception, a shop, games room, laundry and internet gallery. A member of the Best of British group.

Facilities: Good launderette with washing machines, dryers, spin dryer and irons plus a separate drying room and outside lines. Shop (1/4 - 28/10). Near reception is a games room with pool, table tennis and table football.
Off site: Mountain bike hire, riding, golf and fishing within 1 mile.

Tel: (01796) 481263. **Fax:** (01796) 481587.
E-mail: mail@blaircastlecaravanpark.co.uk
Reservations: Contact Park direct, as above.
Open: 1 April - 30 October.

Directions: From A9 just north of Pitlochry take B8079 into Blair Atholl. Park is in grounds of Blair Castle, well signed. O.S.GR: NN868659.

CAMPSITE NAME Blair Castle	Type of Accommodation Mobile Homes Type A	Type of Accommodation Mobile Homes Type B	Type of Accommodation 6 person Mobile Homes
Number of Persons	4 persons	4 persons	6 persons: 4 adults and 2 children
Bedrooms	2 bedrooms: 1 x double, 1 x twin	2 bedrooms: 1 x double, 1 x twin	3 bedrooms: 1 x double, 2 x twin
Lounge/Dining Area	Fully furnished, including teletext T.V. and video	Fully furnished, including colour TV	Fully furnished, including colour TV
Kitchen Area	Fully equipped including cooker, microwave and fridge	Fully equipped, including gas cooker, fridge	Fully equipped, including gas cooker, fridge
Bath/Shower/WC	Washbasin, shower, WC	Washbasin, shower, WC	Washbasin, shower, WC
Other Facilities	Gas/electric heating, Veranda	Gas/electric heating	Gas/electric heating
Bedding	Duvets, pillows, linen, towels provided	Duvets and pillows provided	Duvets and pillows provided
Pets	Not accepted	By prior arrangement	By prior arrangement
Charges **From** (Low Season, per week)	£230	£170	£185
To (High Season, per week)	£370	£310	£335

France

The French Government Tourist Office (FGTO),
178 Piccadilly, London W1V 0AL
Tel: 0906 8244 123 (premium rate)
www.tourist-offices.org.uk/France

Population
57,800,000 (94), density 106 per sq.km.

Capital
Paris.

Climate
France has a temperate climate but it varies considerably, for example, Brittany has a climate similar to that of Devon and Cornwall, whilst the Mediterranean coast enjoys a subtropical climate.

Language
Obviously French is spoken throughout the country but there are many local dialects and variations so do not despair if you have greater problems understanding in some areas than in others. We notice an increase in the amount of English understood and spoken.

Currency
From 1st January 2002 the Euro becomes the official currency of 12 European countries, including France, although you may continue to use French Francs in France until 17th February 2002. See separate article in this guide regarding the Euro.

Banks
Open weekdays 09.00-1200 and 14.00-16.00. Some provincial banks are open Tues-Sat 09.00-12.00 and 14.00-16.00.
Credit Cards: Most major credit cards accepted in most outlets and for motorway tolls.

Post Offices
The French term for post office is either PTT or Bureau de Poste. They are generally open Mon-Fri 08.00-19.00 and Saturday 08.00-12.00 and can close for lunch 12.00-14.00. You can buy stamps with less queuing from Tabacs (tobacconists).

Time
GMT plus 1 (summer BST + 1) but there is a period of about three to four weeks in October when the times coincide.

Telephone
From the UK dial 00 33, followed by the 10 figure local number MINUS the initial "0" - in other words from the UK you will dial 0033 followed by the last NINE digits of the telephone number. To the UK from France dial 0044. Many public phone boxes now only take phone cards. (Telecarte) These can be purchased from post offices, tabacs, and some campsites.

Public Holidays
New Year; Easter Mon; Labour Day; VE Day, 8 May; Ascension; Whit Mon; Bastille Day, 14 July; Assumption, 15 Aug; All Saints, 1 Nov; Armistice Day, 11 Nov; Christmas, 25 Dec.

Shops
Often close on Mon, all or half day and for 2 hours daily for lunch. Food shops open on Sun morning.

Motoring
France has a comprehensive road system from motorways (Autoroutes), Routes Nationales (N roads), Routes Départmentales (D roads) down to purely local C class roads.
Tolls: Payable on the autoroute network which is extensive but expensive. Tolls are also payable on certain bridges such as the one from the Ile de Ré to the mainland and the Pont de St Nazaire.
Speed Restrictions: Built-up areas 31 mph (50 kph), on normal roads 56 mph (90 kph); on dual carriageways separated by a central reservation 69 mph (110 kph), on toll motorways 80 mph (130 kph). In wet weather, limits outside built-up areas are reduced to 50mph (80 kph), 62 mph (100 kph) and 69 mph (110 kph) on motorways. A minimum speed limit of 50 mph (80 kph) exists in the outside lane of motorways during daylight, on level ground and with good visibility.
These limits also apply to private cars towing a caravan, if the latter's weight does not exceed that of the car. Where it does by 30%, limit is 40 mph (65 kph) and if more than 30%, 28 mph (45 kph).
Fuel: Diesel sold at pumps marked 'gaz-oil'.
Parking: Usual restrictions as in UK. In Paris and larger cities, there is a Blue Zone where parking discs must be used, obtainable from police stations, tourist offices and some shops.

Overnighting
Allowed provided permission has been obtained, except near the water's edge or at a large seaside resort. Casual camping is prohibited in state forests, national parks in the Départements of the Landes and Gironde, in the Camargue and also restricted in the south because of the danger of fire. However overnight stops on parking areas of a motorway are tolerated.

Map of the Tourist Regions

Regular readers will see that this year our Site Reports are grouped into sixteen 'tourist regions' and then by the various départements in each of these regions in numerical order.

Regions and départements

For administrative purposes France is actually divided into 23 official Regions, but these do not always coincide with the needs of tourists (for example the area we think of as 'The Dordogne' is split between two of the official Regions. We have, therefore, opted to feature our campsites within unofficial 'tourist regions' although we have of course subdivided these into the official French 'départements', each of which has an official number. For example, the département of Manche is number 50. We have used these département numbers as the first two digits of our campsite numbers, so any campsite in the Manche département will start with the number 50.

Brittany

Major cities: Rennes, Brest
22 Côtes d'Armor, 29 Finistère,
35 Ille-et-Vilaine, 56 Morbihan, 44 Loire
Atlantique.

Strong Celtic roots provide this region with its own distinctive traditions, evident in the local Breton costume and music, the religious festivals and the cuisine, featuring crêpes and cider. Brittany offers 800 miles of rocky coastline with numerous bays, busy little fishing villages and broad sandy beaches dotted with charming seaside resorts. Inland you find wooded valleys, rolling fields, moors and giant granite boulders, but most impressive is the wealth of prehistoric sites, notably the Carnac standing stones. Many castles and manor houses, countless chapels and old villages provide evidence of Brittany's eventful history and wealth of traditions. The Bretons are proud of their culture, very different from the rest of France, and are determined to keep it so. If you are able to attend a 'Pardon' (a religious procession), you will understand some of the Breton history and piety, and see some beautiful traditional costumes. Brittany is a popular destination for families with young children or for those visiting France for the first time. Note: the site reports are laid out by département, in numerical order.

Cuisine of the region
Fish and shellfish are commonplace – lobsters, huitres, langoustes, various sorts of crabs, moules, prawns, shrimps, coquilles St Jacques, for example
Traditional 'crêperies' abound and welcome visitors with a cup of local cider
Other specialties are wafer biscuits and butter biscuits
Agneau de pré-salé – leg of lamb from animals pastured in the salt marshes and meadows
Beurre blanc – sauce for fish dishes made fron a reduction of shallots, wine vinegar and the finest butter (sometimes with dry white wine)
Cotriade – fish soup with potatoes, onions, garlic and butter
Crêpes Bretonnes – the thinnest of pancakes with a variety of sweet fillings
Galette – can be a biscuit, cake or pancake; the latter usually with fillings of mushrooms or ham or cheese or seafood, and called a Galette de blé noir (buckwheat flour)
Gâteau Breton – rich cake with butter, egg yolks and sugar
Poulet blanc Breton – free-range, fine quality, white Breton chicken

Wine
This is cider country! Crêperies serve cider in pottery type cups

Places of interest
Cancale – small fishing port famous for oysters
Carnac – 3,000 standing stones (menhirs), the last erected in 2,000 BC
Concarneau – fishing port, old walled town surrounded by ramparts
Dinan – historical walled town high above the River Rance
La Baule – resort with lovely, sandy bay and beach
Le Croisic – fishing port, Naval museum
Guérande – historic walled town
Perros-Guirec – leading resort of the 'Pink Granite Coast'
Quiberon – boat service to three islands: Belle Ile (largest of the Breton islands), Houat, Hoedic
Rennes – capital of Brittany, medieval streets, half timbered houses; Brittany Museum
St Malo – historical walled city, fishing port and yachting harbour
Tréguier – former Episcopal city, 13th-19th cenzuary St Tugdual cathedral

2900 Camping Les Mouettes
La Grande Grève, 29660 Carantec

Les Mouettes is situated in the north of Brittany less than 15 km from the Roscoff ferry port, so is well situated for those who do not want to travel far. The area has plenty to offer with beautiful bays and many places of interest within easy reach. Les Mouettes is a sheltered site on the edge of an attractive bay with access to the sea at the front of the site. In a wooded setting with many attractive trees and shrubs (located together at the top of the site). The focal point of the site is an impressive heated swimming pool complex comprising a water slide pool and three water slides, 'tropical river', swimming pool and children's pool and a jacuzzi.

Facilities: Laundry facilities. Shop (23/5-13/9, limited hours outside the main season). Takeaway. Centrally located bar (20/5-13/9) overlooking pool complex. Games and TV

rooms. Children's play area. Volleyball, two half-courts for tennis, minigolf and archery (July/Aug). Table tennis. Small fishing lake (only partially fenced). Discos and other entertainment organised in main season.
Off site: Bicycle hire 500 m, riding 6 km. and golf 2 km.

Tel: (0)2.98.67.02.46. **Fax:** (0)2.98.78.31.46.
E-mail: camping.les.mouettes@wanadoo.fr
Reservations: Contact Alan Rogers Travel Service. Tel. 01892 55 98 98
Open: 1 May - 15 September.

Directions: From D58 Roscoff - Morlaix road, turn to Carantec on D173. Site is approx. 4 km. from here on the outskirts of the village, signed to the left at roundabout immediately after passing supermarket on right.

CAMPSITE NAME Les Mouettes	Type of Accommodation Mobile Home Mercure	Type of Accommodation Mobile home Jupiter/Pluton	Type of Accommodation Residences Mobiles
Number of Persons	4 persons	5/6 persons	5/6 persons
Bedrooms	2 bedrooms: 1 x double, 1 x twin	2 bedrooms: 1 x double, 1 x twin, 1x sofa bed in living area	2 bedrooms: 1 x double, 1 x twin, 1 x sofa bed in living area
Lounge/Dining Area	Fully furnished	Fully furnished	Fully furnished
Kitchen Area	Fully equipped including gas hobs and fridge	Fully equipped including gas hobs and fridge	Fully equipped including gas hobs and fridge
Bath/Shower/WC	Washbasin, shower, separate WC	Washbasin, shower, separate WC	Washbasin, shower, separate WC
Other Facilities	Gas heating, double glazing, garden table and chairs, parasol	Gas heating, double glazing, garden table and chairs, parasol	Gas heating, double glazing, garden table and chairs, parasol
Bedding	Blankets and pillows provided Sheets available at a supplement	Blankets and pillows provided Sheets available at a supplement	Blankets and pillows provided Sheets available at a supplement
Pets	Accepted	Accepted	Accepted
Charges **From** (Low Season, per week) **To** (High Season, per week)	2002 €230 €595	2002 €260 €635	2002 €290 €665

2901 Castel Camping Ty Nadan
Route d'Arzano, 29310 Locunolé

Ty Nadan is a well organised site beside the River Elle, set deep in the countryside in the grounds of a country house some 18 km. from the sea. Many activities and clubs are organised all season, particularly sports, exercises, excursions, etc. and including guided mountain bike tours. Canoeing trips are organised which may include some white water stretches more suitable for the experienced (arranged daily in season to Quimperlé, returning by bus). Across the road, by the attractive house and garden in converted Breton outbuildings is a delightful crêperie and a disco.

Facilities: Laundry room with washing machines and dryers. Restaurant, takeaway, bar and shop (all open all season). Heated swimming pool (17 x 8 m), pool with water slides and children's paddling pool. Small beach on the river (unfenced). Tennis courts, table tennis, pool tables, archery and trampolines. Adventure play park. Riding. Small roller skating rink. Bicycle hire. Skateboards, roller skates and boat hire. Fishing.

Tel: (0)2.98.71.75.47. **Fax:** (0)2.98.71.77.31.
E-mail: ty-nadan@wanadoo.fr
Reservations: Contact Alan Rogers Travel Service Tel. 01892 55 98 98 ▰
Open: 15 May - 5 September.

Directions: Make for Arzano which is northeast of Quimperlé on the Pontivy road and turn off D22 just west of village at camp sign. Site is approx. 3 km.

CAMPSITE NAME Ty Nadan	Type of Accommodation Mobile Home	Type of Accommodation Chalets	Type of Accommodation Apartments 6 persons Apartments 8 persons
Number of Persons	4 persons	6 persons	Apartments 6 persons Apartments 8 persons
Bedrooms	2 bedrooms: 1 x double, 1 x twin	2 bedrooms: 1 x double, 1 x twin, 1 x double sofa bed in living area	Apartments 6: 2 bedrooms: 2 x double, 1 x single, 1 x double sofa bed in living area Apartments 8: 3 bedrooms: 2 x double, 1 x twin, 1 x double sofa bed in living area
Lounge/Dining Area	Fully furnished	Fully furnished	Fully furnished including colour TV
Kitchen Area	Fully equipped including gas hobs, coffee machine and fridge	Fully equipped including cooker with oven and electric rings, coffee machine and fridge	Fully equipped including cooker with oven and electric rings, fridge. Apartments 8 also have coffee machine, fridge/freezer and iron
Bath/Shower/WC	Washbasin, shower, WC	Washbasin, shower, WC	Apartments 6: Washbasin, shower, separate WC Apartments 8: washbasin, shower, bath, separate WC
Other Facilities	Electric heating, garden table, parasol,	Electric heating, terrace, garden table, parasol	Electric heating, double glazing, terrace, garden table, parasol
Bedding	Blankets and pillows provided Sheets available at a supplement	Blankets and pillows provided Sheets available at a supplement	Blankets and pillows provided
Pets	Accepted	Accepted	Accepted
Charges **From** (Low Season, per week) **To** (High Season, per week)	2002 €243.6 €595	2002 €304.5 €686	2002 €305.2 } based on €686 } 6 sharing

For latest infomation visit **www.alanrogers.com**

2902 Camping Club du Saint-Laurent

Kerleven, 29940 La Forêt-Fouesnant

Saint-Laurent is a well established site, situated on a sheltered wooded slope bordering one of the many attractive little inlets that typify the Brittany coastline. There is direct access from the site to two small sandy bays, which empty at low tide to reveal numerous rockpools (ideal for children to explore), and the site is on the coastal footpath that leads from Kerleven to Concarneau. The swimming pool (complete with paddling pool and two new water slides) is overlooked by the bar terrace. During July and August daily children's clubs and adult entertainments are organised (in English as well as in French), with discos in the bar each evening. This makes the site an ideal choice for a lively family holiday, particularly for older children.

Facilities: Laundry: washing machines, dryers and ironing facilities in newly refurbished room. Small shop at reception provides essentials. Bar, snack bar and takeaway (all 12/5-10/9). Swimming pools. Gym and sauna. Canoe hire. Basketball, two tennis courts (no charge), and table tennis. Children's play area.

Tel: (02) 98.56.97.65. **Fax:** (02) 98.56.92.51.
Reservations: Contact site direct, as above.
Open: 11 May - 14 September.

Directions: From N165 take D70 Concarneau exit. At first roundabout take first exit D44 (Fouesnant). After 2.5 km. turn right at T junction, follow for 2.5 km, then turn left (Port La Forêt - take care - 200 m. before the junction is a sign that implies Port La Forêt is straight on, and it isn't). Continue to roundabout, straight ahead (Port La Forêt) and after 1 km. turn left (site signed here). In 400 m left turn to site at end of this road.

CAMPSITE NAME Club du Saint Laurent	Type of Accommodation Willerby Cottage	Type of Accommodation Willerby 26 m2	Type of Accommodation Willerby 30 m2
Number of Persons	6 persons	4/6 persons	6 persons
Bedrooms	2 bedrooms: 1 x double, 1 x double sofa bed in living area	2 bedrooms: 1 x double, 1 x twin, 1 double sofa bed in living area	2 bedrooms: 1 x double, 1 x twin, 1 double sofa bed in living area
Lounge/Dining Area	Fully furnished	Fully furnished	Fully furnished
Kitchen Area	Fully equipped including oven, gas hobs and fridge/freezer	Fully equipped including oven, gas hobs and fridge	Fully equipped including oven, gas hobs and fridge
Bath/Shower/WC	Washbasin, shower, separate WC	Washbasin, shower, WC	Washbasin, shower, WC
Other Facilities	Gas heating, garden table, deckchairs, parasol, BBQ	Gas heating, garden table and chairs, deckchairs, parasol, BBQ	Electric heating, garden table, deckchairs, parasol, BBQ
Bedding	Blankets and pillows provided Sheets available at a supplement	Blankets and pillows provided Sheets available at a supplement	Blankets and pillows provided Sheets available at a supplement
Pets	Not accepted	Not accepted	Not accepted
Charges **From** (Low Season, per week) **To** (High Season, per week)	2002 €370 €625	2002 €295 €560	2002 €320 €593

2909 Camping Le Raguénès Plage
19 Rue des Iles à Raguénès, 29920 Névez

Mme Guyader and her family ensure you will receive a warm welcome on your arrival at this well kept and pleasant site. Although the entrance to the site could best be described as more functional than beautiful, once you have passed the reception block you find yourself in an attractive and well laid out campsite with many shrubs and trees. From the far end of the campsite a five minute walk along a path takes you down to a pleasant, sandy beach.

Facilities: Laundry room. Small shop (from 15/5). Bar and restaurant (from 1/6) with outside terrace and takeaway. Reading and TV room, internet access point. Heated pool with sun terrace and children's pool. Sauna (charged). Children's play areas, table tennis, games room and volleyball. Various activities are organised

in July/Aug. Currency and traveller's cheques can be exchanged at reception.
Off site: Supermarket 3 km. Fishing and watersports 300 m, riding 4 km.

Tel: (0)2.98.06.80.69. **Fax:** (0)2.98.06.89.05.
Reservations: Contact Alan Rogers Travel Service Tel. 01892 55 98 98
Open: 13 April - 30 September.

Directions: From N165 take D24 Kerampaou exit. After 3 km turn right towards Nizon and bear right at church in village following signs to Névez (D77). Continue through Névez, following signs to Raguénès. Continue for about 3 km. to site entrance on left (take care - entrance is quite small and easy to miss.)

CAMPSITE NAME Le Raguenes Plage	Type of Accommodation Willerby Cottage No 3	Type of Accommodation Willerby Mobile Home No 2
Number of Persons	5 persons	5 persons
Bedrooms	2 bedrooms: 1 x double, 1 x twin, 1 x double bed settee in living room	2 bedrooms: 1 x double, 1 x single, 1x bunk bed
Lounge/Dining Area	Fully furnished	Fully furnished
Kitchen Area	Fully equipped including gas hobs and fridge/freezer	Fully equipped including gas cooker with oven and with hobs, coffee machine and fridge/freezer
Bath/Shower/WC	Washbasin, shower, WC	Washbasin, small bath, WC
Other Facilities	Electric heating, garden table, parasol, sun loungers and BBQ Washing machine, tumble dryer, hoover and iron are available from the sites laundry block	Gas heating, garden table, parasol, 2 sun loungers and BBQ
Bedding	Blankets and pillows provided Sheets available at a supplement	Blankets and pillows provided Sheets available at a supplement
Pets	Not accepted	Not accepted
Charges From (Low Season, per week) To (High Season, per week)	2001 €320 €541	2001 €275 €518

2905 Castel Camping L'Orangerie de Lanniron

Château de Lanniron, 29336 Quimper Cedex

L'Orangerie is a beautiful and peaceful, family site in 10 acres of a XVIIth century, 42 acre country estate on the banks of the Odet river. It is just to the south of Quimper and about 15 km. from the sea and beaches at Bénodet. The family have a five year programme to restore and rehabilitate the park, the original canal, fountains, ornamental Lake of Neptune, the boat-house and the gardens and avenues. The original outbuildings have been attractively converted around a walled courtyard. The restaurant in the beautiful XVIIth century Orangerie, and the Gardens are both open to the public and in Spring the rhododendrons and azaleas are magnificent, with lovely walks within the grounds. All facilities are available when the site is open.

Facilities: Washing machines and dryers. Shop (all season), Bar, snacks and takeaway, plus restaurant (open daily from 20/5, reasonably priced with children's menu). Heated swimming pool (144 sq.m.) with children's pool. New pool planned. Small play area. Tennis. Minigolf, attractively set among mature trees. Table tennis. Fishing. Archery. Bicycle hire. General reading, games and billiards rooms. TV/video room (cable and satellite). Karaoke. Animation provided including outdoor activities with large room for indoor activities.

Off site: Sea 15 km. Historic town of Quimper under 3 km. Two hypermarkets 1 km.

Tel: (0)2.98.90.62.02. **Fax:** (0)2.98.52.15.56.
E-mail: camping@lanniron.com
Reservations: Contact Alan Rogers Travel Service Tel. 01892 55 98 98
Open: 15 May - 15 September.
Directions: From Quimper follow 'Quimper Sud' signs, then 'Toutes Directions' and general camping signs, finally signs for Lanniron.

CAMPSITE NAME L'Orangerie de Lanniron	Type of Accommodation Studio A La Ferme	Type of Accommodation Mobile Home Jupiter	Type of Accommodation Mobile Home Rapidhome
Number of Persons	2/3 persons	4/6 persons	4/6 persons
Bedrooms	1 bedroom:1 x double, 1 x sofa bed in living area	2 bedrooms: 1 x double, 1 x twin, 1 x double sofa bed in living area	2 bedrooms: 1 x double, 1 x twin, 1 x double bed settee in living area
Lounge/Dining Area	Fully furnished including telephone	Fully furnished	Fully furnished
Kitchen Area	Fully equipped including microwave, electric rings, coffee machine, kettle and fridge	Fully equipped including microwave, gas hobs, coffee machine, kettle and fridge	Fully equipped including microwave, gas hobs, coffee machine, kettle and fridge/ freezer
Bath/Shower/WC	Washbasin, shower, WC	Washbasin, shower, WC	Washbasin, shower, WC
Other Facilities	Electric heating	Gas and electric heating, double glazing, garden table, sun lounger, parasol, BBQ	Electric heating, double glazing, terrace, garden table, sun lounger, parasol and BBQ
Bedding	Blankets and pillows provided	Blankets and pillows provided	Blankets and pillows provided Sheets and towels available at a supplement
Pets	Not accepted	Not accepted	Not accepted
Charges **From** (Low Season, per week) **To** (High Season, per week)	2002 €189 €357	2002 €301 €609	2002 €336 €658

2906 Camping Caravaning Le Pil Koad

Poullan-sur-Mer, 29100 Douarnenez

Pil Koad is an attractive, family run site just back from the sea near Douarnenez in Finistère. The site is on fairly level ground with something of a 'park like' appearance. A large room, the 'Woodpecker Bar', is used for entertainment with discos and cabaret in July/Aug. Gates closed 10.30 - 07.00 hrs. A variety of beaches within easy reach, with the coast offering some wonderful scenery and good for walking.

Facilities: Laundry facilities. Small shop for basics (bread to order all season) and takeaway (both 17/6-2/9). Heated swimming pool and paddling pool (no bermuda-style shorts). Tennis court. Table tennis, minigolf and volleyball. Fishing. Bicycle hire. Children's playground. Weekly outings and clubs for children (30/6-30/8) with charge included in tariff.

Off site: Riding 4 km. Restaurants in village 500 m. Nearest sandy beach 4 km. Douarnenez 6 km.

Tel: (0)2.98.74.26.39. **Fax:** (0)2.98.74.55.97. **E-mail:** camping.pil.koad@wanadoo.fr
Reservations: Contact site direct, as above
Open: 1 May - 15 September.

Directions: Site is 500 m. east from the centre of Poullan on D7 road towards Douarnenez. From Douarnenez take circular bypass route towards Audierne; if you see road for Poullan sign at roundabout, take it, otherwise there is camping sign at turning to Poullan from the D765 road.

CAMPSITE NAME Pil Koad	Type of Accommodation Mobile home IRM	Type of Accommodation Chalet Reve Confort	Type of Accommodation Mobile home Confort
Number of Persons	6 persons	6 persons	4 persons
Bedrooms	2 bedrooms: 1 x double, 1 x twin, 1 x double sofa bed in living area	2 bedrooms: 1x double, 1x twin, 1 x double sofa bed in living area	2 bedrooms: 1 x double, 1 x twin
Lounge/Dining Area	Fully furnished	Fully furnished	Fully furnished
Kitchen Area	Fully equipped including gas hobs, coffee machine and fridge	Fully equipped including cooker with oven and gas hobs, coffee machine and fridge	Fully equipped including gas hobs, coffee machine and fridge
Bath/Shower/WC	Washbasin, shower, separate WC	Washbasin, shower, separate WC	Washbasin, shower, separate WC
Other Facilities	Electric heating, double glazing, terrace, garden table, parasol, BBQ,	Electric heating, double glazing, covered terrace, garden table, parasol, BBQ,	Electric heating, terrace, garden table, parasol, BBQ
Bedding	Blankets and pillows provided Sheets and towels available at a supplement. Laundry service available	Blankets and pillows provided Sheets and towels available at a supplement. Laundry service available	Blankets and pillows provided. Sheets and towels available at a supplement. Laundry service available
Pets	Accepted	Accepted	Accepted
Charges **From** (Low Season, per week) **To** (High Season, per week)	2002 €250 €600	2002 €260 €650	2002 €200 €510

For latest infomation visit **www.alanrogers.com**

2911 Camping Village de la Plage
Rue de Men-Meur, 29730 Le Guilvinec

La Plage is a friendly site located beside a long sandy beach between the fishing town of Le Guilvinec and the watersports beaches of Penmarc'h on the southwest tip of Brittany. It is spacious and surrounded by tall trees, which provide shelter, and is made up of several flat, sandy meadows. There is plenty to occupy one at this friendly site but the bustling fishing harbour at Le Guilvinec and the watersports of Penmarc'h and Pointe de la Torche are within easy travelling distance. A 'Yelloh Village' member.

Facilities: Laundry facilities. Shop. Bright, airy well furnished bar, crêperie and takeaway. Heated swimming pool with paddling pool and water slide. Sauna. Children's play area. TV room. Tennis courts. Volleyball, basketball,

minigolf, badminton, petanque, table tennis, giant chess/draughts. Bicycle hire. Entertainment organised all season for adults and children. Gates locked 23.00 - 06.30 hrs. **Off site:** Fishing and watersports near. Riding 5 km. Golf 20 km.

Tel: (0)2.98.58.61.90. **Fax:** (0)2.98.58.89.06. **E-mail:** info@campingsbretagnesud.com. **Reservations:** Contact Alan Rogers Travel Service on 01892 55 98 98 ▸ **Open:** 4 May - 8 September, with all facilities.

Directions: Site is west of Guilvinec. From Pont l'Abbé, take the D785 road towards Penmarc'h. In Plomeur, turn left on D57 signed Guilvinec. On entering Guilvinec fork right signed Port and camping. Follow road along coast to site on left.

CAMPSITE NAME Village de la Plage	Type of Accommodation Mobile Home	Type of Accommodation Chalet Fabre	Type of Accommodation Cottage Louisiane
Number of Persons	6 persons	7 persons	7 persons
Bedrooms	2 bedrooms: 1 x double, 1 x twin, 1 x double sofa bed in living area	2 bedrooms: 1 x double, 1 x twin with 1 x bunk beds, 1 x double sofa bed in living area	2 bedrooms: 1 x double, 1 x twin with 1 x bunk beds, 1 x double sofa bed in living area
Lounge/Dining Area	Fully furnished	Fully furnished	Fully furnished
Kitchen Area	Fully equipped including oven with gas hobs, fridge	Fully equipped including microwave, gas hobs and fridge	Fully equipped including microwave, gas hobs and fridge
Bath/Shower/WC	Washbasin, shower, separate WC	Washbasin, shower, WC	Washbasin, shower, separate WC
Other Facilities	Electric heating, garden table, parasol, BBQ	Electric heating, terrace, garden table, parasol, BBQ	Electric heating, terrace, garden table, parasol, BBQ
Bedding	Blankets and pillows provided Sheets and towels available at a supplement	Blankets and pillows provided Sheets and towels available at a supplement	Blankets and pillows provided Sheets and towels available at a supplement
Pets	Accepted	Accepted	Accepted
Charges **From** (Low Season, per week) **To** (High Season, per week)	2002 €215 €596	2002 €260 €695	2002 €260 €695

2912 Camping Village Le Manoir de Kerlut
29740 Plobannalec-Lesconil

Le Manoir de Kerlut is a comfortable site in the grounds of a manor house on a river estuary near Pont l' Abbe. The old 'manoir' is not open to the public, but is used occasionally for weddings and private functions. Opened in '89, the campsite has neat, modern buildings and is laid out on flat grass. One area is rather open with separating hedges planted, the other part being amongst more mature bushes and some trees which provide shade. Site amenities are of good quality. A 'Yelloh Village' member.

Facilities: Laundry. Small shop. Takeaway. Large modern bar with TV (satellite) and entertainment all season. Bar in the Manoir. Two heated swimming pools, children's pool and new water slide. Sauna, solarium and small gym. Children's play area. Tennis, volleyball, badminton and petanque. Games room. Bicycle hire. Gates closed 22.30 - 7.30 hrs.
Off site: Fishing 2 km, riding 5 km, golf 15 km.

Tel: (0)2.98.82.23.89 **Fax:** (0)2.98.82.26.49.
E-mail: info@campingsbretagnesud.com
Reservations: Contact Alan Rogers Travel Service. Tel: 01892 55 98 98
Open: 4 May - 15 September, with all services.

Directions: From Pont l'Abbé, on D785, take D102 road towards Lesconil. Site is signed on the left, shortly after the village of Plobannalec.

CAMPSITE NAME Manoir de Kerlut	Type of Accommodation Mobile home	Type of Accommodation Chalet Fabre
Number of Persons	6 persons	7 persons
Bedrooms	2 bedrooms: 1 x double, 1 x twin, 1 x double sofa bed in living area	2 x bedrooms: 1 x double, 1 x twin with 1 x bunk bed, 1 x double sofa bed in living area
Lounge/Dining Area	Fully furnished	Fully furnished
Kitchen Area	Fully equipped including oven with gas hobs, fridge	Fully equipped including oven with gas hobs, fridge
Bath/Shower/WC	Washbasin, shower, separate WC	Washbasin, shower, WC
Other Facilities	Electric heating, garden table, parasol, BBQ	Electric heating, terrace, garden table, parasol, BBQ
Bedding	Blankets and pillows provided Sheets and towels available at a supplement	Blankets and pillows provided Sheets available at a supplement
Pets	Accepted	Accepted
Charges **From** (Low Season, per week) **To** (High Season, per week)	2002 €215 €595	2002 €260 €695

2913 Camping des Abers
Dunes de Ste Marguerite, 29870 Landéda

This delightful 12 acre site is beautifully situated almost at the tip of the Sainte Marguerite peninsula on the north-western shores of Brittany in a wide bay formed between the mouths (Abers) of two rivers, L'Aber Wrac'h and L'Aber Benoit. With soft, white sandy beaches and rocky outcrops and islands at high tide, the setting is ideal for those with younger children and this quiet, rural area provides a wonderful, tranquil escape from the busier areas of France, even in high season. Camping des Abers is set just back from the beach, the lower part sheltered from the wind by high hedges or with panoramic views of the bay from the higher places. The site is arranged in distinct areas, partly shaded and sheltered by mature hedges, trees and flowering shrubs, all planted and carefully tended over 30 years by the Le Cuff family Speaking several languages, they own and run this site with 'TLC' and will make you very welcome.

Facilities: Fully equipped laundry. Mini-market stocks essentials (1/5-15/9). Simple takeaway dishes (1/7-31/8). Pizzeria and restaurant next

door. Table tennis. Good play area (on sand). Indoor TV and games room. Live music, Breton dancing and Breton cooking classes, and guided walks arranged. Splendid beach reached direct from the site with good bathing (best at high tide), fishing, windsurfing and other water sports. Miles of superb coastal walks. Torch useful. Gates locked 22.30-07.00 hrs.

Off site: Tennis and riding close. The nearby town of L'Aber Wrac'h, a well known yachting centre, has many memorable restaurants

Tel: (0)2.98.04.93.35. **Fax:** (0)2.98.04.84.35.
Reservations: Contact Alan Rogers Travel Service Tel 01892 55 98 98
Open: 14 April - 22 September.

Directions: From Roscoff (D10, then D13), cross river bridge (L'Aber Wrac'h) to Lannilis. Go through town taking road to Landéda and from there signs for Dunes de Ste Marguerite, 'camping' and des Abers.

CAMPSITE NAME Des Abers	Type of Accommodation Mobile home Grand Comfort	Type of Accommodation Mobile home Comfort IRM
Number of Persons	4/6 persons	4/6 persons
Bedrooms	2 bedrooms: 1 x double, 1 x twin, 1 x double sofa bed in living area	2 bedrooms: 1 x double, 1 x twin, 1 x double sofa bed in living area
Lounge/Dining Area	Fully furnished	Fully furnished
Kitchen Area	Fully equipped including gas hobs, fridge, coffee machine and kettle	Fully equipped including gas hobs, fridge, coffee machine and kettle
Bath/Shower/WC	Washbasin, shower, separate WC	Washbasin, shower, separate WC
Other Facilities	Electric heating, double glazing, garden table and chairs, deckchair, parasol	Electric heating, double glazing, garden table and chairs, deckchair, parasol
Bedding	Blankets and pillows provided Sheets and towels available at a supplement	Blankets and pillows provided Sheets and towels available at a supplement
Pets	Accepted	Accepted
Charges **From** (Low Season, per week) **To** (High Season, per week)	2002 €230 €400	2002 €250 €450

2914 Haven Domaine de Kerlann
Land Rosted, 29930 Pont-Aven

Starting with a small original site, Haven Europe have invested imaginatively with much care for the existing environment and thoughtful planning on the infrastructure side. The result is that a large number of mobile homes blend into the new landscaping and the many carefully retained original trees. The 'piece de resistance' of the site is the amazing pool complex comprising three outdoor pools with separate toboggan, attractively landscaped with sunbathing terraces, and an indoor tropical style complex complete with jacuzzi and its own toboggan. Much evening holiday camp style entertainment (with a French flavour) takes place. On the bar terrace with its raised stage which overlooks the complex. If you tire of activity on site, the nearby town of Pont-Aven with its Gauguin connection, art galleries and museums is well worth visiting or there is a range of safe beaches and small ports and villages to enjoy.

Facilities: Laundry. Shop. French style restaurant, snack restaurant, takeaway and bar. Impressive pool complex including indoor and outdoor pools with lifeguards. Well equipped play areas. All weather multi-sports court, tennis courts, minigolf. Video games room, pool tables and satellite TV in the bar. Three children's clubs for different age groups.

Tel: (0)2.98.06.01.77.
Fax: (0)2.98.06.18.50.
Reservations: Contact site or Haven Europe in the UK (quoting this guide as a reference) on 0870 242 7777.
Open: 7 April - 26 October.

Directions: From Tregunc - Pont-Aven road, turn south towards Névez and site on right.

CAMPSITE NAME Domaine de Kerlann	Type of Accommodation Standard Mobile Homes	Type of Accommodation Luxury Mobile Homes	Type of Accommodation Chalets/Lodges/Apartments
Number of Persons	4-8 persons	7-8 persons	4-8 persons
Bedrooms	2-3 bedrooms: 2 x double, 1 x twin, 1 x double sofa bed in living area	2-3 bedrooms: 2 x double, 1 x twin, 1 x double sofa bed in living area	1-3 bedrooms: 2 x double, 1 x twin, 1 x double sofa bed in living area
Lounge/Dining Area	Fully furnished	Fully furnished	Fully furnished
Kitchen Area	Fully equipped including full cooker and fridge	Fully equipped including microwave, full cooker and fridge/freezer, some include dishwasher	Fully equipped including microwave, full cooker and fridge/freezer, some include dishwasher
Bath/Shower/WC	Washbasin, shower, WC	Washbasin, shower, WC	Washbasin, shower, WC
Other Facilities	Gas fire, garden table and chairs, BBQ	Gas fire, garden table and chairs, BBQ	Central heating, garden table and chairs, BBQ
Bedding	Blankets and pillows provided	Blankets and pillows provided	Blankets and pillows provided
Pets	Not accepted	Not accepted	Not accepted
Charges **From** (Low Season, per week) **To** (High Season, per week)	2002 £183 - £260 £662 - £872 Haven have a wider range of accommodation than can be featured here. Please phone Haven for details	2002 £260 - £330 £886 - £1054	2002 £190 - £393 £668 - £1166

2926 Camping La Plage
Kérambechennec, 29950 Bénodet

Considering its position within easy walking distance of the town centre and beach, this is a surprisingly pretty, green and tranquil site, catering equally in two fairly distinct parts for clients in mobile homes and independent campers and caravanners. The quite large swimming pool complex is close to the mobile homes. A good range of facilities are housed in some quite attractive buildings close to the entrance. The main attraction of this site must be its close proximity to a popular and quite stylish resort, and the fact that one could combine this with staying in fairly tranquil surroundings.

Facilities: Laundry facilities Large bar. Takeaway. Children's play area, games room and two billiards/pool tables. Swimming pool, paddling pools and toboggan.

Tel: (0)2.98.57.00.55. **Fax:** (0)2.98.57.12.60.
Reservations: Contact site direct, as above.
Open: 1 June - 30 September.

Directions: From Bénodet Plage follow signs to site.

CAMPSITE NAME La Plage	Type of Accommodation Chalet Le Cottage	Type of Accommodation Mobile home	Type of Accommodation Chalet Le Club
Number of Persons	6 persons	4/6 persons	5 persons
Bedrooms	2 bedrooms: 1 x double, 1 x twin with 1 x bunk beds	2 bedrooms: 1 x double, 1 x twin, 1 x double sofa bed	2 bedrooms: 1 x double, 1 x twin, 1 x single bunk bed
Lounge/Dining Area	Fully furnished	Fully furnished	Fully furnished
Kitchen Area	Fully equipped including microwave, gas hobs, coffee machine and fridge	Fully equipped including microwave, gas hobs, coffee machine, fridge	Fully equipped including microwave, gas hobs, coffee machine and fridge
Bath/Shower/WC	Washbasin, shower, separate WC	Washbasin, shower, bath, separate WC	Washbasin, shower, WC
Other Facilities	Garden table and chairs, deckchairs, parasol, BBQ	Electric heating, garden table and chairs, deckchairs, parasol, BBQ	Electric heating, garden table and chairs, deckchairs, parasol, BBQ
Bedding	Blankets and pillows provided Sheets available at a supplement	Blankets and pillows provided Sheets available at a supplement	Blankets and pillows provided
Pets	Accepted	Accepted	Accepted
Charges **From** (Low Season, per week) **To** (High Season, per week)	2001 €305 €503	2001 €366 €549	2001 €305 €503

2929 Camping Village Le Grand Large

48 route du Grand Large, Mousterlin, 29170 Fouesnant

This is a good site on the Pointe de Mousterlin for those searching for a beach situation in natural surroundings. The site is separated from the beach by the road that follows the coast around the point. It is also protected from the wind by an earth bank with trees and a fence. The beach itself looks over the bay towards the Isles de Glénan. A small river runs through the site but it is fenced. Benodet (7 km) and Fouesnant (5 km) are near in different directions and the sandy beach is just up the steps and across the road. In season this is a bustling family site with plenty going on, but it would also suit walkers and nature lovers in the low season as it is adjacent to a large tract of protected land, Marais de Mousterlin, ideal for walking, cycling and bird watching.

Facilities: Laundry. Bar overlooks the sea with attractive terrace and a crêperie/grill restaurant

that also provides takeaway food. Swimming pool with paddling pool, water slides in a separate pool, tennis court and a multi-sport court where it is possible to play 5-a-side football, badminton, volleyball, handball or basketball. Small children's play area. TV room and games room with table tennis and billiards.

Tel: (0)2.98.56.04.06. **Fax:** (0)2.98.56.58.26.
E-mail: info@campingsbretagnesud.com
Reservations: Contact Alan Rogers Travel Service Tel 01892 55 98 98
Open: 4 May - 8 September, with all facilities.

Directions: Site is 7 km. south of Fouesnant. Turn off N165 expressway at Coat Conq, signed Concarneau and Fouesnant. At Fouesnant take A45 signed Beg Meil, then follow signs to Mousterlin. In Mousterlin turn left and follow camping signs.

CAMPSITE NAME Village Le Grand Large	Type of Accommodation Mobile home
Number of Persons	6 persons
Bedrooms	2 bedrooms: 1x double, 1x twin, 1x double sofa bed in living area
Lounge/Dining Area	Fully furnished
Kitchen Area	Fully equipped including microwave, gas hobs and fridge
Bath/Shower/WC	Washbasin, shower, separate WC
Other Facilities	Electric heating, garden table, parasol, BBQ
Bedding	Duvets and pillow provided Sheets and towels available at a supplement
Pets	Accepted
Charges **From** (Low Season, per week) **To** (High Season, per week)	2002 €215 €595

3502 Castel Camping Domaine des Ormes

Epiniac, 35120 Dol-de-Bretagne

This impressive site is in the northern part of Brittany, about 30 kilometres from the old town of St Malo, within the grounds of the Château des Ormes. In an estate of wooded parkland and lakes it has a pleasant atmosphere, busy in high season, almost a holiday village, but peaceful at other times, with a wide range of facilities. A marvellous 'Aqua Park' with pink stone and palms and a variety of pools, toboggans, waterfalls and jacuzzi (free) is set just above the small lake with pedaloes and canoes for hire. A pleasant bar and terrace overlooks the pools and a grass sunbathing area surround them - almost a touch of the Caribbean! The original pools are sheltered by the restaurant building, parts of which are developed from the 600 year old water mill. A particular feature is an 18-hole golf course; also a golf practice range and a beginner's 5-hole course. A new hotel with pool and restaurant is

now part of the complex. A popular site with British visitors, and consequently very busy with much organised entertainment.

Facilities: Shop, bar, restaurant and takeaway. Games room, bar and disco. Two traditional heated swimming pool and Aqua park. Golf. Bicycle hire. Fishing. Riding. Minigolf, two tennis courts, sports ground with volleyball, etc, paintball, archery and a cricket club.

Tel: (0)2.99.73.53.00.
Fax: (0)2. 99.73.53.55.
E-mail: info@lesormes.com
Reservations: Contact site direct, as above.
Open: 15 May - 10 September.

Directions: Access road leads off main D795 about 7 km. South of Dol-de Bretagne,north of Combourg.

Campsite name Domaine des Ormes	Type of Accommodation Mobile home	Type of Accommodation Chalet
Number of Persons	4/6 persons	4/6 persons
Bedrooms	2 bedrooms: 1 x double, 1 x twin, 1 x double sofa bed in living area	2 bedrooms: 1 x double, 1 x twin, 1 x double sofa bed in living area
Lounge/Dining Area	Fully furnished	Fully furnished
Kitchen Area	Fully equipped including gas hobs, microwave, coffee machine and fridge/ freezer	Fully equipped including electric rings, mini oven, coffee machine and fridge/ freezer
Bath/Shower/WC	Washbasin, shower, separate WC	Washbasin, shower, WC
Other Facilities	Electric heating, garden table, parasol, BBQ	Electric heating, garden table, parasol, BBQ
Bedding	Blankets & pillows provided	Blankets and pillows provided Sheets available at a supplement
Pets	Accepted	Accepted
Charges **From** (Low Season, per week) **To** (High Season, per week)	2002 €271 €613	2002 €345 €722

3504 Camping Le P'tit Bois
St Jouan-des-Guérêts, 35430 St Malo

On the outskirts of St Malo, this neat, family oriented site is very popular with British visitors. Behind reception, an attractive, sheltered terraced area around the pools provides a focus for the site, containing a bright snack bar with takeaway food, small bar, TV room and games rooms.

Facilities: Small shop (from 15/5). Bar where entertainment and discos are organised. Snack bar with takeaway, small bar, TV room (large screen for sports events) and games rooms. Swimming pool complex with standard pool, two paddling pools and two water slides (from 15/5). Indoor pool planned for 2002. Children's playground and multi-sports court. Tennis court, minigolf, table tennis, and outdoor chess. Charcoal barbecues are not permitted. Card operated security gates (deposit).
Off site: Fishing 1.5 km, bicycle hire or riding 5 km, golf 7 km.

Tel: (0)2.99.21.14.30. **Fax:** (0)2.99.81.74.14.
E-mail: camping.ptitbois@wanadoo.fr
Reservations: Contact Alan Rogers Travel Service on 01892 55 98 98 ▮
Open: 29 March - 14 September.

Directions: St Jouan is west off the St Malo - Rennes road (N137) just outside St Malo. Site is signed from the N137 (exit St Jouan or Quelmer).

CAMPSITE NAME Le P'tit Bois	Type of Accommodation Residence Mobile 6 places Maxi Grand Confort	Type of Accommodation Residence Mobile 4 places
Number of Persons	6 persons	4 persons
Bedrooms	2 bedrooms: 1 x double, 1 x twin, 1 x double sofa bed in living area	2 bedrooms: 1 x double, 1 x twin
Lounge/Dining Area	Fully furnished	Fully furnished
Kitchen Area	Fully equipped including microwave, gas hobs and fridge	Fully equipped including oven with gas hobs and fridge
Bath/Shower/WC	Washbasin, shower, separate WC	Washbasin, shower, WC
Other Facilities	Electric heating, double glazing, garden table, sun loungers and chairs, parasol, BBQ, vacuum cleaner	Gas heating, garden table, sun loungers, parasol, BBQ, vacuum cleaner
Bedding	Blankets and pillows provided Sheets available at a supplement	Blankets and pillows provided Sheets available at a supplement
Pets	Accepted (only with proof of vaccination) €30 per week	Accepted (only with proof of vaccination) €30 per week
Charges **From** (Low Season, per week) **To** (High Season, per week)	2002 €430 €670	2002 €300 €560

3506 Camping La Touesse
35800 Dinard-St Lunaire

This family campsite was purpose built and has been developed since 1987 by Alain Clement who is keen to welcome more British visitors. Set just back from the coast road, 300 m. from a sandy beach it is in a semi-residential area. It is, nevertheless, an attractive sheltered site with a range of trees and shrubs. The plus factor of this site, besides its proximity to Dinard, is the nearby fine sandy beach which is sheltered – so useful in early season – and safe for children. The owners speak English.

Facilities: Laundry facilities. Shop for basics (1/4 - 15/9). Pleasant bar/restaurant (or clubhouse as it is called) with TV. Volleyball, table tennis and video games for children. Sauna.
Off site: Many amenities near. Bicycle hire 1 km. Fishing 300 m. Riding 500 m. Golf 2 km. Sandy beach 4 minutes walk.

Tel: (0) 2.99.46.61.13. **Fax:** (0) 2.99.16.02.58.
E-mail: camping.la.touesse@wanadoo.fr
Reservations: Contact Alan Rogers Travel Service on 01892 55 98 98
Open: 1 April - 30 September.

Directions: From Dinard take D786 coast road towards St Lunaire; watch for site signs to the left.

CAMPSITE NAME La Touesse	Type of Accommodation Willerby Mobile Home	Type of Accommodation Mobile Home O'Hara	Type of Accommodation Mobile Home Louisiane
Number of Persons	6 persons	4/6 persons	6 persons
Bedrooms	2 bedrooms: 1 x double, 1 x twin, 1 x double sofa bed in living area	2 bedrooms: 1 x double, 1 x twin, 1 x double sofa bed in living area	2 bedrooms: 1 x double, 1 x twin, 1 x double sofa bed
Lounge/Dining Area	Fully furnished	Fully furnished	Fully furnished
Kitchen Area	Fully equipped including gas hobs, coffee machine and fridge	Fully equipped including gas hobs, coffee machine and fridge	Fully equipped including gas hobs, coffee machine and fridge
Bath/Shower/WC	Washbasin, shower, WC	Washbasin, shower, WC	Washbasin, shower, separate WC
Other Facilities	Gas heating, garden table and chairs	Electric heating, double glazing, garden table and chairs, parasol	Electric heating, double glazing, garden table and chairs, parasol
Bedding	Blankets and pillows provided	Blankets and pillows provided	Blankets and pillows provided
Pets	Accepted	Accepted	Accepted
Charges 2001	2001	2001	2001
From (Low Season, per week)	€185	€244	€260
To (High Season, per week)	€485	€505	€520

4401M Camping du Petit Port
21 Bvd. du Petit Port, 44300 Nantes

This modern site, which is within the town limits, in a park-like area with mature trees, is well maintained and of good quality. The tram system within the town is cheap and reliable (tickets available from reception) and the site is easily reached by bus or tram from the railway station. This is a surprisingly peaceful situation for a site within the limits of so large a city, and it makes an ideal base for exploring the area, visiting La Rochelle etc.

Facilities: Launderette. Shop for basics (1/6 -30/8). Children's play area. TV room. Bicycle hire.

Off site: Heated swimming pool (free for campers), ice rink (discount), bowling alley and café very close, bakery 100 m. and English-owned restaurant opposite. Golf course easily accessible via new tramway and site offers an all-inclusive golfing package.

Tel: (0)2.40.74.47.94. **Fax:** (0)2.40.74.23.06.
E-mail: nge@nge-nantes.fr
Reservations: Contact site direct, as above.
Open: all year.

Directions: Site is on northern edge of the town on Bvd. Petit Port, near the university (ring road east). From express road use exit signed for Porte de la Châpelle and follow signs for Petit Port and university. Alternatively follow signs 'Porte de Rennes'.

CAMPSITE NAME Petit Port	Type of Accommodation Willerby – ABI Mobile Home	Type of Accommodation Mobile Home O'Hara
Number of Persons	4 persons	4 persons
Bedrooms	2 bedrooms: 1 x double, 1 x twin	2 bedrooms: 1 x double, 1 x twin
Lounge/Dining Area	Fully furnished	Fully furnished
Kitchen Area	Fully equipped including gas hobs and fridge	Fully equipped including gas hobs and fridge
Bath/Shower/WC	Washbasin, shower, WC	Washbasin, shower, WC
Other Facilities	Electric heating, garden table	Electric heating, some with terrace, garden table
Bedding	Blankets and pillows provided	Blankets and pillows provided
Pets	Not accepted	Not accepted
Charges	2002	2002
From (Low Season, per week)	€182.94	€205.81
To (High Season, per week)	€282.79	€298.80

4409 Castel Camping Château du Deffay
B.P. 18, Sainte Reine, 44160 Pontchâteau

A family managed site, Château de Deffay is a refreshing departure from the usual Castel formula in that it is not over organised or supervised and has no tour operator units. The landscape is natural right down to the molehills, and the site blends well with the rural environment of the estate, lake and farmland which surround it. For these reasons it is enjoyed by many. However, with the temptation of free pedaloes and the fairly deep, unfenced lake, parents should ensure that children are supervised. The facilities are situated within the old courtyard area of the smaller château (that dates from before 1400). The larger château (built 1880) and another lake stand away from this area providing pleasant walking. Some of the chalets overlook the lake and fit well with the environment.

Facilities: Washing machines, and dryer. Extra facilities are in the courtyard area where the well stocked shop, bar, small restaurant with takeaway and solar heated swimming pool and paddling pool are located (all 15/5-15/9). Play area for children. TV in the bar, separate room for table tennis. English language animation in season including children's mini club. Torches useful.
Off site: Golf 5 km. Close to the Brière Regional Park, the Guérande Peninsula, and La Baule with its magnificent beach.

Tel: (0)2.40.88.00.57. **Fax:** (0)2.40.01.66.55.
Reservations: Contact Alan Rogers Travel Service on 01892 55 98 98
Open: 1 May - 21 September.

Directions: Site is signed from D33 Pontchâteau - Herbignac road near Ste. Reine. Also signed from the D773 and N165.

CAMPSITE NAME Chateau du Deffay	Type of Accommodation 2 persons chalet	Type of Accommodation 4 persons Chalet
Number of Persons	2 persons	4 persons
Bedrooms	1 bedroom: 1 x twin	2 bedrooms: 1 x double, 1 x twin
Lounge/Dining Area	Fully furnished	Fully furnished
Kitchen Area	Fully equipped including electric rings, coffee machine, kettle and fridge	Fully equipped including electric rings, coffee machine, kettle and fridge
Bath/Shower/WC	Washbasin, shower, WC	Washbasin, shower, separate WC
Other Facilities	Electric heating, terrace, garden table and chairs, parasol	Electric heating, terrace, garden table and chairs, parasol
Bedding	Blankets and pillows provided Sheets and towels available at a supplement	Blankets and pillows provided Sheets and towels available at a supplement
Pets	Accepted	Accepted
Charges **From** (Low Season, per week) **To** (High Season, per week)	2002 €99 €256.15	2002 €149 €448.20

4410 Camping Caravaning International Le Patisseau
29 Rue du Patisseau, 44210 Pornic

Le Patisseau is rurally situated 2.5 km. from the sea. It is quite a relaxed site, which can be very busy and pretty lively in high season due to its popularity with young families and teenagers. The older part of the site has an attractive woodland setting. A railway line runs along the bottom half of the site with trains two or three times a day, but they do finish at 10.30 pm. and the noise is minimal. The site's restaurant and bar (1/4-30/8) have been rebuilt to overlook a new indoor pool and spa area. This is a happy, busy site and the Morice family work very hard to maintain a friendly atmosphere, but don't expect it to be too neat and tidy with everything run like clockwork - they want people to enjoy themselves. Pornic itself is a delightful fishing village and the coastline is interesting with secluded sandy coves and inlets.

Facilities: Laundry room. Shop (all season). New bar, restaurant and takeaway. Indoor heated pool (with sauna, jacuzzi and spa) and outdoor pools with water slides (1/5-30/8). Children's play area. Volleyball and table tennis. Bicycle hire. **Off site:** Fishing 1.5 km, golf 5 km.

Tel: (0)2.40.82.10.39. **Fax:** (0)2.40.82.22.81. **E-mail:** contact@lepatisseau.com. **Reservations:** Contact Alan Rogers Travel Service on 01892 55 98 98 ☎ **Open:** 1 April - 15 September.

Directions: The site is to the east of D213 road and from the south there is no exit to take you over the D213. It is necessary to go towards the town and pick up campsite signs in the direction of Le Clion-sur-Mer to take you back over the D213.

CAMPSITE NAME Le Patisseau	Type of Accommodation Mobile Home Grand Luxe	Type of Accommodation Chalet	Type of Accommodation Mobile home
Number of Persons	6 persons	6 persons	6 persons
Bedrooms	2 bedrooms: 1 x double, 1 x twin, 1 x double sofa bed in living area	2 bedrooms: 1 x double, 1 x twin, 1 x double sofa bed in living area	2 bedrooms: 1 x double, 1 x twin, 1 x double sofa bed in living area
Lounge/Dining Area	Fully furnished	Fully furnished	Fully furnished
Kitchen Area	Fully equipped including, gas hobs and fridge	Fully equipped including gas hobs and fridge	Fully equipped including gas hobs and fridge
Bath/Shower/WC	Washbasin, shower, separate WC	Washbasin, shower, separate WC	Washbasin, shower, separate WC
Other Facilities	Electric heating, terrace, garden table, parasol, BBQ	Electric heating, covered terrace, garden table, parasol, BBQ	Electric heating, terrace, garden table, parasol, BBQ
Bedding	Blankets and pillows provided	Blankets and pillows provided	Blankets and pillows provided
Pets	Not accepted	Not accepted	Not accepted
Charges **From** (Low Season, per week) **To** (High Season, per week)	2002 €320 €686	2002 €320 €686	2002 €290 €641

Major cities: Caen, Rouen
Départements: 14 Calvados, 27 Eure, 50 Manche, 61 Orme, 76 Seine Maritime

Normandy is a pastoral region – or, in fact, the dairy of France providing rich cream, butter, and fine cheeses such as Camembert and 'Pont l'Evêque'. Contented cows graze the apple orchards – the apples are used in producing cider and the well known 'Calvados', Normandy's apple brandy. Normandy also has a superb coast line including the Cotentin Peninsula, the cliffs of the Côte d'Albâtre and the fine beaches and fashionable resorts of the Côte Fleurie.

The history of Normandy is closely linked with our own as in 1066 the Norman Duke William defeated the Saxon King Harold in the battle of Hastings and was crowned King of England, his exploits well chronicled on the famous Bayeux Tapestry. In more recent times, June 1944, the Allied Forces landed on the Normandy coast. Many museums, exhibitions, sites and monuments, including the Caen Memorial Museum, commemorate operations that took place between 6 June and August of 1944.

Note: the site reports are laid out by département in numerical order not by region.

Cuisine of the region

Andouillette de Vire – small chitterling (tripe) sausage
Barbue au cidre – brill cooked in cider and Calvados
Douillons de pommes à la Normande – baked apples in pastry
Escalope (Vallée d'Auge) – veal sautéed and flamed in Calvados and served with cream and apples
Ficelle Normande – pancake with ham, mushrooms and cheese
Marnite Dieppoisse – fish soup with some or all of the following: sole, turbot, rouget, moules, crevettes, onions, white wine, butter and cream
Poulet (Vallée d'Auge) – chicken cooked in the same way as Escalope Vallée d'Auge
Tripes à la Mode de Caen – stewed beef tripe with onions, carrots, leeks, garlic, cider and Calvados

Wine

Cider usually accompanies a meal
Trou Normand Calvados – a 'dram' drunk in one gulp, between courses; claimed to restore the appetite

Places of interest

Alençon – famous for lace, fine art museum, birthplace of Ste Thérèse
Bagnoles-de-l'Orne – spa resort and casino, guided tours of Arthurian land of Lancelot
Bayeux – home to the famous tapestry; 15th-18th century houses, cathedral, museums
Caen – feudal castle, Museum of Normandy, Museum for Peace
Omaha Beach – D-Day beaches, Landing site monuments commemorating the Allied Forces, American Cemetery
Deauville – internationally famous seaside resort and horse racing centre
Giverny – home of impressionist painter Claude Monet, Monet Museum
Honfleur – picturesque port city with old town and bridge
Lisieux – pilgrimage site, shrine of Ste Thérèse, Basilic and Carmelite convent
Mont St Michel – world famous abbey on island which becomes isolated by incoming tide
Rouen – Joan of Arc Museum; Gothic churches, cathedrals, abbey, clock tower

1407 Camping de la Vallée
Rue de la Vallée, 14510 Houlgate

Camping de la Vallée is an attractive site with good, well maintained facilities. Situated on a grassy hillside overlooking Houlgate. Part of the site is sloping, the rest level, with gravel or tarmac roads. An old farmhouse has been converted to house a new bar and comfortable TV lounge and billiards room. English is spoken in season, when the site can become very busy.

Facilities: Laundry with machines, dryers and ironing boards (no washing lines allowed). Shop (from 1/5). Bar. Small snack bar with takeaway in season (from 15/5). Heated swimming pool (from 15/5; no shorts). Children's playground. Bicycle hire. Volleyball, football field, tennis, petanque. Organised entertainment in Jul/Aug. **Off site:** Beach 1 km, town 900 m. Fishing 1 km. Riding 500 m. Championship golf course 2 km.

Tel: (0)2.31.24.40.69. **Fax:** (0)2.31.28.08.29.
E-mail: camping.lavallee@wanadoo.fr
Open: 1 April - 30 September.
Reservations: Contact site direct as above
Directions: From A13 take exit for Cabourg and follow signs for Dives/Houlgate going straight on at roundabout. Follow road straight on at roundabout, and then four sets of traffic lights. Turn left along seafront. After 1 km. at lights turn right, carry on for about 1 km. and over mini-roundabout – look for site sign and flag poles on right.

CAMPSITE NAME La Vallee	Type of Accommodation Mobile home
Number of Persons	4/6 persons
Bedrooms	2 bedrooms: 1x double, 1x twin, 1x double sofa bed in living area
Lounge/Dining Area	Fully furnished
Kitchen Area	Fully equipped including gas hobs, coffee machine, kettle, fridge, tumble dryer
Bath/Shower/WC	Shower, separate WC
Other Facilities	Electric heating, double glazing, terrace, garden table and chairs, parasol
Bedding	Blankets and pillows provided
Pets	Not accepted
Charges **From** (Low Season, per week) **To** (High Season, per week)	€275 €488

5000 Camping L'Etang des Haizes
La Haye-du-Puits, 50250 St Symphorien-le-Valois

This already appealing and friendly site has added a new swimming pool complex with four lane slides, jacuzzi and a paddling pool. The lake offers good coarse fishing for huge carp (we are told!), pedaloes, a small beach, ducks and, believe it or not, a turtle can sometimes be seen on a fine day! Gate locked 22.00 - 07.00 hrs.

Facilities: Small laundry. Milk, bread and takeaway snacks are available on site. Bar with TV and terrace overlooking the lake and pool complex (all 20/5-10/9).Two children's play areas. Bicycle hire. Table tennis, pool table, petanque and volleyball. Entertainment and activities organised for all ages, including treasure hunts, archery and food tasting.
Off site: La Haye-du-Puits (1 km) has two supermarkets, good restaurants and a market on Wednesdays. Good sandy beach 8 km. Normandy landing beaches 25 km.

Tel: (0)2.33.46.01.16. **Fax:** (0)2.33.47.23.80.
Reservations: Contact site direct, as above.
Open: 1 April - 15 October.

Directions: From Cherbourg follow N13 (Mont St Michel) road as far as Valognes, then the D2 to St Sauveur-le-Vicomte. Continue on the D900 for La Haye-du-Puits, go straight on at new roundabout on the outskirts of town and site is signed almost immediately on the right.

CAMPSITE NAME L'Etang des Haizes	Type of Accommodation Mobile home Anglais	Type of Accommodation Chalet Fabre
Number of Persons	4/6 persons	4/6 persons
Bedrooms	2 bedrooms: 1 x double, 1 x twin, 1 x double sofa bed in living area	2 bedrooms: 1 x double, 1 x twin, 1 x double settee in living area
Lounge/Dining Area	Fully furnished	Fully furnished
Kitchen Area	Fully equipped including gas hobs, kettle and fridge	Fully equipped including microwave, gas hobs, kettle and fridge
Bath/Shower/WC	Washbasin, shower, WC	Washbasin, shower, WC
Other Facilities	Gas heating, picnic table, sun loungers	Electric heating, double glazing, terrace, garden table
Bedding	Blankets and pillows available Sheets available at a supplement	Blankets and pillows provided
Pets	Not accepted	Not accepted
Charges From (Low Season, per week) To (High Season, per week)	2002 3-4 persons: €299 5-6 persons: €329 3-4 persons: €529 5-6 persons: €582	2002 3-4 persons: €299 5-5 persons: €329 3-4 persons: €529 5-6 persons: €582

Vendée ~ Charentes

We have exercised a little license with this area taking one département from the official WESTERN LOIRE region, namely number 85 Vendée, and one from the Poitou-Charentes region, number 17 Charente-Maritime.

The Vendée along with the coastal area stretching down from La Rochelle past Rochefort to Royan, ie. Charente-Maritime, has become well known as a tourist destination. It is popular with British visitors because of its micro climate and marvellous sandy beaches yet within a fairly easy drive from the Normandy or Brittany ferry ports.

The Vendée was the centre of the counter-revolutionary movement between 1793 and 1799 and a two hour 'son et lumiere' extravaganza held at the Chateau Puy-du-Fou from mid June to end of August (Fri and Sat) tells the whole story with the aid of ultra-modern technology. On the Ile de Noirmoutier, mimosa blooms in February, so mild is its climate. Les Sables d'Olonne is its main resort renowned for its excellent sandy beach and it also has a thriving sardine fishing industry.

The area between the Vendée and Charentes, the Marais Poitevin, is one of the most unusual in France - a vast tract of marshland with a thousand or more tree-lined canals and streams where everything is moved by punt, including the animals. Further south the port of La Rochelle, once a Protestant stronghold, with massive medieval towers, buzzes with life. The islands of Ré (toll bridge), a haven for cyclists, and Oléron (free toll bridge 2 miles long) are popular with those seeking beaches and small, quiet ports. Royan is the leading seaside resort at the confluence of the Gironde estuary and the Atlantic ocean and is said to have launched the fashion for sea bathing in the 19th century. La Palmyre, where pine forests planted to stabilise the dunes flank the beaches, is popular with the British .

Note: the site reports are laid out by département in numerical order.

Cuisine of the region

Fish predominates, both fresh water (eel, trout, pike), and sea water (shrimps, mussels etc), and 'huitres' – oysters!

Cagouilles – snails from Charentes
Chaudrée – ragout of fish cooked in white wine, shallots and butter
Chevrettes – local name for crevettes (shrimps)
Mouclade – mussels cooked in wine, egg yolks and cream, served with Pineau des Charentes
Soupe de moules à la Rochelaise – soup of various fish, mussels, saffron, garlic, tomatoes, onions and red wine
Sourdons – cockles from the Charentes

Wine

Light fruity wines from Haut-Poitou, Deux-Sèvres and Charente
Very popular – Cognac and Pineau des Charentes (an aperitif of grape juice and Cognac)

Places of interest

Marais Poitevin – marshes known as the 'Green Venice'
Angoulême – Hill-top town surrounded by ramparts; cathedral, Renaissance château
La Rochelle – port, Porte de la Grosse Horloge (clock gate), Museum of the New World
Le Puy-du-Fou – 15th-16th century castle, sound and light show involving over 700 participants
Les Sables d'Olonne – fishing port and seaside resort
Noirmoutier – linked to the mainland by a 3 mile bridge
Saint Savin – 17th century abbey, mural painting

1701 Camping Bois Soleil
2 Avenue de Suzac, 17110 St Georges-de-Didonne

Close to the sea and the resort of St Georges, Bois Soleil is a fairly large site in three separate parts. The sandy beach here is a wide public one, sheltered from the Atlantic breakers although the sea goes out some way at low tide. Two of the three parts of the site are for tourers, while the third and largest part, 'La Forêt', is mainly for mobile homes (some privately owned) This lively site offers something for everyone, with plenty of activities or as a haven for the quieter life - it is best to book early as it's very popular.

Facilities: Launderette. Nursery for babies. Supermarket, bakery (July/Aug) and beach shop. Upstairs restaurant and bar with terrace, excellent takeaway facility (from April). Little swimming pool for small children. 'Parc des Jeux' with tennis, table tennis, minigolf, bicycle hire, boules and children's playground. TV room and library. Comprehensive tourist information and entertainment office. Charcoal barbecues are not permitted but gas ones can be hired by the evening. Dogs or other animals are not accepted.

Off site: Fishing and riding within 500 m, golf 2 km.

Tel: (0)5.46.05.05.94. **Fax:** (0)5.46.06.27.43.
E-mail: camping.bois.soleil@wanadoo.fr
Reservations: Contact Alan Rogers Travel Service, Tel. 01892 55 98 98
Open: 1 April - 15 November.

Directions: From Royan centre take coast road (D25) along the sea-front of St Georges-de-Didonne towards Meschers. Site is signed at roundabout at end of the main beach.

CAMPSITE NAME Bois Soleil	Type of Accommodation Grand Cottage	Type of Accommodation Cottage de Charme
Number of Persons	6 persons	6 persons
Bedrooms	2 bedrooms: 1 x double, 1 x twin, 1 x double sofa bed in living area	2 bedrooms: 1 x double, 1 x twin, 1 x double sofa bed in living area
Lounge/Dining Area	Fully furnished	Fully furnished
Kitchen Area	Fully equipped including microwave, gas hobs, fridge, coffee machine	Fully equipped including microwave, oven with gas hobs, fridge, coffee machine
Bath/Shower/WC	Shower, separate WC	Shower, separate WC
Other Facilities	Electric heating, double glazing, terrace, garden table, parasol	Electric heating, double glazing, terrace, garden table, parasol
Bedding	Blankets and pillows provided	Blankets and pillows provided
Pets	Not accepted	Not accepted
Charges **From** (Low Season, per week) **To** (High Season, per week)	2002 €180 €580	2002 €300 €830

1702 Airotel Le Puits de l'Auture
La Grande Côte, 17420 St Palais sur Mer

This popular region has a very sunny climate and Le Puits de l'Auture is well situated with the sea outside the gates, just across the road, and a long sandy beach starting 400m. away. As soon as you enter the site there is a feeling that it is well cared for, with an abundance of flower beds at the entrance. Considering its close proximity to the beach and its popularity, there is a remarkably calm and relaxed atmosphere and it is well worth considering.

Facilities: Washing machines and laundry. Well stocked shop, takeaway food and bar (all 10/6-25/9). Three swimming pools with sunbathing

areas which are most attractive with banana plants making a backdrop with a difference. Volleyball, table tennis and games room. Play area. Bicycle hire. Barbecues only allowed in special area.
Off site: Riding and golf 800 m. Several restaurants nearby specialising in sea food.

Tel: (0)5.46.23.20.31. **Fax:** (0)5.46.23.26.38.
E-mail: camping-lauture@wanadoo.fr
Reservations: Contact site direct, as above.
Open: 1 May - 30 September.

Directions: Site is on coast, 2 km. from St Palais and 8 km. from Royan. From Royan take D25 past St Palais following signs for La Palmyre. At two lane junction system turn back left signed Grande Côte and St Palais and site is 800 m.

CAMPSITE NAME Puits De L'Auture	Type of Accommodation Willerby Cottage (Mobile home model 2)	Type of Accommodation Willerby Cottage (Mobile home model 5)	Type of Accommodation Cottage style (Mobile home model 7)
Number of Persons	6 persons	6 persons	7 persons
Bedrooms	2 bedrooms: 1 x double, 1 x triple, 1 x double sofa bed in living area	2 bedrooms: 1 x double, 1 x triple, 1 x single sofa bed in living area	2 bedrooms: 1 x double, 1 x triple, 1 x double bed settee in living area
Lounge/Dining Area	Fully furnished including colour T.V	Fully furnished	Fully furnished
Kitchen Area	Fully equipped including microwave, gas hob, coffee machine, kettle and fridge	Fully equipped including gas hobs, coffee machine and fridge	Fully equipped including gas hobs, coffee machine, kettle and fridge/freezer
Bath/Shower/WC	Washbasin, shower, separate WC	Washbasin, shower, separate WC	Washbasin, shower, separate WC
Other Facilities	Electric heating, terrace with garden table, parasol.	Electric heating, terrace, garden table, parasol	Electric heating, terrace, garden table, parasol
Bedding	Blankets and pillows provided. Sheets available at a supplement	Blankets and pillows provided. Sheets available at a supplement	Blankets and pillows provided. Sheets available at a supplement
Pets	Not accepted	Not accepted	Not accepted
Charges From (Low Season, per week) To (High Season, per week)	€352 €664	€275 €472	€432 €791

1704 Camping International Bonne Anse Plage
17570 La Palmyre

On the edge of the Forêt de la Coubre, just beyond the popular resort of La Palmyre, Bonne Anse has a lovely setting amongst pine trees, just a short stroll from an extensive tidal inlet. It is a spacious, gently undulating site, carefully designed. The site's amenities are centred around the entrance and reception building and include a restaurant and bar with a spacious outdoor terrace. This forms the social focus of the site and overlooks the boules area with the pool complex opposite. With plenty to do for the active, the site is perhaps a little impersonal. English is spoken.

Facilities: Launderette. Shopping centre (all season) includes a supermarket, excellent delicatessen and takeaway, crêperie, shops for bread and pastries, holiday goods and papers, plus visiting traders' stalls (wines, seafood, etc) in high season. Restaurant and bar (20/6-30/8). Splendid, lively swimming pool complex with heated pool (35 x 25 m); three water toboggans and a water slide. Children's playground, large video games room, TV (satellite), minigolf and table tennis. Enclosed area with an all-weather surface for football, volleyball or basketball. Direct access to cycle tracks (bicycle hire available) that avoid the main road. Entertainment in season. Gas barbecues available to hire.

Off site: Fishing or riding 1 km, golf 5 km, plus facilities for watersports and tennis nearby. Supervised, safe beaches close by, also fitness track.

Tel: (0)5.46.22.40.90. **Fax:** (0)5.46.22.42.30.
E-mail: Bonne.Anse@wanadoo.fr.
Reservations: Contact Alan Rogers Travel Service on 01892 55 98 98 ▶
Open: 18 May - 8 September.

Directions: Leave A10 autoroute at Saintes and head for Royan (N150). In Royan take signs for La Palmyre (D25). At La Palmyre roundabout follow signs for Ronce-les-Bains and site is 1km on the left.

CAMPSITE NAME Bonne Anse Plage	Type of Accommodation 6 person Mobile home	Type of Accommodation 4 person Mobile home	Type of Accommodation Cottage
Number of Persons	6 persons	4 persons	6 persons
Bedrooms	2 bedrooms: 1 x double, 1 x twin, 1 x double sofa bed in living area	2 bedrooms: 1 x double, 1 x twin	2 bedrooms: 1 x double, 1 x triple, 1 x single sofa bed
Lounge/Dining Area	Fully furnished	Fully furnished	Fully furnished
Kitchen Area	Fully equipped including gas hobs and fridge	Fully equipped including gas hobs and fridge	Fully equipped including microwave, gas hobs, kettle and fridge/ freezer
Bath/Shower/WC	Washbasin, shower, separate WC	Washbasin, shower, separate WC	Washbasin, shower, separate WC
Other Facilities	Garden table, deckchairs, parasol, BBQ available for hire	Garden table, deckchairs, parasol, BBQ available for hire	Terrace, garden table, deckchairs, parasol, BBQ available for hire
Bedding	Blankets and pillows provided	Blankets and pillows provided	Blankets and pillows provided
Pets	Not accepted	Not accepted	Not accepted
Charges **From** (Low Season, per week) **To** (High Season, per week)	2001 €305 €686	2001 €229 €610	2001 €336 €747

1714 Castel Camping Séquoia Parc
17320 Saint Just-Luzac

Approached by an impressive avenue of flowers, shrubs and trees, Séquoia Parc is a top class site set in the grounds of La Josephtrie, a striking château with beautifully restored outbuildings and a spacious courtyard. The site itself is designed to a high specification with reception in a large, light and airy room retaining its original beams and leading to the courtyard area where you find the shop, bar and restaurant. This is a popular site and reservation is necessary in high season. A 'Yelloh Village' member.

Facilities: Laundry room. Shop. Restaurant/ bar and takeaway. Impressive swimming pool complex with paddling pool. Tennis, volleyball, football field. Games and TV rooms. Bicycle hire. Pony trekking. Organised entertainment in July/ Aug.

Tel: (0)5.46.85.55.55. **Fax:** (0)5.46.85.55.56.
E-mail: sequoia.parc@wanadoo.fr
Reservations: Contact site direct, as above.
Open: 18 May - 9 September.

Directions: Site is 2.5 km. southeast of Marennes. From Rochefort take D733 south for 12 km. Turn west on D123 to Ile d'Oléron. Continue for 12 km. and turn southeast on D728 towards Saintes. Site clearly signed, in 1 km. on the left.

CAMPSITE NAME Sequoia Park	Type of Accommodation Mobile home
Number of Persons	6 persons
Bedrooms	2 bedrooms: 1 x double, 1 x twin, 1 x double sofa bed
Lounge/Dining Area	Fully furnished
Kitchen Area	Fully equipped including gas hobs, coffee machine and fridge
Bath/Shower/WC	Washbasin, shower, WC, (some have separate WCs)
Other Facilities	Terrace, garden table and chairs, deckchair, parasol
Bedding	Blankets and pillows provided
Pets	Accepted
Charges	2001
From (Low Season, per week)	€175
To (High Season, per week)	€651

1718 Camping-Caravaning La Pignade

Avenue des Monards, 17390 Ronce-les-Bains

La Pignade is a Haven Europe owned park set in a pine forest, where the river Suedre meets the Atlantic, on the edge of the seaside resort of Ronce-les-Bains with its sandy beaches. The central area of the park is impressive with its water fountain, neat paved area, well-tended bushes and colourful shrubs. Tall pines also provide shade. The entrance opens up to a large courtyard piazza around which all the main amenities are grouped. In the evening it is particularly alive with the buzz of activity and chatter. The large and brightly decorated bar has plenty of seating inside and outside on the courtyard, similarly at the restaurant. Around the pools are paved areas for sunbathing, backed by tall pines allowing some cooling breezes on hot days. Entertainment is especially good for children of all ages with many organised activities.

Facilities: Shop open daily with wide range of provisions and essential holiday items. Bar. Restaurant serving local specialities, together with reasonably priced set menus. Large heated swimming pool with shallow end for children and water chute with its own splash pool. Large play area. Volleyball, table tennis, minigolf. golf driving net and archery. Children's clubs (PAWs, Tiger and TGO) with organised games.

Tel: (0)5.46.36.25.25. **Fax:** (0)5.46.36.34.14. **Reservations:** Contact site direct or Haven Europe in the UK (quoting this guide as a reference) on 0870 242 7777.
Open: 28 April - 14 September.

Directions: Site is signed 250m. south of the town of Ronce-les-Bains off the D25 La Tremblade road.

CAMPSITE NAME La Pignade	Type of Accommodation Standard Mobile Homes	Type of Accommodation Luxury mobile Homes	Type of Accommodation Chalets/Lodges/Apartments
Number of Persons	4-8 persons	7-8 persons	4-8 persons
Bedrooms	2-3 bedrooms: 2 x double, 1 x twin, 1 x double sofa bed in living area	2-3 bedrooms: 2 x double, 1 x twin, 1 x double sofa bed in living area	1-3 bedrooms: 2 x double, 1 x twin, 1 x double sofa bed in living area
Lounge/Dining Area	Fully furnished	Fully furnished	Fully furnished
Kitchen Area	Fully equipped including full cooker and fridge	Fully equipped including microwave, full cooker and fridge/freezer. Some include dishwasher	Fully equipped including microwave, full cooker and fridge freezer. Some include dishwasher
Bath/Shower/WC	Washbasin, shower, WC	Washbasin, shower, WC	Washbasin, shower, WC
Other Facilities	Gas fire, garden table and chairs, BBQ	Gas fire, garden table and chairs, BBQ	Central heating, garden table and chairs, BBQ
Bedding	Blankets and pillows provided	Blankets and pillows provided	Blankets and pillows provided
Pets	Not accepted	Not accepted	Not accepted
Charges **From** (Low Season, per week) **To** (High Season, per week)	2002 £183- £260 £662- £872	2002 £260 - £330 £886 - £1054	2002 £190 - £393 £669 - £1166
	Haven have a wider range of accommodation than can be featured here. Please phone Haven for details		

8503 Camping La Loubine
1 Route de la Mer, 85340 Olonne-sur-Mer

La Loubine is an attractive, lively family site with friendly atmosphere and good facilities for teenagers. The buildings around a pleasant courtyard overlooking the impressive pool complex have been tastefully converted to provide the bar etc. and it is here that evening entertainment takes place (of the disco/karaoke variety). There is a night security barrier. This is a busy site, popular with families with children and teenagers.

Facilities: Washing machines, dryers, washing lines and irons. Ample supply of laundry sinks. Shop, bar, takeaway and restaurant (all 15/5-15/9). Indoor pool with jacuzzi, sauna and fitness room (free). Outdoor pools (from 1/5; no bermuda style shorts) consisting of two heated outdoor pools with five water slides and children's pool. Large children's play area. Tennis (free in low season). Table tennis, minigolf, badminton. Bicycle hire. Activities and sports organised. Daily club for children in July/Aug.
Off site: Riding 200 m, golf 3 km, fishing 3 km. The beach at Sauveterre is 1.8 km, Les Sables d'Olonne 5 km.

Tel: (0)2.51.33.12.92. **Fax:** (0)2.51.33.12.71.
E-mail: camping.la.loubine@wanadoo.fr
Reservations: Contact site direct, as above.
Open: 1 April - 30 September (full facilities from 15/5).

Directions: Site is west of Olonne beside the D80 road. Turn towards the coast at traffic lights, signed La Forêt d'Olonne and site (75 m).

CAMPSITE NAME La Loubine	Type of Accommodation Mobil-home	Type of Accommodation Chalet Gîtotel	Type of Accommodation Cottage mobil-home
Number of Persons	4/6 persons	4/6 persons	4/6 persons
Bedrooms	2 bedrooms: 1 x double, 1 x twin or bunk bed, 2 x sofa bed in living area	2 bedrooms: 1 x double, 1x twin, 1 x bunk bed	2 bedrooms: 1 x double, 1 x twin or bunk bed, 2 x sofa bed in living area
Lounge/Dining Area	Fully furnished	Fully furnished	Fully furnished
Kitchen Area	Fully equipped including oven and microwave (on request), gas hobs, coffee machine, kettle and fridge/freezer	Fully equipped including oven and microwave (on request), gas hobs, coffee machine, kettle and fridge/freezer,	Fully equipped including oven and microwave (on request), gas hobs, coffee machine, kettle and fridge/freezer
Bath/Shower/WC	Washbasin, shower, separate WC	Washbasin, shower, WC	Washbasin, shower, separate WC
Other Facilities	Electric or gas heating, double glazing, garden table, deckchairs, parasol, BBQ, T.V on request	Electric or gas heating, double glazing, garden table, deckchairs, parasol, BBQ, T.V on request	Electric or gas heating, double glazing, garden table, deckchairs, parasol, BBQ, T.V on request
Bedding	Blankets, pillows and sheets provided	Blankets, pillows and sheets provided	Blankets and pillows provided Sheets available at a supplement
Pets	Not accepted	Not accepted	Not accepted
Charges From (Low Season, per week) To (High Season, per week)	2002 (based on 4 persons) €260 €595	2002 (based on 4 persons) €214 €519	2002 (based on 4 persons) €214 €519

8540 Camping and Caravaning Bois Soleil

85340 Olonne-sur-Mer

This family run site has a very French feel and the majority of the population when we visited seemed to be French. The main buildings house a small reception, as well as the bar and attached shop. There is an excellent new swimming pool complex with sunbathing areas, paddling pool and a separate pool for the two water slides and impressive flume. In July and August a range of daily activities is organised for adults and children.

Facilities: Laundry sinks and washing machines. Shop in July and August only, with 'eat in' or takeaway food service; bread (and cooked chicken) must be ordered the previous

day. Swimming and paddling pools. Sandy children's play area (caged), trampoline and table tennis. **Off site:** beaches are just 2km. The thriving resort of Les Sables d'Olonne is 5km along the coast.

Tel: (0)2.51.33.11.97. **Fax:** (0)2.51.33.14.85. **Reservations:** Contact site direct, as above. **Open:** 1 May- 16 September. **Directions:** Site is off the D80 coast road from Olonne-sur-Mer and is clearly signed on the inland side.

CAMPSITE NAME Bois Soleil	Type of Accommodation Chalet Gîtotel	Type of Accommodation Mobile Home
Number of Persons	4/5 persons	6 persons
Bedrooms	2 bedrooms: 1 x double, 1 x single, 1 x bunk bed	2 bedrooms: 1 x double, 1 x twin, 1 x double sofa bed in living area
Lounge/Dining Area	Fully furnished	Fully furnished some include TV
Kitchen Area	Fully equipped including oven and microwave (on request), gas hobs, coffee machine, kettle and fridge	Fully equipped including oven and microwave (on request), gas hobs, kettle, coffee machine and fridge/freezer
Bath/Shower/WC	Washbasin, shower, WC	Washbasin, shower, WC
Other Facilities	Electric heating, garden table and deckchairs, parasol, BBQ	Electric heating, double glazing, garden table and deckchairs, BBQ
Bedding	Blankets and pillows provided Sheets available at a supplement	Blankets and pillows provided Sheets available at a supplement
Pets	Accepted	Accepted
Charges **From** (Low Season, per week) **To** (High Season, per week)	2002 (based on 4 persons) €214 €473	2002 (based on 4 persons) €244 €533

8504 Castel Camping
La Garangeoire

St Julien-des-Landes, 85150 La Mothe-Achard

La Garangeoire is one of a relatively small number of seriously good sites in the Vendée, situated some 15 km. inland near the village of St Julien des Landes. One of its more memorable qualities is the view of the château through the gates as you drive in. Imaginative use has been made of the old Noirmoutiers 'main road' which passes through the centre of the site and now forms a delightful, quaint thoroughfare, nicknamed the Champs Elysée. Providing a village like atmosphere, it is busy at most times with the facilities opening directly off it. The site is set in the 200 ha.of parkland which surrounds the small château of La Garangeoire. The peaceful fields and woods, where visitors may walk, include three lakes, one of which is used for fishing and boating (life jackets supplied from reception). The site has a spacious, relaxed atmosphere and many use it as a quiet base.

Facilities: Good laundry facilities. Good shop. Full restaurant, takeaway and a separate crêperie, with bars and attractive courtyard terrace overlooking the swimming pool complex with water slides, fountains and a children's pool. Large playing field with play equipment for children's activities, whether organised or not. Games room. Two tennis courts. Bicycle hire. Table tennis, crazy golf, archery and volleyball. Riding in July/Aug. Fishing and boating. **Off site:** Beaches 15 km.

Tel: (0)2.51.46.65.39. **Fax:** (0)2.51.46.69.85. **E-mail:** garangeoire@wanadoo.fr **Reservations:** Contact Alan Rogers Travel Service on 01892 55 98 98 ■ **Open:** 15 May - 15 September.

Directions: Site is signed from St Julien; the entrance is to the north off the D21 road.

CAMPSITE NAME La Garangeoire	Type of Accommodation Mobile home O'Hara	Type of Accommodation Chalet Fabre
Number of Persons	4/6 persons	7 persons
Bedrooms	2 bedrooms: 1 x double, 1 x twin, 1 x bunk bed	2 bedrooms: 1 x double, 1 x bunk bed, 1 x double sofa bed
Lounge/Dining Are	Fully furnished	Fully furnished
Kitchen Area	Fully equipped including oven with gas hobs, coffee machine, kettle, fridge	Fully equipped including oven with electric rings, coffee machine, kettle, fridge
Bath/Shower/WC	Washbasin, shower, separate WC	Washbasin, shower, separate WC
Other Facilities	Electric heating, garden table and chairs, deckchair, parasol, BBQ	Electric heating, covered terrace, garden table and chairs, deckchair, parasol, BBQ
Bedding	Blankets and pillows provided	Blankets and pillows provided Sheets available at supplement
Pets	Accepted	Accepted
Charges From (Low Season, per week) To (High Season, per week)	2002 €260 €610	2002 €275 €640

8507 Camping Les Biches
85270 St Hilaire-de-Riez

Les Biches is a popular, quality site 4 km. from the sea. It is set in a pinewood so nearly everywhere has shade. A very attractive pool complex is near the site entrance, overlooked by the bar and terraces. Various activities such as boules tournaments and sporting events are organised during high season. It is a useful site for families with children and it tends to be busy and active all season.

Facilities: Washing machines and dryers. Shop (all season) with ice service. Large bar (all season). Restaurant and crèperie (1/6-9/9).Takeaway (20/5-16/9). Two heated swimming pools (unsupervised), children's pool, water slide with splash pool, jacuzzi and indoor pool. Tennis courts. Volleyball, table tennis and minigolf. Games room with amusement machines. Large adventure type children's playground. Bicycle hire. Disco. TV room with satellite TV. Internet terminal.
Off site: Private fishing lake 2.5 km, riding 4.5 km. and golf 6 km. Beach 4 km.

Tel: (0)2.51.54.38.82. **Fax:** (0)2.51.54.30.74.
E-mail: campingdesbiches@wanadoo.fr
Reservations: Contact Alan Rogers Travel Service on 01892 55 98 98
Open: 15 May - 15 September.

Directions: Site is about 2 km. north of St Hilaire, close to and well signed from the main D38 road.

CAMPSITE NAME Les Biches	Type of Accommodation 4/6 Person Mobile Home	Type of Accommodation Mobile Home IRM	Type of Accommodation Chalet Gitotel
Number of Persons	4/6 persons	4 persons	4/6 persons
Bedrooms	2 bedrooms: 1 x double, 1 x twin, 1 x double sofa bed in living area	2 bedrooms: 1 x double, 1 x twin	2 bedrooms: 1 x double, 1 x double with 1 x bunk bed
Lounge/Dining Area	Fully furnished	Fully furnished	Fully furnished
Kitchen Area	Fully equipped including microwave, gas hobs, kettle, fridge/freezer	Fully equipped including microwave, gas hobs, kettle and fridge/freezer,	Fully equipped including microwave, gas hobs, coffee machine, kettle and fridge/freezer
Bath/Shower/WC	Washbasin, shower, separate WC	Washbasin, shower, separate WC	Washbasin, shower, separate WC
Other Facilities	Gas heating, double glazing, garden table and chairs, deckchair	Gas heating, double glazing, garden table and chairs, deckchair	Gas heating, double glazing, garden table and chairs, deckchair
Bedding	Blankets and pillows provided Sheets available at a supplement	Blankets and pillows provided Sheets available at a supplement	Blankets and pillows provided Sheets available at a supplement
Pets	Accepted	Accepted	Accepted
Charges **From** (Low Season, per week) **To** (High Season, per week)	2002 €270 €665	2002 €225 €620	2002 €320 €715

8510 Haven Le Bois Dormant
Rue des Sables, 85160 St Jean-de-Monts

Owned by Haven Europe and with a good range of facilities, Le Bois Dormant is on the outskirts of the pleasant, modern resort of St Jean de Monts, 3 km. from the beach. This site can be expected to be very busy for most of the season, with many organised activities for children of all ages.

Facilities: Washing machines and dryers. Small shop. Bar/restaurant, also serves takeaway snacks. Large (200 sq.m.) swimming pool, paddling pool and water slides (no bermuda style shorts). Games room, minigolf, table tennis, multi-sport sports pitch with track and tennis courts.

Off site: All the facilities of the site's larger, busier sister site Le Bois Masson are available to campers here.

Tel: (0)2.51.58.01.30. **Fax:** (0)2.51.59.35.30.
Reservations: Contact site direct or Haven Europe in the UK (quoting this guide as a reference) on 0870 242 7777.
Open: 7 April - 14 September.
(visitors may use the facilities at Le Bois Masson until 28 April when all facilities a Le Bois Dormant open).

Directions: Site is well signed from roundabout at southeast end of the St Jean de Monts bypass (CD38). Follow signs off the roundabout to 'centre ville' and site is about 500 m. on the left.

CAMPSITE NAME Le Bois Dormant	Type of Accommodation Standard Mobile Homes	Type of Accommodation Luxury Mobile Homes	Type of Accommodation Chalets/Lodges/Apartments
Number of Persons	4-8 persons	7-8 persons	4-8 persons
Bedrooms	2-3 bedrooms: 2 x double, 1 x twin, 1x double sofa bed	2-3 bedrooms: 2 x double, 1 x twin, 1 x double sofa bed in living area	1-3 bedrooms: 2 x double, 1 x twin, 1 x double sofa bed in living area
Lounge/Dining Area	Fully furnished	Fully furnished	Fully furnished
Kitchen Area	Fully equipped including full cooker and fridge	Fully equipped including microwave, full cooker and fridge/freezer. Some include dishwasher	Fully equipped including microwave, full cooker, fridge/freezer. Some include dishwasher
Bath/Shower/WC	Washbasin, shower, WC	Washbasin, shower, WC	Washbasin, shower, WC
Other Facilities	Gas fire, garden table and chairs, BBQ	Gas fire, garden table and chairs, BBQ	Central heating, garden table and chairs, BBQ
Bedding	Blankets and pillows provided	Blankets and pillows provided	Blankets and pillows provided
Pets	Not accepted	Not accepted	Not accepted
Charges **From** (Low Season, per week) **To** (High Season, per week)	2002 £183 - £260 £662 - £872 Haven have a wider range of accommodation than can be featured here. Please phone Haven for details	2002 £260 - £330 £886 - £1054	2002 £190 - £ 393 £669 - £1166

8515 Camping La Yole
Chemin des Bosses, Orouet, 85160 St Jean de Monts

La Yole is an attractive, popular and well run site, 1 km. from a sandy beach. The pool complex is surrounded by a paved sunbathing area and overlooked by a new bar and restaurant which have a large terrace. A pleasant walk through pinewoods then by road leads to two sandy beaches. The security barrier is closed at night. A Sites et Paysages member. This is a friendly, popular site with welcoming owners.

Facilities: Laundry with washing machine, dryer and iron. Well stocked shop. Takeaway. Bar (all season) and restaurant (18/5-31/8). Internet point. Swimming pool with water slide, paddling pool and an indoor heated pool with jacuzzi. Children have exceptional space with a play area on sand, large field for ball games, picnics and a club room. Tennis. Table tennis, pool and video games. Organised entertainment in high season. Only gas barbecues are permitted.

Off site: Fishing, golf and watersports 6 km. at St Jean.

Tel: (0)2.51.58.67.17. **Fax:** (0)2.51.59.05.35. **E-mail:** camping-layole@wanadoo.fr
Reservations: Contact site direct, as above.
Open: 8 May - 15 September.

Directions: Signed off the D38, 6 km. south of St Jean de Monts in the village of Orouet.

CAMPSITE NAME La Yole	Type of Accommodation Mobile home, Cottage Willerby
Number of Persons	6 persons
Bedrooms	2 bedrooms: 1 x double, 1 x twin, 1 x double bed settee in living area
Lounge/Dining Area	Fully furnished including Hi Fi
Kitchen Area	Fully equipped including microwave, gas hobs and fridge/freezer
Bath/Shower/WC	Washbasin, shower, separate WC, hairdryer
Other Facilities	Electric heating, double glazing, garden table, 2 x sun lounger, parasol
Bedding	Blankets and pillows provided
Pets	Not accepted
Charges **From** (Low Season, per week) **To** (High Season, per week)	2002 €343,01 €612,85

8517 Camping Caravaning Le Bois Tordu

Route de La Pege, 85270, St Hilaire de Riez

Set in a popular holiday area, with a full range of amenities close to hand, Le Bois Tordu is a small but busy site. Although it is close to a large and inviting beach, 300 m. across the road, the site also has its own swimming pool, paddling pool and splash pool for the water slide.

Facilities: Laundry. Swimming pool. New indoor pool, water slides and jacuzzi for 2002. Children's play area. Covered table tennis table. **Off site:** Beside the front entrance are a supermarket, bar, snack bar, bakery, newsagent, currency exchange and bicycle hire - open all season.

Tel: (0)2.51.54.33.78. **Fax:** (0)2.51.54.08.29. **Reservations:** Contact site direct, as above. **Open:** 1 April - 15 October.

Directions: Driving south on D38 St Jean de Monts - St Gilles road, turn right at L'Oasis hotel/ restaurant in Orouet (6 km. outside St Jean de Monts), signed to Les Mouettes. After 1.5 km. you come to a roundabout. Turn left here signed to St Hilaire de Riez and site is 1.5 km. on the left.

CAMPSITE NAME Bois Tordu	Type of Accommodation Mobile home
Number of Persons	4/6 persons
Bedrooms	2 bedrooms: 1 x double, 1 x twin, 1 x double sofa bed in living area
Lounge/Dining Area	Fully furnished
Kitchen Area	Fully equipped including oven with gas hobs, coffee machine, kettle and fridge
Bath/Shower/WC	Washbasin, shower, separate WC
Other Facilities	Electric heating, double glazing, garden table, deckchair, parasol
Bedding	Blankets and pillows provided Sheets available at a supplement
Pets	Not accepted
Charges From (Low Season, per week) To (High Season, per week)	2001 €259.16 €579.30

8526 Village de La Guyonnière
85150 St Julien-des-Landes

La Guyonnière is a spacious, rural site, away from the hectic coast. It is popular for many reasons, the main ones being the free and easy atmosphere and its reasonable pricing. It is Dutch owned and the majority of its customers are Dutch, but English is spoken and British visitors are made very welcome. The Bar/restaurant facilities are housed in the original farm buildings which have been attractively converted. Entertainment is provided in the bar on high season evenings. A perfect place for families, with large play areas on sand and grass, and paddling pond with shower. Being in the country it is a haven for cyclists and walkers, with many signed routes from the site. A pleasant 500 m. walk takes you to the Jaunay lake where fishing is possible (permits from the village), canoeing (lifejackets from reception) and pedaloes to hire. There are no tour operators and, needless to say, no road noise.

Facilities: Laundry sinks. Small shop (1/5 - 30/9) order bread from reception outside these dates). Bar with TV and pool table and pleasant restaurant (1/5 - 30/9). Pizzeria with takeaway. Small swimming pool, new heated pool with jacuzzi and slide, very attractive and can be covered in cool weather. Paddling pool. Children's play areas, sand pit. Table tennis, volleyball and football fields. Bicycle hire. **Off site:** Riding 3 km, golf 8 km, beaches 10 km.

Tel: (0)2.51.46.62.59. **Fax:** (0)2.51.46.62.89. **E-mail:** pierre.jaspers@wanadoo.fr
Reservations: Contact site direct, as above.
Open: 1 May- 30 October.

Directions: Site is off the D12 road (La Mothe Achard - St Gilles Croix de Vie), approx. 4 km. west of St Julien-des-Landes. It is signed about 1 km. from the main road.

CAMPSITE NAME La Guyonniere	Type of Accommodation Mobile home
Number of Persons	6 persons
Bedrooms	2 bedrooms: 1 x double, 1 x twin, 1 x double sofa bed in living area
Lounge/Dining Area	Fully furnished
Kitchen Area	Fully equipped including gas hobs, coffee machine and fridge
Bath/Shower/WC	Washbasin, shower, separate WC
Other Facilities	Electric heating, double glazing, terrace, garden table, parasol
Bedding	Blankets and pillows provided. Sheets available at a supplement
Pets	Not accepted
Charges **From** (Low Season, per week) **To** (High Season, per week)	2001 €205,80 €472, 59

N8533 Camping Naturiste Cap Natur'

151 Avenue de la Faye, 85270 St Hilaire de Riez

Situated on the northern outskirts of the busy resort of St Hilaire-de-Riez, and only about 1 kilometre from the nearest beach (6 km. from the nearest official naturist beach beside Plage des 60 Bornes) This family campsite for naturists is in an area of undulating sand dunes and pine trees. The modern facilities are excellent and include both open air and indoor pools, and a jacuzzi. Around the pool is an ample paved sunbathing area, including a stepped 'solarium'. The whole of the indoor complex is a designated non-smoking area. In season a regular Saturday evening 'soirée' is held with a set Vendéen meal, wine and entertainment. There is an air of peace and quiet about this site which contrasts with the somewhat frenzied activity which pervades many of the resorts in this popular tourist area, with a friendly, warm welcome from the family that own it. Member France4 Naturisme.

Facilities: Small shop and restaurant (menu includes some local specialities), good sized bar, with TV, pool tables and various indoor table games. Indoor and outdoor swimming pools. Children's play area on soft sand. Volleyball and archery. Torches useful.

Tel: (0)2.51.60.11.66 **Fax:** (0)2.51.60.17.48
E-mail: info@cap-natur.com
Reservations: Contact Alan Rogers Travel Service on 01892 55 98 98
Open: 24 March - 3 November (possibly 11th depending on French holidays).

Directions: Site is on the north side of St Hilaire-de-Riez. From Le Pissot roundabout go south on the D38, follow signs for St Hilaire at first roundabout you come to (first exit off roundabout), then at second roundabout (garage) turn right signed 'Terre Fort'. At third Y-shaped junction turn right again signed 'Parée Prèneau' (also site sign here). The site is 2 km along this road on the left.

CAMPSITE NAME Cap Natur' (Naturist)	Type of Accommodation Mobile Home	Type of Accommodation Residenes
Number of Persons	4/5 persons	6 persons
Bedrooms	2 bedrooms: 1 x double, 1 x twin, 1 x double sofa bed in living area	2 bedrooms: 1 x double, 1 x twin or 1 x bunk bed, 1 x double sofa bed
Lounge/Dining Area	Fully furnished	Fully furnished
Kitchen Area	Fully equipped including gas hobs and fridge	Fully equipped including microwave, electric rings, coffee machine and fridge
Bath/Shower/WC	Washbasin, shower, separate WC	Washbasin, shower, separate WC
Other Facilities	Double glazing, garden table and chairs, parasol, BBQ	Terrace, garden table and chairs, deckchair, parasol, BBQ
Bedding	Blankets and pillows provided Sheets available at a supplement	Blankets and pillows provided
Pets	Accepted	Accepted
Charges From (Low Season, per week) To (High Season, per week)	2002 ¤ 329 ¤ 630	2002 From ¤ 304.5 to ¤ 399.7 From ¤ 530 to ¤ 672

Loire Valley

We have taken the liberty of enlarging the official Loire Valley region to make a more easily identifiable tourist region which the British understand. The area includes all the Loire Valley.

Loire Valley
Major cities: Orleans, Tours.
Departements: 18 Cher, 28 Eure-et-Loir, 36 Indre, 37 Indre-et-Loire, 41 Loir-et-Cher, 45 Loiret

Western Loire
From this offical region we include the following départements:
49 Maine-et-Loire, 53 Mayenne, 72 Sarthe.

Poitou-Charentes
From this offical region we include the following départements:
79 Deux Sevres, 86 Vienne.

For centuries the Loire Valley was frequented by French royalty and the great River Loire winds its way past some of France's most magnificent châteaux. Known as the Garden of France, it is a most productive and lush area with large farms and a mild climate making it a favourite with visitors. Well known for its wines, over 100 different ones are produced from vineyards stretching along the 1,000 km (620 mile) course of the River Loire. Imposing abbeys, troglodyte caves, tiny Romanesque churches, woodlands such as the Sologne and sleepy, picturesque villages reward exploration. Cities like Blois and Tours are elegant with fine architecture and museums and Paris is only one hour by the TGV. Today Poitiers is home to Futuroscope, the 'museum of the moving image'. Note: Reports are laid out by département in numerical order not by region.

Cuisine of the region
Wild duck, pheasant, hare, deer, and quail are classics and fresh water fish such as salmon, perch and trout are favourite. A tasty 'beurre blanc' is the usual sauce with fish.
This is the home of Tarte Tatin – upside down tart of caramelised apples and pastry
Tarte a la citrouille – pumpkin tart
Bourdaines – apples stuffed with jam and baked
Such specialties as rillettes, andouillettes, tripes, mushrooms and the regional cheeses of Trappiste d' Entrammes and Cremet d' Angers, Petit Sable and Ardoises d'Angers cookies.

Places of interest
Amboise – château by the river, Clos Lucé and Leonardo da Vinci museum with scale models of his inventions
Azay-le-Rideau – Renaissance château
Beauregard – château near Chambord, famous for its Delft tiled floors and timbered ceilings
Blois – château with architecture from Middle Ages to Neo-Classical periods
Chambord – Renaissance château, park and terraces, grandiose creation of François I
Chartres – cathedral with famous stained glass windows
Chaumont-sur-Loire – annual International Garden Festival with about 30 themed landscape gardens.
Chenonçeau – château with great gallery and bridge
Cheverny – delightful privately owned château
Chinon – old town, Pavillon de l'Horloge, Joan of Arc museum
Langeais – château and tapestry collection
Loches – old town, château and its fortifications
Orléans – Holy Cross cathedral, house of Joan of Arc
Tours – Renaissance and Neo-Classical mansions, cathedral of St Gatien, museums of archeology and modern art
Vendôme – Tour St Martin, La Trinité
Villandry – famous renaissance gardens

4102 Castel Camping Château de la Grenouillère

41500 Suevres

Château de la Grenouillère is a comfortable site with good amenities on the N152 midway between Orléans and Tours. It is well situated for visiting many of the Loire châteaux and there are enough attractions on site and locally to make it suitable for a longer stay holiday. It is set in a 28-acre park with wooded areas, orchards and meadows.

Facilities: Washing machines and dryers in a small laundry. Shop. Bar. Pizza takeaway. Restaurant. Swimming pool complex of four outdoor pools and a water slide. A covered, heated pool is planned for 2002. Tennis, squash, table tennis, pool, baby foot and video games. Internet point. Bicycle and canoe hire (July/Aug). Guided tours organised once a week.

Tel: (0)2.54.87.80.37. **Fax:** (0)2.54.87.84.21.
E-mail: la.grenouillere@wanadoo.fr
Reservations: Contact site direct, as above.
Open: 15 May - 10 September.

Directions: Site is between Suevres and Mer on north side of N152 and is well signed.

CAMPSITE NAME Chateau la Grenouillere	Type of Accommodation Chalets Gitotel
Number of Persons	5 persons
Bedrooms	2 bedrooms: 2 x double, 1 x bunk bed
Lounge/Dining Area	Fully furnished
Kitchen Area	Fully equipped including microwave, gas hobs, coffee machine and fridge
Bath/Shower/WC	Washbasin, shower, separate WC
Other Facilities	Electric heating, terrace, garden table and chairs, BBQ
Bedding	Blankets, pillows and sheets provided
Pets	Not accepted
Charges From (Low Season, per week) To (High Season, per week)	2002 €270 €700

4103 Sologne Parc des Alicourts
Domaine des Alicourts, 41300 Pierrefitte sur Sauldre

A secluded holiday village set in the heart of the forest and with many sporting facilities, Parc des Alicourts is midway between Orléans and Bourges, to the east of the A71. All facilities are open all season and the leisure amenities are exceptional. Competitions are organised for adults as well as children and, in high season organised activities include a club for children with an entertainer twice a day, a disco once a week and a dance for adults. An inviting water complex (all season) includes two swimming pools, a pool with wave machine and beach area, three water slides and a spa.

Facilities: Washing machines and dryers. Shop with good range of produce in addition to the basics (the nearest good-sized town is some distance). Restaurant with traditional cuisine at reasonable prices, plus a takeaway service in a pleasant bar with terrace. Water complex. 7 hectare lake with fishing, bathing, canoes, pedaloes and children's play area. Five hole golf course (very popular). Football pitch, volleyball, tennis, minigolf, table tennis, boules. Roller skating/skateboard area (bring your own equipment). Bicycle hire with cyclo-cross and mountain bikes and a way-marked path for walking and cycling.

Tel: (0)2.54.88.63.34. **Fax:** (0)2.54.88.58.40.
E-mail: parcdesalicourts@wanadoo.fr
Reservations: Contact Alan Rogers Travel Service on 01892 55 98 98
Open: 18 May - 10 September.

Directions: From A71, take the Lamotte Beuvron exit (no 3) or from N20 Orléons to Vierzon (which runs parallel with the A71) turn left on to D923 towards Aubigny. After 14 km, turn right at camping sign on to D24E. Site is clearly marked from there in about 4 km.

CAMPSITE NAME Sologne Parc des Alicourts	Type of Accommodation Mobile Home Ophea	Type of Accommodation 6 persons Chalet Gitotel	Type of Accommodation 4 persons Chalet Gitotel
Number of Persons	5 persons	6 persons	4 persons
Bedrooms	2 bedrooms: 1 x double, 3 bunk beds	3 bedrooms: 1 x double, 2 x bunk beds	2 bedrooms: 1 x double, 1 x twin
Lounge/Dining Area	Fully furnished	Fully furnished	Fully furnished
Kitchen Area	Fully equipped including microwave, gas hobs and fridge	Fully equipped including microwave, electric rings and fridge	Fully equipped including microwave, electric rings and fridge
Bath/Shower/WC	Washbasin, shower, separate WC	Washbasin, shower, separate WC	Washbasin, shower, separate WC
Other Facilities	Gas heating, garden table, deckchair, parasol	Electric heating, garden table, deckchair	Electric heating, garden table, deckchair
Bedding	Blankets, pillows and sheets provided	Blankets, pillows and sheets provided	Blankets, pillows and sheets provided
Pets	Not accepted	Not accepted	Not accepted
Charges **From** (Low Season, per week) **To** (High Season, per week)	2002 €384 €735	2002 €426 €770	2002 €342 €658

4908 Camping l'Ile d'Offard
Rue de Verden, 49400 Saumur

Perched on an island between the banks of the Loire and just 2 km. from the centre of Saumur, this site is a popular base from which to visit the numerous châteaux in the region. As the site only closes from mid December until mid January, it is ideal for winter travellers. The adjacent municipal swimming pools and mini golf (open in July and August) are free for visitors.

Facilities: Well equipped laundry. Snack bar and takeaway, restaurant and bar (end April - early Sept). Table tennis, volleyball. Children's play area. Entertainment in July/Aug. with kid's club, themed meals, wine tastings, canoeing. **Off site:** Riding 5 km. Fishing in the Loire. Thursday market 500 m, Saturday morning market 2 km.

Tel: (0)2.41.40.30.00. **Fax:** (0)2.41.67.37.81. **E-mail:** iledoffard@wanadoo.fr

Reservations: Contact Alan Rogers Travel Service on 01892 55 98 98
Open: 15 January - 15 December.

Directions: From all directions follow the unnamed camping signs in the centre of Saumur.

CAMPSITE NAME Ile d'Offard	Type of Accommodation Mobile home IRM	Type of Accommodation Mobile home Louisiane
Number of Persons	6 persons	6 persons
Bedrooms	2 bedrooms: 1 x double, 1 x twin or 1 x bunk bed, 1x double sofa bed in living area	2 bedrooms: 1 x double, 1 x twin, 1 x double sofa bed in living area
Lounge/Dining Area	Fully furnished	Fully furnished
Kitchen Area	Fully equipped including gas hobs, coffee machine and fridge	Fully equipped including microwave, gas hobs, coffee machine and fridge
Bath/Shower/W	Washbasin, shower, WC	Washbasin, shower, separate WC
Other Facilities	Electric heating, garden table and chairs, deckchair, parasol	Electric heating, garden table and chairs, deckchair, parasol
Bedding	Blankets and pillows provided. Sheets and towels available at a supplement	Blankets and pillows provided. Sheets and towels available at a supplement
Pets	Accepted	Accepted
Charges From (Low Season, per week) To (High Season, per week)	2002 €267 €476	2002 €294 €581

Major city: Dijon
Départements: 21 Côte d'Or, 58 Nièvre, 71 Saône-et-Loire, 89 Yonne

Burgundy (Bourgogne), in the rich heartland of France, is an historic region, once a powerful independent state and important religious centre. Its golden age is reflected in the area's magnificent art and architecture – the grand palaces and art collections of Dijon, the great pilgrimage church of Vézelay, the Cistercian Abbaye de Fontenay and the evocative abbey remains at Cluny, once the most powerful monastery in Europe.

However Burgundy is best known for its wine including some of the world's finest, produced from the great vineyards of the Côte d'Or and Chablis, and perhaps for its rich cuisine including such dishes as 'Boeuf Bourguignon'.

No-one can visit Burgundy without going to the 15th century Hotel Dieu at Beaune. It is both an attractive home for the elderly and where the annual Burgundy wine auctions are held. Once inside, take the conducted tour and you will see the wonderful patterned tile roofs and even the old hospital wards where patients were laid two to a bed.

The area is criss-crossed by navigable waterways and also includes the 'Parc Régional du Morvan' good walking country. It is interesting to note that Dijon itself is only an hour and a half from Paris on the TGV.

Note: the site reports are laid out by département in numerical order.

Cuisine of the region

Many dishes are wine based, eg. 'Coq au Chambertin' and 'Poulet au Meursault'
Dijon is known for its spiced honey-cake (pain d'épice) and spicy mustard
Boeuf Bourguignon – braised beef simmered in a red wine-based sauce
Charolais (Pièce de) – steak from the excellent Charolais cattle
Garbure – heavy soup, a mixture of pork, cabbage, beans and sausages
Gougère – cheese pastry based on Gruyère
Jambon persillé – parsley-flavoured ham, served cold in jelly
Matelote – fresh-water fish soup, usually based on a red wine sauce
Meurette – red wine-based sauce with small onions, used with fish or poached egg dishes

Wine

Burgundy is produced mainly from vineyards in the sheltered valleys that stretch south from Dijon to Lyon. The region is further subdivided into five main areas (north to south): Chablis, Côte d'Or, Côte Chalonnaise, Mâconais and Beaujolais. It is the Côte d'Or region centred around Beaune that produces the great wines on which Burgundy's reputation depends

Places of interest

Autun – 12th century St Lazare cathedral.
Beaune – medieval town; its Hospices are a masterpiece of Flemish-Burgundian architecture; Museum of Burgundy Wine
Cluny – Europe's largest Benedictine abbey
Dijon – Palace of the Dukes, Fine Arts Museum, Burgundian Folklore Museum. Unfortunately development has ruined much of the original medieval city centre
Fontenay – Fontenay Abbey and Cloister
Joigny – medieval town
Mâcon – Maison des Vins (wine centre)
Paray-le-Monial – Romanesque basilica, pilgrimage centre
Sens – historic buildings, museum with fine Gallo-Roman collections
Vézelay – fortified medieval hillside, Magdalene Basilica

2100 Camping Lac de Panthier
21320 Vandenesse en Auxois

An attractively situated lakeside site in Bungundy countryside, Camping Lac de Panthier is in fact two distinct campsites – one where the site activities take place and the other where the reception and other facilities can be found. The site has a swimming pool complex but the most obvious attraction is its proximity to the lake with its many watersports facilities. This site is in beautiful countryside within 2 km. of the lovely Canal de Bourgogne, which links the Seine and the Saône rivers.

Facilities: Shop, bar and restaurant (all 15/5-22/9). Swimming pool complex with adults' pool, children's pool and water-slide (15/5-15/9). Watersports.
Off site: Boat excursions from Pouilly en Auxois (8 km). Dijon, Autun and Beaune are also within easy reach.

Tel: (0)3.80.49.21.94. **Fax:** (0)3.80.49.25.80.
E-mail: info@lac-de-panthier.com

Reservations: Contact site direct as above.
Open: 20 April - 29 September.

Directions: From the A6 use exit 24 (where the A6 joins the A38). Take the N81 towards Arnay Le Duc (back over the A6), then almost immediately turn left on D977 for 5 km. Fork left again for Vandenesse en Auxois. Continue through village on D977 for 2.5 km, turn left again and site is on left.

CAMPSITE NAME Lac de Panthier	Type of Accommodation Mobile Home	Type of Accommodation Chalet Gitotel
Number of Persons	6 persons	5 persons
Bedrooms	2 bedrooms: 1 x double, 1 x twin, 1 x sofa bed in living area	2 bedrooms: 1 x double, 1 x twin, 1 x sofa bed in living area
Lounge/Dining Area	Fully furnished	Fully furnished
Kitchen Area	Fully equipped including gas hobs, coffee machine and fridge	Fully equipped including microwave, gas hobs, coffee machine and fridge
Bath/Shower/WC	Washbasin, shower, WC	Washbasin, shower, separate WC
Other Facilities	Gas/electric heating, terrace, parasol	Gas/electric heating, terrace, parasol
Bedding	Blankets and pillows provided Sheets and towels available at a supplement	Blankets and pillows provided Sheets available at a supplement
Pets	Accepted	Accepted
Charges **From** (Low Season, per week) **To** (High Season, per week)	€175 €531	€195 €559

For latest infomation visit **www.alanrogers.com**

7102M Le Village des Meuniers
71520 Dompierre-les-Ormes

In a tranquil setting with panoramic views, the neat appearance of the reception building sets the tone for the rest of this attractive site. It is an excellent example of current trends in French tourism development. The site enjoys stunning views of the surrounding countryside – the Beaujolais, the Maconnais, the Charollais and the Clunysois. An extensive sunbathing area surrounds the attractively designed swimming pool complex. This is a superior municipal site, tastefully landscaped, with a high standard of cleanliness in all areas. As the hedges and

trees mature they will offer more shade. This is an area well worth visiting, with attractive scenery, interesting history, excellent wines and good food.

Facilities: Café, bar, shop and takeaway. Swimming pool complex with three heated pools and toboggan run (from 1/6). Children's activities organised in high season.
Off site: Fishing 1.5 km, riding 10 km. Village 500m. offers all services (banks and some shops, closed Sun/Mon).

Tel: (0)3.85.50.36.60.
Fax: (0)3.85.50.36.61.
E-mail: levillagedesmeuniers@wanadoo.fr
Reservations: Contact Alan Rogers Travel Service on 01892 55 98 98
Open: 15 May - 15 September.

Directions: Town is 35 km. west of Macon. Follow N79/E62 (Charolles/Paray/Digoin) road and turn south onto D41 to Dompierre-les-Ormes (3 km). Site is clearly signed through village.

CAMPSITE NAME Le Village des Meuniers	Type of Accommodation Chalet
Number of Persons	6/8 persons
Bedrooms	3 bedrooms: 1 x double, 2 x twin, 1 x double sofa bed or 2 x double, 1 x twin, 1 x double sofa bed
Lounge/Dining Area	Fully furnished
Kitchen Area	Fully equipped including microwave, electric rings, coffee maker and fridge
Bath/Shower/WC	Washbasin, shower, separate WC
Other Facilities	TV, electric heating, double glazing, garden table and chairs, BBQ
Bedding	Blankets and pillows provided Sheets and towels provided
Pets	Accepted
Charges **From** (Low Season, per week) **To** (High Season, per week)	2002 €290 €450

Franche Comté

Major city: Besançon
Départements: 25 Doubs, 39 Jura, 70 Haute-Saône, 90 Tre. de Belfort

Geographically Franche-Comté is really two regions. The high valley of the Saône is wide, gently rolling country with a certain rustic simplicity, while the Jura mountains are more rugged with dense forests, sheer cliffs, deep gorges and torrents of water. In winter this means cross-country skiing over 2,000 km of marked trails and, in the summer, rafting along the gentle Lison and Loue rivers or the more challenging Saône or Doubs. Nature lovers can climb, bike and hike in the mountains or explore the hills honeycombed with over 4,000 caves. The streams and lakes provide world-class fishing. The spa towns of Salins les Bains and Besançon offer relaxation and a chance to 'take the waters'. The Region's position, bordering Switzerland and close to Germany, is reflected in its culture and the great diversity of architectural style in the many fine buildings.

Cuisine of the region

Freshwater fish such as trout, grayling, pike and perch are local specialities
Brési – wafer-thin slices of dried beef; many local hams
Jésus de Morteau – fat pork sausage smoked over pine and juniper
Poulet au vin jaune – chicken, cream and 'morilles' (chestnuts) cooked in 'vin jaune'
Gougère – hot cheese pastry based on the local 'Comté' cheese

Wine

The region has a rare wine known as 'vin de paille' as well as vin jaune (deep yellow and very dry) and vin du jura, Jura wine
Pontarlier – aniseed liqueur
Kirsh – cherry flavoured liqueur

Places of interest

Arbois – Pasteur Family Home and Museum, Museum of Wine and Wine Growing
Belfort – sandstone lion sculpted by Bartholdi; castle and Vauban fortifications; Memorial and Museum of the French Resistance
Besançon – citadel with good views over the city; cathedral is a mixture of influences ranging from a Roman altar to a 19th century astronomic clock
Champlitte – Museum of Folk Art and Franche Comté Traditions
Dole – lovely old town, Louis Pasteur's birthplace
Gray – Baron Martin Museum
Luxeuil-les-Bains – Tour des Echevins Museum and Abbey
Morez – Eyeglass Museum
Morteau – Watch Museum
Morains-en-Montagne – the House of Toys
Ornans – Gustave Courbet birthplace and museum
Ronchamp – Chapel of Notre-Dame du Haut de Ronchamp designed by Le Corbusier
Saline – Royale d'Arc et Senans Royal Salt Works
Salins-les-Bains – Salt mines and tunnels
Sochaux – Peugeot Museum

3904 Camping La Pergola
Lac de Chalain, 39130 Marigny

Close to the Swiss border and overlooking the sparkling waters of Lac de Chalain, La Pergola is a neat, tidy and terraced site set amongst the rolling hills of the Jura. It awaits discovery as it is not on the main tourist routes. A tall fence protects the site from the public footpath that separates the site from the lakeside but there are frequent access gates. The entrance is very attractive and the work that Mme. Gicquaire puts into the preparation of the flower-beds is very evident. The bar/restaurant terrace is beautiful, featuring grape vines for welcome shade and a colourful array of spectacular flowers leading on to a landscaped waterfall area next to the three swimming pools and entertainment area. English is spoken.

Facilities: Washing machines and dryers. Bar. Restaurant. Pool complex, two pools heated.

Good children's play area and children's club. Table tennis and volleyball. Water sports include windsurfing, pedaloes and small boats for hire. Organised programme in high season includes cycle tours, keep fit sessions and evening entertainment with disco twice weekly. **Off site:** Riding 3 km.

Tel: (0)3.84.25.70.03. **Fax:** (0)3.84.25.75.96. **E-mail:** contact@lapergola.com. **Reservations:** Contact Alan Rogers Travel service on 01892 55 98 98 **Open:** 13 May - 16 September.

Directions: Site is 2.5 km. north of Doucier on Lake Chalain road D27.

CAMPSITE NAME La Pergola	Type of Accommodation Mobile Home
Number of Persons	6/7 persons
Bedrooms	2 bedrooms: 1 x double, 1x twin, 1 x single sofa bed, 1 x double sofa bed
Lounge/Dining Area	Fully furnished
Kitchen Area	Fully equipped including microwave, gas hobs, coffee machine, fridge/freezer and dishwasher
Bath/Shower/WC	Washbasin, shower, separate WC
Other Facilities	Electric and gas heating, double glazing, wood terrace, garden table and chairs, parasol, BBQ
Bedding	Blankets, pillows and sheets provided
Pets	Accepted
Charges **From** (Low Season, per week) **To** (High Season, per week)	2002 €297 €629

2503 Camping du Bois de Reveuge
25680 Huanne-Montmartin

Bois de Reveuge was opened in 1992, but it still has a new look about it, in as much as there is little shade yet from the young trees. Being on a hillside, the site is terraced with good views across the surrounding countryside and leading down to two lakes which may be used for fishing and canoeing. The site also has private use of a 10 hectare lake set in a park 10 km. away where there is a watersports school and boating opportunities. Tall trees have been left standing at the top of the hill where the site's own mobile homes are located. The enthusiastic owner has installed a good solar heated swimming pool (15/5-15/9) which can be covered in cool weather and another pool with four water slides. Several supervisors are in attendance during the summer who, as well as acting as a lifeguards, sometimes offer swimming lessons.

Facilities: Kiosk for basic food supplies and restaurant with terrace (both 1/6-3/9). Swimming pools (20/4-15/9). Three children's play areas. High season 'baby club' with a large tent for wet weather, large video screen and some music and other entertainment for adults. Groups may request activities such as orienteering. A package deal includes use of canoes as well as archery, fishing, bicycle hire and pedaloes.

Tel: (0)3.81.84.38.60 (winter (0)3.81.84.12.42). **Fax:** (0)3.81.84.44.04.
Reservations: Contact Alan Rogers Travel Service Tel. 01892 55 98 98
Open: 20 April - 20 September.

Directions: Site is well signed from the D50. From A36 autoroute south of the site, take exit for Baume-les-Dames and head north on D50 towards Villersexel for about 7 km. to camp signs

CAMPSITE NAME Le Bois de Reveuge	Type of Accommodation Chalet Gitotel	Type of Accommodation Mobile Home
Number of Persons	5 persons	5 persons
Bedrooms	2 bedrooms: 1 x double, 1 x single, 1 x double sofa bed in living area	2 bedrooms: 1 x double, 1 x single, 1 x double sofa bed in living area
Lounge/Dining Area	Fully furnished	Fully furnished
Kitchen Area	Fully equipped including gas hobs and fridge	Fully equipped including gas hobs and fridge
Bath/Shower/WC	Washbasin, shower, separate WC	Washbasin, shower, separate WC
Other Facilities	Electric heating, double glazing, garden table and chairs, BBQ	Gas/electric heating, garden table and chairs, BBQ
Bedding	Blankets and pillows provided	Blankets and pillows provided
Pets	Not accepted	Not accepted
Charges **From** (Low Season, per week) **To** (High Season, per week)	2002 €255 €639	2002 €224 €569

Major city: Grenoble
Départements: 38 Isère, 73 Savoie, 74 Haute-Savoie

L ying between the Rhône Valley and the Alpine borders with Switzerland and Italy are the old provinces of Savoie and Dauphine. This is an area of enormous granite outcrops, deeply riven by spectacular glacier hewn and river etched valleys. It has become one of the world's leading wintersport playgrounds and in the summer provides a range of outdoor activities. From Chambéry, north to the shores of Lac Léman (Lake Geneva) are many towns and villages that, since Roman times, attracted visitors to take the waters. Aix-les-Bains, Evian and Annecy were three major lakeside spa resorts of the Victorians; while Chamonix, under Mont Blanc, and Grenoble, capital of Dauphine, attracted the more active (often British) 19th century travellers who pioneered modern ski-ing and 'alpinism'. Today's modern ski resorts are Tignes, Val d'Isère, Megeve and Courchevel, whilst Grenoble is a bustling town with academic eminence in high technology and industry. To the north is the region of Chartreuse famous for its monastery, and liqueur! Italy and Switzerland are within easy reach for day excursions.

Cuisine of the region
'Plat gratine' applies to a wide varity of dishes; in the Alps this means cooked in breadcrumbs; gratins of all sorts show how well milk, cream and cheese combine together.
Farcement (Farçon Savoyard) – potatoes baked with cream, eggs, bacon, dried pears and prunes; a hearty stomach filler
Féra – a freshwater lake fish
Fondue – hot melted cheese and white wine; a classic of the region
Gratin Dauphinois – a classic potato dish with cream, cheese and garlic
Gratin Savoyard – another classic potato dish with cheese and butter
Lavaret – a freshwater lake fish, like salmon
Longeole – a country sausage
Lotte – a burbot, not unlike an eel
Omble chevalier – a char, it looks like a large salmon trout
Tartiflette – potato, bacon, onions and Reblochon cheese

Places of interest
Aix-les-Bains – spa resort on the Lac du Bourget, boat excursions to the Royal Abbey of Hautecombe
Albertville – 1992 Winter Olympics, museum, now has an active night-life!
Annecy – canal-filled lakeside town, 12th century château, old quarter
Bourg-St-Maurice – centre of Savoie café society
Chambéry – old quarter, Dukes of Savoie château, Savoie museum.
Chamonix – site of first Winter Olympics in 1924; world capital of mountain climbing; Mont Blanc tunnel, 11.6 km. long (for many years the longest tunnel in the world – closed at present after a disastrous fire)
Evian-les-Bains – spa and casino on Lake Geneva, home of Evian water
Grenoble – University city; a cable car takes visitors across the River Isère and up to the Fort de la Bastille, from where there are panoramic views of the city and mountains beyond.
Mont Blanc – mountain visible 99 miles away in Lyon. Its sheer size explains why it still challenges climbers generations after it was first conquered

3801 Le Coin Tranquille
38490 Les Abrets en Dauphine

Set in the Dauphiny countryside north of Grenoble, Le Coin Tranquille is truly a 'quiet corner', especially outside school holiday times, although it is popular with families in high season. Les Abrets is well placed for visits to the Savoy regions and the Alps. Very much a family affair, the original small site was developed by Martine's parents, who are still very active about the site. Now Martine runs the site and her husband Gilles is the chef of the restaurant which is to be recommended. The pitches are separated by well maintained hedges of hydrangea, flowering shrubs and walnut trees to make a lovely environment

doubly enhanced by the rural aspect and marvellous views across to the mountains. This is a popular site with a warm welcome, that makes a wonderful base for exploring the area, especially in low season – the Chartreuse caves at Voiron are well worth a visit.

Facilities: Laundry room. Busy shop. Excellent restaurant, open all year (closed two days weekly in low season) and attracting local clientele. Swimming pool and paddling pool (15/5-30/9; no bermuda shorts) with sunbathing areas. Children's play area. TV/video room with balcony, games room and quiet reading room. Supervised games for children, slide shows of the region's attractions and weekly entertainment for adults including live music (not discos) arranged in high season. Bicycle hire. **Off site:** Fishing 5 km. riding 6 km.

Tel: (0)4.76.32.13.48. **Fax:** (0)4.76.37.40.67.
E-mail: contact@coin-tranquille.com
Reservations: Contact site direct, as above.
Open : 1 April - 31 October.

Directions: Site is northeast of Les Abrets. From the town take N6 towards Chambery, turning left after about 2 km. where site is signed.

CAMPSITE NAME Le Coin Tranquille	Type of Accommodation Chalet Fabre Detente
Number of Persons	6 persons
Bedrooms	2 bedrooms: 1 x double, 1 x twin, 1 x single, 1 x double sofa bed in living area
Lounge/Dining Area	Fully furnished
Kitchen Area	Fully equipped including gas hobs, coffee machine and fridge,
Bath/Shower/WC	Washbasin, shower, separate WC
Other Facilities	Electric heating, double glazing, covered terrace, garden table and chairs, deckchair, BBQ
Bedding	Blankets and pillows provided Sheets available at supplement
Pets	Accepted
Charges **From** (Low Season, per week) **To** (High Season, per week)	2002 €315 €620

We have taken the coastal départements of the official French region of Aquitaine, stretching from Bordeaux in the north to the Pyrenees and the Spanish border in the south to make our 'tourist' region.

Major city: Bordeaux
Departements: 33 Gironde, 40 Landes, 64 Pyrenees Atlantiques

The Landes stretches north from Biarritz to Arcachon. The most notable features are the uninterrupted line of sandy beaches, over 100 miles long, and the giant pine forests in the hinterland. Water also plays a feature in the many 'etangs' which lie just behind the beaches and provide and attractive situation for many campsites. Dax on the banks of the Adour is a spa town.

The département of the Gironde covers the area from the Bassin d'Arcachon, famed for its oysters, and Europe's highest sand dune to the Gironde estuary and Bordeaux. The vineyards of Bordeaux are world famous and especially well known for their Medoc, Sauternes, and St Emilion wines.

The Pays Basque area (Pyrénées Atlantiques) in the south west corner is much influenced by Spain. The most famous Basque towns are Biarritz, Bayonne and the picturesque old port of St-Jean-de-Luz. Further inland and nearer the Pyrénées is the attractive town of St-Jean-Pied-de-Port on the pilgrims' route to northern Spain and Santiago de Compostela and only 20 km from the forest of Iraty with its lakes and ski runs. Look for the high, unusually shaped walls used for the Basque game of 'pelota'; St-Jean is one of the strongest centres of the sport.

Note: the site reports are arranged by département in numerical order.

Cuisine of the region
Foie Gras – specially prepared livers of geese and ducks, seasoned and stuffed with truffles
Confits – (preserved goose and duck) are a key ingredient in a number of dishes
Fish and seafood – like carp stuffed with foie gras, mullet in red wine and besugo (sea bream)
Chorizos – spicy sausages
Jambon de Bayonne – raw ham, cured in salt and sliced paper thin
Lamproie – eel-like fish with leeks, onions and red Bordeaux wine
Gâteau Basque – shallow custard pastry, often with fruit fillings
Cèpes – fine, delicate mushrooms; sometimes dried
Chou farci – stuffed cabbage, sometimes aux marrons (with chestnuts)

Wine
Three distinctive areas: Médoc, famous for fine red wines, Graves and Sauternes left of the Garonne and Saint-Emilion and its surroundings – for Entre-Deux-Mers and Côtes de Blaye

Places of interest
Bayonne – old streets and fortifications; Basque Museum
Bordeaux – see the 14,000 piece Bohemian glass chandelier in the foyer of the Grand Theatre, and the 29 acre Esplanade des Quinconces
Pau – famous motor racing circuit on (closed) public highway; stadium for the Basque game of pelota
St Emilion – visit the castle ramparts or drink premier cru St Emilion at pavement cafés
St Jean-de-Luz – seaside resort and fishing village
St Jean-Pied-de-Port – ancient city with citadel; bright Basque houses in steep streets

3306 Camping Le Palace

B.P. 33, Bvd. Marsan de Montbrun,
33780 Soulac-sur-Mer

Le Palace is close to the beach south of Royan across the estuary. It is a traditional site, large and level. A wide range of amenities is arranged around a lush green roundabout with a fountain at the centre of the site. Dancing and concerts take place here in the main season. A wide, sandy beach is 400 m. from the site gates and swimming, said not to be dangerous in normal conditions, is controlled by lifeguards. English is spoken.

Facilities: Washing machines. Supermarket and other shops (from 10/6). Restaurant and bar (from 10/6). Swimming pool (20 x 10 m), with lifeguards. Supervised children's playground with paddling pool. Bicycle hire. Programme of sports, entertainments and excursions in July/Aug. Winter caravan storage. **Off site:** Tennis courts adjacent, riding 400 m.

Tel: (0)5.56.09.80.22. **Fax:** (0)5.56.09.84.23.
E-mail: campingpalace@libertysurf.fr.
Reservations: Contact site direct, as above.
Open: 1 May - 15 September.

Directions: Site is 1 km. south of Soulac and well signed. The shortest and simplest way is via the ferry which runs from Royan across the Gironde estuary to the Pointe de Grave. Alternatively make the trip via Bordeaux.

CAMPSITE NAME Le Palace	Type of Accommodation Mobile home O'Hara	Type of Accommodation Chalet Fun
Number of Persons	4/5 persons	4/5 persons
Bedrooms	2 bedrooms: 1x double, 1x twin, 1x single sofa bed in living area	2 bedrooms: 1x double, 1x twin, 1x single bunk bed
Lounge/Dining Area	Fully furnished	Fully furnished
Kitchen Area	Fully equipped including electric rings and fridge	Fully equipped including gas hobs and fridge
Bath/Shower/WC	Washbasin, shower, separate WC	Washbasin, shower, WC
Other Facilities	Electric heating, garden table and chairs, BBQ	Garden table and chairs, BBQ
Bedding	Blankets and pillows provided Sheets proivded	Blankets and pillows provided Sheets provided
Pets	Not accepted	Not accepted
Charges **From** (Low Season, per week) **To** (High Season, per week)	2002 ¤486.77 ¤549.58	2002 ¤471.07 ¤533.88

3311 Airotel Camping de la Côte d'Argent
33990 Hourtin-Plage

Spread over 20 hectares of undulating sand-based terrain and in the midst of a pine forest, this large site is well placed and well equipped for leisurely family holidays. It also makes an ideal base for walkers and cyclists, with over 100 km. of cycle lanes leading through the Medoc countryside. Hourtin-Plage is a pleasant invigorating resort on the Atlantic coast and a popular location for watersports enthusiasts, or those who prefer spending their days on the beach. More appealing though may be to stay on site, for Côte d'Argent's top attraction is its swimming pool complex with wooden bridges connecting the pools and islands, on which there are sunbathing patios and children's play areas. Due to the work on the site the access roads

were in a poor condition, but we were told would be repaired in the near future.

Facilities: Plenty of laundry machines. Large supermarket. Restaurant, takeaway and pizzeria bar. Four swimming pools, waterslides and flumes. Two tennis courts, pool tables and four play areas. Mini-club and organised entertainment in season. Charcoal barbecues are not permitted.
Off site: Walkway to the beach.

Tel: (0)5.56.09.10.25. **Fax:** (0)5.56.09.24.96.
E-mail: info@camping-cote-dargent.com
Reservations: Contact site direct, as above.
Open: 11 May - 15 September.

Directions: Turn off D101 Hourtin-Soulac road 3 km. north of Hourtin. Then join D101E signed Hourtin-Plage. Site is 300 m. from the beach.

CAMPSITE NAME Cote d'Argent	Type of Accommodation 4 person Mobile Home	Type of Accommodation 4/6 person Mobile Home	Type of Accommodation Mobile home luxe
Number of Persons	4 persons: 2 x adults, 2 x children (under 12 years only)	4/6 persons	4/6 persons
Bedrooms	2 bedrooms: 1 x double, 1 x twin (under 12 years only)	2 bedrooms: 1 x double, 1 x twin, 1 x double sofa bed in living area	2 bedrooms: 1 x double, 1 x twin, 1 x double sofa bed in living area
Lounge/Dining Area	Fully furnished	Fully furnished	Fully furnished
Kitchen Area	Fully equipped including gas hobs and fridge	Fully equipped including gas hobs and fridge	Fully equipped including gas hobs and fridge
Bath/Shower/WC	Washbasin, shower, WC	Washbasin, shower, WC	Washbasin, shower, WC
Other Facilities	Terrace, picnic table	Terrace, picnic table	Terrace, garden table, parasol
Bedding	Blankets and pillows provided Sheets available at a supplement	Blankets and pillows provided Sheets available at a supplement	Blankets and pillows available. Sheets available at a supplement
Pets	Not accepted	Not accepted	Not accepted
Charges **From** (Low Season, per week) **To** (High Season, per week)	2002 €328 €601	2002 €343 €624	2002 €351 €671

3331 Yelloh village Le Panorama
Route de Biscarosse
33115 Pyla sur mer

According to our French agent, Le Panorama is not just another family campsite…while you can expect most of the services associated with a top quality campsite; there is also "a special spirit" about this site… "A classical concert every evening in high season, a fantastic view of the sunset over the ocean while you are eating local food at the restaurant terrace make your holiday a little different, maybe more romantic". Le Panorama is a 15 ha site situated south of La Dune du Pyla in a pinewood, with direct access to the ocean by a long wood staircase over the sand dunes. So for swimming you can choose between the sea or one of the 4 heated swimming pools. A sauna and Jacuzzi are also provided. All activities are free of charges except the tennis court. The site provides a large range of activities and entertainment for everyone including children, teenagers and adults, but the activities don't seem to detract from the quietness and the cleanliness. Security is good, with a warden on site. The "charm" associated with this site stems from its situation in the pinewoods and you can use a bike on the many cycle routes around this area to visit many of

the surrounding villages, such as Pyla, Teste and Arachon. Bordeaux is about 50 minutes away by car. Member 'Yelloh Village'.

Facilities: Washing machines. Shop. Bar and Restaurant. Four swimming pools, aquagym, sauna, Jacuzzi and hydro-massage. Children's play area. Tennis. Mini golf

Tel: (0)5 56 22 10 44   **Fax:** (0)5 56 22 10 12
E-mail: mail@ camping-panorama.com
Reservations: Contact site direct, as above.
Open: 1 May – 30 September.
Directions: The new D259 signed from the N250 to Biscarrosse and Dune du Pilat, just before La Teste, avoids Pyla-sur-Mer. At end of new road turn left at roundabout onto D218 coast road. Site is signposted from here.

CAMPSITE NAME Panorama	Type of Accommodation Grand Club Gitotel	Type of Accommodation Chalet Mobile Louisiane
Number of Persons	5 persons	5 persons
Bedrooms	2 bedrooms: 1x double, 1x twin, 1x bunk bed	2 bedrooms: 1x double, 1x twin, 1x bunk bed
Lounge/Dining Area	Fully furnished	Fully furnished
Kitchen Area	Fully equipped including microwave, gas hobs and fridge	Fully equipped including microwave, gas hobs and fridge
Bath/Shower/WC	Washbasin, shower, separate WC	Washbasin, shower, separate WC
Other Facilities	Double glazing, terrace, garden table, deckchair	Electric heating, double glazing, terrace, garden table, deckchair
Bedding	Blankets and pillows provided Sheets available at a supplement	Blankets and pillows provided Sheets available at a supplement
Pets	Not accepted	Not accepted
Charges **From** (Low Season, per week) **To** (High Season, per week)	2002 ¤ 340 ¤ 725	2002 ¤ 340 ¤ 725

For latest infomation visit **www.alanrogers.com**

4004 Yelloh Village La Paillotte
Azur, 40140 Soustons

La Paillotte, in the Landes area of southwest France is a site with a character of its own. The campsite buildings (reception, shop, and restaurant) are all Tahitian in style, circular and constructed from local woods with the typical straw roof (and layer of waterproof material underneath). Some are now being replaced but still in character. It lies right beside the Soustons Lake, 1.5 km. from Azur village, and has its own sandy beach. This is particularly suitable for young children because the lake is shallow and slopes extremely gradually. For boating the site has a small private harbour where you can keep your own non-powered boat (of shallow draught). La Paillotte is an unusual site with its own atmosphere which appeals to many regular clients. Member 'Sites et Paysages', 'Camping Qualité Plus' and 'Yelloh Village'.

Facilities: Washing machines and dryers. Shop (1/6 - 6/9). Good restaurant with pleasant terrace overlooking the lake and bar (all 12/5-10/9). Takeaway (high season). New swimming pool complex (from 1/5, no bermuda style shorts). Sports, games and activities organised for children and adults. 'Mini-club' room, with 'mini' equipment. TV room, library and amusement room with juke box. Fishing. Bicycle hire. Table tennis. Sailing, windsurfing (with lessons),

rowing boats and pedaloes for hire. Torches useful.
Off site: Riding 5 km, golf 10 km. Atlantic beaches 10 km.

Tel: (0)5.58.48.12.12. **Fax:** (0)5.58.48.10.73.
E-mail: info@paillotte.com
Reservations: Contact Alan Rogers Travel Service on 01892 55 98 98
Open: 1 June - 29 September.

Directions: Coming from the north along N10, turn west on D150 at Magescq. From south go via Soustons. In Azur turn left before church (site signed).

CAMPSITE NAME La Paillotte	Type of Accommodation Fare	Type of Accommodation Oasis	Type of Accommodation Oasis Cottage
Number of Persons	6 persons	6 persons	6 persons
Bedrooms	3 bedrooms: 2 x double, 1 x twin	2 bedrooms: 1 x double, 1 x twin, 1 double sofa bed	2 bedrooms: 1 x double, 1 x twin, 1 double sofa bed
Lounge/Dining Area	Fully furnished	Fully furnished	Fully furnished
Kitchen Area	Fully equipped including microwave	Fully equipped	Fully equipped
Bath/Shower/WC	Washbasin, shower, WC	Washbasin, shower, WC	Washbasin, shower, WC
Other Facilities	Heating, covered terrace	Heating, garden table	Heating, garden table
Bedding	Blankets and pillows provided	Blankets and pillows provided	Blankets and pillows provided
Pets	Not accepted	Not accepted	Not accepted
Charges	2002	2002	2002
From (Low Season, per week)	€330	€200	€170
To (High Season, per week)	€930	€695	€675

N3330 Domaine Residential Naturiste du village de la Jenny
Route de la Jenny, 33680 La Porge

Situated in the heart of Europe's largest forest, yet within walking distance through the forest to the Atlantic beaches, La Jenny provides an ideal spot for a quiet and peaceful holiday, yet with the advantage of plenty of possibilities for those who want to be more active.

With four pools, one of 1000sq m., a wide range of sports facilities, including golf, tennis and archery there are plenty of opportunities, with many activities for children, including a "kiddie club" in the main season, and an extensive programme of evening entertainment as well.

Facilities: Shop. Restaurant, pizzeria and bar. Golf clubhouse. Hairdressers. Newsagent. Body Care. Bicycle hire. Launderette. Heated pool (from April). Tennis. Archery. Yoga. Aquagym. Pony Club. Golf lessons. Tennis lessons. Fitness centre. Sauna. Diving.

Tel: (0)5 56 26 56 90 **Fax:** (0)5 56 26 56 51
E-mail: info@lajenny.fr
Reservations: Contact Suzanne Piper in the UK on 01797 364315, or the site direct.
Open: 1 April - 15 September.

Directions: RN 10 to Bordeaux, thence via the Aquitaine suspension bridge on the Bordeaux by-pass to Exit 7, following directions to Lacanau on the D107 via Le Temple and La Porge, thence via Lege Cap Ferret/Ares on the D3 to La Jenny.

CAMPSITE NAME La Jenny	Type of Accommodation Chalet Louisan	Type of Accommodation Chalet Tourterelle	Type of Accommodation Gite Fregate
Number of Persons	6/8 persons	4/6 persons	2/3 persons
Bedrooms	3 bedrooms: 2x double, 1x bunk beds, 1x double sofa bed in living area	2 bedrooms: 1x double, 1x twin, 1x double sofa bed in living area	1 bedroom: 1x double, 1x single sofa bed in living area
Lounge/Dining Area	Fully furnished	Fully furnished	Fully furnished
Kitchen Area	Fully equipped including cooker with oven and electric rings and fridge	Fully equipped including electric rings and fridge	Fully equipped including cooker with oven and electric rings and fridge
Bath/Shower/WC	Washbasin, shower, separate WC	Washbasin, shower, WC	Washbasin, shower, WC
Other Facilities	Double glazing, covered terrace, garden table	Terrace, garden table and chairs	Terrace, garden table and sun lounger
Bedding	Blankets and pillows provided	Blankets and pillows provided Sheets available at a supplement	Blankets and pillows provided Sheets available at a supplement
Pets	Accepted	Accepted	Accepted
Charges **From** (Low Season, per week) **To** (High Season, per week)	2001 €504 €1110	2001 €336 €750	2001 €280 €560

4010 Camping du Domaine de la Rive

40600 Biscarrosse

Set in pinewoods, La Rive has a superb beach-side location on Lac de Sanguient. The swimming pool complex is wonderful, with various pools linked by water channels and bridges, the four-slide pool having a wide staircase to the top to speed up enjoyment. There is also a Jacuzzi, paddling pool and two large, unusually shaped swimming pools, all surrounded by paved sunbathing areas and decorated with palm trees. An indoor pool is planned. The beach is excellent, shelving gently to provide safe bathing for all ages. There are windsurfers and small craft can be launched from the site's slipway. This is a friendly site with a good mix of nationalities.

Facilities: Well stocked shop (15/5-15/9). Bar serving snacks and takeaway. Games room adjoining. Restaurant with reasonably priced family meals (1/6-15/9). Swimming pool complex supervised July/Aug (15/5-15/9). Children's play area. Two tennis courts. Bicycle hire. Hand-ball or basketball court, table tennis, boules, archery and football. Fishing. Water skiing. Water sports equipment may be hired and tournaments in various sports are arranged in July/Aug. Discos and karaoke evenings organised outside bar with stage and tiered seating. Mini-club for children twice daily.
Off site: Riding 5 km, golf 10 km.

Tel: (0)5.58.78.12.33. **Fax:** (0)5.58.78.12.92.
E-mail: larive@wanadoo.fr
Reservations: Contact Alan Rogers Travel Service on 01892 55 98 98
Open: 1 April - 30 October.

Directions: Take D652 from Sanguinet to Biscarrosse and site is signed on the right in about 6 km.

CAMPSITE NAME Domaine de la Rive	Type of Accommodation Chalet	Type of Accommodation Mobile home O'Hara
Number of Persons	6 persons	6 persons
Bedrooms	2 bedrooms: 1 x double with1 x bunk bed 1 x double	2 bedrooms: 1 x double, 1 x twin, 1 x sofa bed in living area
Lounge/Dining Area	Fully furnished	Fully furnished
Kitchen Area	Fully equipped including gas hobs, coffee machine and fridge	Fully equipped including gas hobs, coffee machine and fridge
Bath/Shower/WC	Washbasin, shower, separate WC	Washbasin, shower, separate WC
Other Facilities	Double glazing, terrace, garden table and chairs, parasol, BBQ	Electric heating, double glazing, terrace, garden table and chairs, parasol, BBQ
Bedding	Blankets and pillows provided Sheets available at a supplement	Blankets and pillows provided Sheets available at a supplement
Pets	Not accepted	Not accepted
Charges From (Low Season, per week) To (High Season, per week)	2002 €288 €749	2002 €252 €693

N4012 Domaine Naturiste Arnaoutchot

40560 Vielle-Saint-Girons

'Arna' is a large naturist site with extensive facilities and direct access to the beach. The centrally located amenities are extensive and of excellent quality. The site has the advantage of direct access to a large, sandy naturist beach, although access from some parts of the site may involve a walk of perhaps 600-700 m. The 'Arna Club' provides more than 30 activities and workshops (in the main season). English is spoken. Member France4 Naturisme. Arna's 30th anniversary is in 2002, with special celebrations during the season

Facilities: Laundry. Large supermarket and a range of other shops. Bar/restaurant, pizzeria and tapita (fish) bar. Pizza delivery to accommodation or to telephone point on beach. Heated indoor swimming pool with solarium, whirlpool and slide. Outdoor pool and terraced sunbathing area. Health centre with sauna, steam, whirlpool and massage treatments. Arna Club (main season) including riding, archery, golf practise, tennis, petanque, swimming, rambling, cycling, sailing school, handicrafts, excursions and special activities for children. TV, video and games rooms. Cinema. Library. Hairdresser and chiropodist. Cash point. Internet point. Bicycle hire. Fishing on site. Torches useful.
Off site: Riding or golf 5 km.

Tel: (0)5.58.49.11.11. **Fax:** (0)5.58.48.57.12.
E-mail: contact@arna.com
Reservations: Contact Alan Rogers Travel Service on 01892 55 98 98 ▓
Open: 1 April - 15 September.

Directions: Site is signed off D652 road at Vielle-Saint-Girons - follow D328 for 3-4 km.

CAMPSITE NAME Arnaoutchot	Type of Accommodation Chevreuil B	Type of Accommodation Mobile home Helios	Type of Accommodation Cottage 30
Number of Persons	4/5 persons	4/5 persons	6 persons
Bedrooms	2 bedrooms: 1 x double, 1 x twin, 1 x double sofa bed	2 bedrooms: 1 x double, 1 x twin, 1 x single sofa bed	2 bedrooms: 1 x double, 1 x twin, 1 x bunkbed, 1 x single sofa bed
Lounge/Dining Area	Fully furnished	Fully furnished	Fully furnished
Kitchen Area	Fully equipped including electric hobs and fridge	Fully equipped including gas hobs and fridge	Fully equipped including gas hobs and fridge
Bath/Shower/WC	Washbasin, shower, separate WC	Washbasin, shower, WC	Washbasin, shower, separate WC
Other Facilities	Electric heating, garden table, BBQ	Electric heating, garden table, BBQ	Electric heating, double glazing, garden table, BBQ
Bedding	Blankets and pillows provided	Blankets and pillows provided	Blankets and pillows provided
Pets	Not accepted	Not accepted	Not accepted
Charges **From** (Low Season, per week) **To** (High Season, per week)	2002 €287 €784	2002 €203 €602	2002 €287 €721

4014 Camping-Caravaning Lou P'tit Poun

Avenue du Quartier Neuf, 40390 St Martin de Seignanx

The manicured grounds surrounding Lou P'tit Poun give it a well-kept appearance, a theme carried out throughout this very pleasing site. It is only after arriving at the car park that you feel confident it is not a private estate. Beyond this point the site unfolds to reveal an abundance of thoughtfully positioned shrubs and trees. Behind a central sloping flower bed lies the open plan reception area. The jovial owners not only make their guests welcome, but extend their enthusiasm to organising weekly entertainment for young and old during high season. A Sites et Paysages member.

Facilities: Laundry facilities with washing machine and dryer. Café and shop (both 1/7 - 31/8). Swimming pool (1/6 - 15/9) Children's play area. Games room, TV. Half court tennis. Table tennis. Bicycle hire. **Off site:** Fishing or riding 7 km, golf 10 km. Bayonne 6 km. Sandy beaches of Basque coast ten minute drive.

Tel: (0)5.59.56.55.79. **Fax:** (0)5.59.56.53.71. **E-mail:** ptitpoun@club-internet.fr
Reservations: Contact Alan Rogers Travel Service on 01892 55 98 98
Open: 15 June - 15 September:

Directions: Leave A63 at exit 6 and join N117 in the direction of Pau. Site is signed at Leclerc supermarket. Continue on N117 for approx. 5.5 km. and site is then clearly signed on right.

CAMPSITE NAME Lou P'tit Poun	Type of Accommodation Mobile home	Type of Accommodation Chalet Havitat
Number of Persons	5 persons	5 persons
Bedrooms	2 bedrooms: 1 x double, 1 x twin, 1 x single sofa bed	2 bedrooms: 1 x double, 1 x twin, 1 x single sofa bed
Lounge/Dining Area	Fully furnished	Fully furnished
Kitchen Area	Fully equipped including gas hobs, coffee machine and fridge	Fully equipped including gas hobs, coffee machine and fridge
Bath/Shower/WC	Washbasin, shower, WC	Washbasin, shower, WC
Other Facilities	Electric heating, garden table and chairs, deckchair, parasol	Double glazing, covered terrace, garden table and chairs
Bedding	Blankets and pillows provided Sheets available at a supplement	Blankets and pillows provided Sheets available at a supplement
Pets	Not accepted	Not accepted
Charges **From** (Low Season, per week) **To** (High Season, per week)	2002 €249 €619	2002 €259 €649

4017 Camping La Reserve
40160 Parentis-en-Born

La Reserve was featured in our Alan Rogers Good Camps Guide for camping and caravanning until it was sold a few years ago. It has now been taken over by Haven Europe. A big site set in a pinewood, it has access to a large lake with a beach and small harbour (Atlantic beaches are nearby). The lake shelves very gradually so provides good bathing for children and good facilities for windsurfing and sailing; powered boats for water skiing are also permitted here. Much organised entertainment and sports activities for children and adults in the Haven tradition.

Facilities: Washing machines. Well-stocked supermarket. Restaurant and large bar where entertainment is organised all season. Heated swimming pool, another unheated outdoor pool (350 sq.m), and paddling pool. Children's club for all ages, two tennis courts (floodlit in the evening), minigolf, table tennis and volleyball. Boats for hire (including powered ones), windsurfing courses and water skiing. TV room, general room and amusement machines.

Tel: (0)5.58.09.75.96. **Fax:** (0)5.58.09.76.13.
Reservations: Contact site direct or Haven Europe in the UK (quoting this guide as a reference) on 0870 242 7777.
Open: 28 April - 14 September.

Directions: Turn west off D652 Gastes - Mimizan road 3 km. south of Gastes by camp sign.

CAMPSITE NAME La Reserve	Type of Accommodation Standard Mobile Homes	Type of Accommodation Luxury Mobile Homes	Type of Accommodation Chalets/Lodges/Apartements
Number of Persons	4-8 persons	7-8 persons	4-8 persons
Bedrooms	2-3 bedrooms: 2 x double, 1 x twin, 1 x double sofa bed in living area	2-3 bedrooms: 2 x double, 1 x twin, 1 x double sofa bed in living area	1-3 bedrooms: 2 x double, 1 x twin, 1 x double sofa bed in living area
Lounge/Dining Area	Fully furnished	Fully furnished	Fully furnished
Kitchen Area	Fully equipped including full cooker and fridge	Fully equipped including microwave, full cooker and fridge/freezer. Some include dishwasher	Fully equipped including microwave, full cooker and fridge/freezer. Some include dishwasher
Bath/Shower/WC	Washbasin, shower, WC	Washbasin, shower, WC	Washbasin, shower, WC
Other Facilities	Gas fire, garden table and chairs, BBQ	Gas fire, garden table and chairs, BBQ	Central heating, garden table and chairs, BBQ
Bedding	Blankets and pillows provided	Blankets and pillows provided	Blankets and pillows provided
Pets	Not accepted	Not accepted	Not accepted
Charges **From** (Low Season, per week) **To** (High Season, per week)	2002 £183 - £260 £662 - £872 Haven have a wider range of accommodation than can be featured here.Please phone Haven for details	2002 £260 - £330 £886 - £1054	2002 £190 - £393 £669 - £1166

6411 Camping du Col d'Ibardin
64122 Urrugne

This family owned site at the foot of the Basque Pyrénées is highly recommended and deserves praise. It is well run with emphasis on personal attention, the smiling Madame, her staff and family ensuring that all are made welcome and is attractively set in the middle of an oak wood. Behind the forecourt, with its brightly coloured shrubs and modern reception area, various roadways lead to the accommodation. From this site you can enjoy the mountain scenery, be on the beach at Socoa within minutes or cross the border into Spain approximately 14 km. down the road.

Facilities: Laundry unit with washing machine and dryer. Small shop selling basic foodstuffs, with orders taken for bread (1/5-15/9). Catering and takeaway service in July/Aug. Bar and occasional evening entertainment which

includes Flamenco dancing. Swimming pool and paddling pool. Children's playground and club with adult supervision. Tennis courts, boules, table tennis, video games. Bicycle hire.
Off site: Fishing 5 km, riding 2 km, golf 7 km. Large supermarket and shopping centre 5 km.

Tel: (0)5.59.54.31.21. **Fax:** (0)5.59.54.62.28.
E-mail: info@col-ibardin.com.
Reservations: Contact site direct, as above.
Open: 1 April - 30 September.

Directions: Leave A63 autoroute at St Jean-de-Luz sud, exit no. 2 and join the RN10 in the direction of Urrugne. Turn left at roundabout (signed Col d'Ibardin) on the D4 and site is on right after 5 km. Do not turn off to the Col itself, but carry on towards Ascain.

CAMPSITE NAME Col d'Ibardin	Type of Accommodation Mobile Home O'Hara	Type of Accommodation Mobile home
Number of Persons	4/5 persons	4/5 persons
Bedrooms	2 bedrooms: 1 x double, 1 x twin, 1 x double sofa bed in living area	2 bedrooms: 1 x double, 1 x twin, 1 x double sofa bed in living area
Lounge/Dining Area	Fully furnished	Fully furnished
Kitchen Area	Fully equipped including gas hobs, coffee machine and fridge	Fully equipped including gas hobs, coffee machine and fridge
Bath/Shower/WC	Washbasin, shower, separate WC	Washbasin, shower, WC
Other Facilities	Electric heating, double glazing, garden table and chairs, parasol	Garden table and chairs, parasol
Bedding	Blankets and pillows provided	Blankets and pillows provided
Pets	Not accepted	Not accepted
Charges **From** (Low Season, per week) **To** (High Season, per week)	2002 €220 €510	2002 €200 €490

Dordogne/Aveyron

We have again rearranged the French départements and regions to give us what we believe the British think of as 'the Dordogne' and have lifted the following départements from these official French regions:

Aquitaine Départements:
24 Dordogne, 47 Lot et Garonne
Midi-Pyrénées Départements:
12 Aveyron, 46 Lot
Poitou-Charentes Département:
16 Charente

The history of the Dordogne goes back many thousands of years when man lived in the caves of the Périgord and left cave paintings at sites such as Les Eyzies and Lascaux. The ancient dukedom of Aquitaine was ruled by the English for 300 years following the marriage of Eleanor of Aquitaine to Henry Plantagenet, who became King of England in 1154. The fortified villages and castles of the area bear evidence of the resulting conflict between the French and English for control of Aquitaine, and today add charm and character to the countryside. Monpazier is the best surviving example of the bastides (fortified towns). It is a diverse region of mountains, vineyards, and fertile river valleys, rolling grasslands and dense forests. Within its boundaries are the beautiful valleys of the Dordogne and Vézère.

To the south of the cultivated fields and cliff-side villages beside the river Lot lie the higher, stony lands of the Quercy Causse and the rocky gorges of the Rivers Aveyron and Tarn. Centred around Millau, there are tortuous gorges and valleys, spectacular rivers, underground caves and grottes, and thickly forested mountains. This is the home of Roquefort cheese.

To the northwest is the old province of Poitou, or Charente, heartland of the domains of Eleanor, Duchess of Aquitaine, where the river Charente was once a busy industrial waterway bringing armaments from Angoulême to the naval shipyards of Rochefort. Today it is Cognac beside the River Charente which springs to mind. Untouched by any recession 80% of the production is exported. The Remy Martin tastings are worth a visit.

Note: Reports are laid out by département in numerical order not by region.

Cuisine of the region

Cagouilles – snails from Charentes
Foie Gras – specially prepared livers of geese and ducks, seasoned and stuffed with truffles
Cassoulet – a hearty stew of duck, sausages and beans
Confit de Canard (d'oie) – preserved duck meat (goose)
Magret de canard – duck breast fillets
Confits – (preserved goose and duck) are a key ingredient in a number of dishes
Fish and seafood – like carp stuffed with foie gras, mullet in red wine and besugo (sea bream)
Chorizos – spicy sausages
Cèpes – fine, delicate mushrooms; sometimes dried
Chou farci – stuffed cabbage, sometimes aux marrons (with chestnuts)
Huile de noix (walnut oil) – many magnificent walnut trees in the Dordogne area
Mouclade – mussels cooked in wine, egg yolks and cream, served with Pineau des Charentes

Places of interest

Agen – rich agricultural area, famous for its prunes
Angoulême – Hill-top town surrouded by ramparts; cathedral, Renaissance château
Cognac – the most celebrated 'eau de vie' in the world, cellars, Valois Castle
Cordes – medieval walled hilltop village
Monflanquin – well preserved fortified village
Rocamadour – cliffside medieval pilgrimage site
Saint Cirq-La Popie – medieval village perched on a cliff
Sarlat – the Saturday market is wonderful (arrive by 9.30 to find a parking space!)

For latest infomation visit **www.alanrogers.com**

1201 Castel Camping Val de Cantobre

12230 Nant d'Aveyron

This attractive, terraced site has been imaginatively and tastefully developed by the Dupond family over a 25 year period. In particular, the magnificent carved features in the bar create a delightful ambience, complemented by a recently built terrace. The pools have a new surround, bedecked by flowers and crowned by a large urn which dispenses water into the paddling pool. But it is the activity programme that is unique at Val de Cantobre, supervised by qualified instructors, some arranged by the owners and some at a fair distance from the site. Passive recreationists appreciate the scenery, especially Cantobre, a medieval village that clings to a cliff in view of the site. Nature lovers will be delighted to see the vultures wheeling in the Tarn gorge alongside more humble rural residents. Butterflies in profusion, orchids, huge edible snails, glow worms, families of beavers and the natterjack toad all live here. It is easy to see why – the place is magnificent. A warm welcome awaits from the Dupond family.

Facilities: Shop, although small, offers a wide variety of provisions; including many regional specialities (comparing well with local shops and

markets). Bar, restaurant, pizzeria and takeaway facility. Three adjoining swimming pools. **Off site:** Around 15 types of activity including river rafting, white water canoeing, rock climbing or jumps from Millau's hill tops on twin seater steerable parachutes. All weather sports pitch. Fishing. Torch useful.

Tel: (0)5.65.58.43.00. **Fax:** (0)5.65.62.10.36. **Reservations:** Contact site direct, as above. **Open:** 18 May - 15 September, with all facilities.

Directions: Site is 4 km. north of Nant, on D991 road to Millau. From Millau direction take D991 signed Gorge du Dourbie.

CAMPSITE NAME Val de Cantobre	Type of Accommodation 4 person Mobile Home	Type of Accommodation Chalet Fabre
Number of Persons	4 persons	5 persons
Bedrooms	2 bedrooms: 1x double, 1x twin	2 bedrooms: 1x double, 1x triple
Lounge/Dining Area	Fully furnished	Fully furnished
Kitchen Area	Fully equipped including gas hobs, coffee machine, fridge	Fully equipped including microwave, gas and electric hobs, coffee machine and fridge
Bath/Shower/WC	Washbasin, shower, WC	Washbasin, shower, separate WC
Other Facilities	Electric heating, garden table, deckchairs, parasol, BBQ	Electric heating, terrace, garden table, deckchairs, parasol, BBQ
Bedding	Blankets and pillows provided Sheets available at a supplement	Blankets and pillows provided Sheets available at a supplement
Pets	Accepted	Accepted
Charges **From** (Low Season, per week) **To** (High Season, per week)	2002 €229 €566	2002 €287 €630

1208 Camping Club Les Genêts

Lac de Pareloup, 12410 Salles Curan

This family run site is on the shores of Lac de Pareloup and offers both family holiday and watersports facilities. The site slopes gently down to the beach and lake with facilities for all watersports including waterskiing. A full animation and activities programme is organised in high season, and there is much to see and do in this very attractive corner of Aveyron. A 'Sites et Paysages' member.

Facilities: Laundry room. Very well stocked shop. Bar and restaurant. Snack bar serving pizzas and other snacks in main season. Swimming pool and spa pool (both 1/6-15/9; unsupervised). Children's playground. Minigolf, volleyball and boules. Bicycle hire. Pony riding and Red Indian style tee-pees. Hire of pedaloes, windsurfers and kayaks. Fishing licences available.

Tel: (0)5.65.46.35.34. **Fax:** (0)5.65.78.00.72. **E-mail:** contact@camping-les-genets.fr **Reservations:** Contact Alan Rogers Travel Service, Tel. 01892 55 98 98 **Open:** 1 June - 15 September.

Directions: From Salles-Curan take D577 for 4 km. approx., turning right into a narrow lane immediately after a sharp right hand bend. Site is signed at junction.

CAMPSITE NAME Les Genets	Type of Accommodation Mobile Home	Type of Accommodation Chalet Détente
Number of Persons	4/6 persons	4/6 persons
Bedrooms	2 bedrooms: 1 x double, 1 x twin, 1 x double sofa bed in living area	2 bedrooms: 1 x double, 1 x twin, 1 x double sofa bed in living area
Lounge/Dining Area	Fully furnished TV for hire in low season	Fully furnished TV for hire in low season
Kitchen Area	Fully equipped including oven with gas hobs, coffee machine and fridge/freezer	Fully equipped including oven with gas hobs, coffee machine, fridge/ freezer and dishwasher
Bath/Shower/WC	Washbasin, shower, separate WC	Washbasin, shower, separate WC
Other Facilities	Electric heating, double glazing, terrace, garden table, parasol	Electric heating, double glazing, terrace, garden table,
Bedding	Blankets and pillows provided Sheets available at a supplement	Blankets and pillows provided Sheets available at a supplement
Pets	Accepted	Accepted
Charges **From** (Low Season, per week) **To** (High Season, per week)	2002 €215 €600	2002 €305 €670

For latest infomation visit **www.alanrogers.com**

2411 Camping-Caravaning Aqua Viva
Carsac, 24200 Sarlat

This site is divided into two sections, separated by the access road. One side is very quiet and spacious with some touring pitches and 32 chalets terraced in woodland. The other half contains touring pitches only. Canoe lessons and guided trips on the Dordogne are organised by the site, as are many other sporting activities. The site is ideally situated for visits to Rocamadour and Padirac, as well as the many places of interest in the Dordogne region. It is also close to Sarlat for markets and hypermarkets. The site is very popular with families, especially those with pre-teen and younger teenage children. English is spoken.

Facilities: Small shop and takeaway. Small reasonably priced restaurant. Bar and terrace where evening entertainment is arranged in season. Excellent, heated swimming pool and

children's pool. Small lake (for fishing). Table tennis. Floodlit basketball and boules area. High quality minigolf. Children's tennis court and under 7s play park. Bicycle hire and fishing on site. **Off site:** Riding 1 km, golf 5 km.

Tel: (0)5.53.31.46.00. **Fax:** (0)5.53.29.36.37. **E-mail:** aqua_viva@perigord.com. **Reservations:** Contact site direct,as above. **Open:** Easter - 30 September.

Directions: Site is 6 km. from Sarlat on the D704 road from Sarlat to Souillac. Coming from Sarlat, the entrance on the left is not easy to see.

CAMPSITE NAME Aqua Viva	Type of Accommodation 2/3 person Chalet Havitat	Type of Accommodation 4/5 person Chalet Havitat	Type of Accommodation 6 person Chalet Havitat
Number of Persons	2/3 persons	4-5 persons	6 persons
Bedrooms	1 bedroom: 1x double, 1x single sofa bed in living area	2 bedrooms: 1x double, 1x twin, 1x single sofa bed in living area	2 bedrooms: 1x double, 1x triple, 1x single sofa bed in living area
Lounge/Dining Area	Fully furnished	Fully furnished including colour T.V in some	Fully furnished including colour T.V in some
Kitchen Area	Fully equipped including gas hobs, coffee machine and fridge	Fully equipped including gas hobs, coffee machine and fridge	Fully equipped including gas hobs, coffee machine and fridge
Bath/Shower/WC	Washbasin, shower, WC	Washbasin, shower, WC	Washbasin, shower, separate WC
Other Facilities	Electric heating, terrace, garden table, parasol and sun lounger	Electric heating, double glazing, terrace, garden table, parasol and sun lounger	Electric heating, terrace
Bedding	Blankets and pillows provided	Blankets and pillows provided Sheets available at a supplement	Blankets and pillows provided. Sheets available at a supplement
Pets	Accepted	Accepted	Accepted
Charges **From** (Low Season, per week) **To** (High Season, per week)	2002 ¤189 ¤ 464	2002 ¤275 ¤ 621	2002 ¤307 ¤ 691

2412 Camping La Palombière
Sainte Nathalène, 24200 Sarlat

This is a spacious site, set in a peaceful valley east of Sarlat, with a quiet and tranquil atmosphere. A large recreation area provides high quality sports facilities and a range of amenities are arranged on a various terraced levels. This is an ideal site for families where children are at an age where they need a wide range of activities, but it nevertheless preserves a relaxed ambience and general tranquillity.

Facilities: Laundry. Well stocked shop (12/5-22/9). Bar and restaurant complex, with good range of meals (1/5-22/9). Good sized, heated swimming pool and children's pool. Children's play area (under

8 yrs). Boules pitches, small football pitch, tennis and volleyball courts. Minigolf. Bicycle hire. Canoe trips reserved at reception. Sports competitions and evening activities are organised in season, including talent shows, weekly disco, cabaret and even giant scrabble! **Off site:** Fishing 3 km, riding or golf 10 km.

Tel: (0)5.53.59.42.34. **Fax:** (0)5.53.28.45.40.
E-mail: la.palombiere@wanadoo.fr.
Reservations: Contact site direct, as above.
Open: 14 April - 19 September.

Directions: Take D47 east from Sarlat to Ste Nathalène. Site is signed from village and is reached by taking a left turn just beyond it.

CAMPSITE NAME La Palombiere	Type of Accommodation Willerby T23 Mobile home Willerby T28 mobile home	Type of Accommodation Mediterranee mobile home Flores mobile home	Type of Accommodation Chalet Eden Chalet Reve confort
Number of Persons	T23: 4 persons T28: 5 persons	Mediterranee: 5 persons Flores: 7 persons	Eden: 5 persons Reve confort: 7 persons
Bedrooms	T23: 2 bedrooms: 1x double, 1x twin T28: 2 bedrooms: 1x double, 1x triple	Mediterranee: 2 bedrooms: 1 x double, 1x triple Flores: 2 bedrooms: 1x double, 1x triple, 1x double sofa bed in living area	Eden: 2 bedrooms: 1x double, 1x triple, Reve confort: 2 bedrooms: 1x double, 1x triple, 1x double sofa bed in living area
Lounge/Dining Area	Fully furnished	Fully furnished	Fully furnished
Kitchen Area	Fully equipped including gas hobs, kettle, fridge and tumble dryer	Fully equipped including microwave, gas hobs, coffee machine, fridge and tumble dryer Flores: as above but no coffee machine, or kettle	Eden: Fully equipped including microwave, gas hobs, coffee machine, kettle, fridge and tumble dryer Reve confort: as above but no microwave
Bath/Shower/WC	T23: Washbasin, shower, WC T28: washbasin, shower, separate WC	Mediterranee: Washbasin, shower, WC Flores: washbasin, shower, separate WC	Eden: Washbasin, shower, WC Reve confort: shower, separate WC
Other Facilities	Gas and electric heating, garden table, sun lounger, parasol, BBQ	Electric heating, double glazing, terrace, garden table, sun lounger, parasol, BBQ	Electric heating, double glazing, terrace, garden table, sun lounger, parasol, BBQ
Bedding	Blankets and pillows provided. Sheets available at a supplement	Blankets and pillows provided. Sheets available at a supplement	Blankets and pillows provided. Sheets available at a supplement
Pets	Accepted	Accepted	Accepted
Charges **From** (Low Season, per week) **To** (High Season, per week)	2002 T23: €170 T28: €190 T23: €540 T28: €610	2002 Mediterranee: €190 Flores: €240 Mediterranee: €610 Flores: €670	2002 Eden: €240 Reve Confort: €290 Eden: €670 Reve Confort: €750

2416 Camping-Caravaning Le Grand Dague

Atur, 24750 Périgueux

Le Grand Dague is a good quality site on the outskirts of Périgueux. Having negotiated the narrow access road, the site is found to be very spacious, clean and attractive. The main building houses reception, a small shop, and the very attractive restaurant and bar with its shady terrace. A takeaway service and an appetising restaurant menu make the most of this provision. A swimming pool, water slide and paddling pool enjoy a sunny location. The site is approximately 6 km. from Périgueux and also close to hypermarkets and tennis. A 'Sites et Paysages' member.

Facilities: Laundry sinks. Small shop for essentials (15/5-30/9). Attractive restaurant with

appetising menu, bar and takeaway (all from June). Swimming pool, water slide and paddling pool (from early May). Football, volleyball, badminton, petanque, minigolf and table tennis. Fishing. Bicycle hire. **Off site:** Riding 5 km, golf 10 km.

Tel: (0)5.53.04.21.01. **Fax:** (0)5.53.04.22.01.
E-mail: info@legranddague.fr
Reservations: Contact site direct, as above.
Open: Easter - 30 September.

Directions: Site is signed from N89 south of Périgueux. From centre of Périgueux take Brive road, then road to Atur. Site is well signed.

CAMPSITE NAME Le Grand Dague	Type of Accommodation Mobile home AB	Type of Accommodation Chalet Havitat	Type of Accommodation Mobile Home O'Hara
Number of Persons	5/6 persons	6 persons	6 persons
Bedrooms	2 bedrooms: 1 x double, 1 x twin, 1 x double sofa bed in living area	2 bedrooms: 1x double, 1 x twin, 1 x double sofa bed in living area	2 bedrooms: 1 x double, 1 x twin, 1 x double sofa bed in living area
Lounge/Dining Area	Fully furnished	Fully furnished	Fully furnished
Kitchen Area	Fully equipped including gas hobs, coffee machine and fridge	Fully equipped including gas hobs, coffee machine and fridge	Fully equipped including gas hobs, coffee machine and fridge
Bath/Shower/WC	Washbasin, shower, separate WC	Washbasin, shower, separate WC	Washbasin, shower, separate WC
Other Facilities	Electric heating, garden table and chairs, parasol	Electric heating, garden table and chairs, parasol	Electric heating, garden table and chairs, parasol
Bedding	Blankets and pillows provided	Blankets and pillows provided	Blankets and pillows provided
Pets	Accepted	Accepted	Accepted
Charges **From** (Low Season, per week) **To** (High Season, per week)	2002 €205 €545	2002 €252 €590	2002 €252 €590

4601 Castel Camping de la Paille Basse

46200 Souillac-sur-Dordogne

Lying some 8 km. from Souillac, this family owned, high quality site is easily accessible from the N20 and well placed to take advantage of excursions into the Dordogne. It is part of a large domaine of 80 hectares, which is available to campers for walks and recreation. The site is quite high up and there are excellent views over the surrounding countryside. Activities and entertainment are organised in season (animation was of a very high standard when we stayed). For good reason, the site can get very busy in high season.

Facilities: Laundry facilities. Shop for essentials. Good restaurant, bar with terrace and takeaway. Crêperie. Good swimming pool complex, with main pool (25 x 10 m), second one (10 x 6 m) and paddling pool (unheated). Solarium. Sound-proofed disco room (twice weekly in season). TV rooms (with satellite).

Cinema room below swimming pool area. Archery, tennis (charged), football, volleyball and table tennis. Children's playground. Off site: Golf 4 km.

Tel: (0)5.65.37.85.48. Fax: (0)5.65.37.09.58. E-mail: paille-basse@wanadoo.fr. Reservations: Contact site direct, as above. Open: 15 May - 15 September.

Directions: From Souillac take D15 road leading northwest towards Salignac-Eyvignes and after 6 km. turn right at camp sign on 2 km. approach road.

CAMPSITE NAME Le Paille Basse	Type of Accommodation 6 Person Mobile Home	Type of Accommodation 4 Person Mobile Home
Number of Persons	6 persons	4 persons
Bedrooms	2 bedrooms: 1x double, 1x twin, 1x double sofa bed in living area	2 bedrooms: 1x double, 1x twin
Lounge/Dining Area	Fully furnished	Fully furnished
Kitchen Area	Fully equipped including oven with gas hobs, fridge	Fully equipped including gas hobs and fridge
Bath/Shower/WC	Washbasin, shower, WC	Washbasin, shower, WC
Other Facilities	Gas heating, garden table and chairs, parasol, deckchair	Gas heating, garden table and chairs, parasol, deckchair
Bedding	Blankets and pillows provided	Blankets and pillows provided
Pets	Not accepted	Not accepted
Charges From (Low Season, per week) To (High Season, per week)	2002 €230 €565	2002 €170 €495

4701 Camping-Caravaning Moulin du Périé

Sauveterre- la-Lémance, 47500 Fumel

Set in a quiet area and surrounded by woodlands, this peaceful little site is well away from much of the tourist bustle. The picturesque old mill buildings, now home to the restaurant etc are adorned with flowers and creepers and the food is to be recommended. The owner has an extensive knowledge of wine that he is pleased to share with visitors. The attractive front courtyard is complemented by an equally pleasant terrace at the rear. A quiet, friendly site with regular visitors.

Facilities: Laundry. Shop for essentials. Bar/ reception and restaurant (including takeaway). Two small, clean swimming pools (no bermuda-style shorts) overlook a shallow, spring water lake, ideal for inflatable boats and paddling. Bordering the lake, a large grass field is popular for football and volleyball. Boules, table tennis, outdoor chess. New children's playground and

trampoline. Small, indoor play area. Bicycle hire. In season various activities, on and off site are arranged; including canoeing, riding, wine tasting visits, sight seeing trips plus weekly barbecues and gastronomic meals.

Off site: Fishing 1 km. Small supermarket in village and larger stores in Fumel.

Tel: (0)5.53.40.67.26. **Fax:** (0)5.53.40.62.46.
E-mail: moulinduperie@wanadoo.fr
Reservations: Contact Alan Rogers Travel Service on 01892 55 98 98
Open: 4 May - 24 September.

Directions: Sauveterre-la -Lémance lies by the Fumel - Périgueux (D710) road, midway between the Dordogne and Lot rivers. From D710, cross railway line, straight through village and turn left (northeast) at far end on C201 minor road signed Château Sauveterre, Loubejec and site. Site is 3 km. up this road on right.

CAMPSITE NAME Le Moulin du Perie	Type of Accommodation Mobile home IRM	Type of Accommodation Chalet Havitat
Number of Persons	6 persons	7 persons
Bedrooms	2 bedrooms: 1 x double, 1 x bunk bed, 1 x double sofa bed in living area	2 bedrooms: 1 x double, 1 x bunk bed, 1 x single, 1 x double sofa bed in living area
Lounge/Dining Area	Fully furnished	Fully furnished
Kitchen Area	Fully equipped including gas hobs, coffee machine and fridge	Fully equipped including gas hobs, coffee machine and fridge
Bath/Shower/WC	Washbasin, shower, separate WC	Washbasin, shower, separate WC
Other Facilities	Electric heating, double glazing, garden table and chairs, deckchair, parasol	Electric heating, double glazing, terrace, garden table and chairs
Bedding	Blankets and pillows provided Sheets available at a supplement	Blankets and pillows provided Sheets available at a supplement
Pets	Not accepted	Not accepted
Charges **From** (Low Season, per week) **To** (High Season, per week)	2002 €168 - €305 €488 - €580	2002 €200 - €304 €610

Rhône Valley

Major city: Lyon
Départements: 01 Ain, 07 Ardèche, 26 Drôme, 42 Loire, 69 Rhône

The Rhône Valley is one of Europe's main arteries – this traditional route carries millions of travellers and millions of tons of freight by rail (TGV), by autoroute and by water to the Mediterranean. However, either side of this busy corridor are areas of great interest and natural beauty. From the sun-baked Drôme, with its ever-changing landscapes, culminating in the isolated mountains of the Vercors; the deep gorges and high plateaux of the Ardèche, studded with prehistoric caves to lush valleys filled with orchards and the vineyards of the Beaujolais and the Rhône Valley.

The region's 2,000 year history as a cultural crossroads has blessed the area with a rich blend of customs, architecture and sights of interest. The city of Lyon was developed by the Romans as a trading centre, and was once the capital. It is now the second largest city of France. Although heavily industrialised, it has a charming old quarter and is renowned for its gastronomy. The Place de la Terreur in the centre of the city is where the guillotine was placed during the French revolution – until it wore out through over-use. There are also reminders of the city's role in World War 2 as a resistance centre.

Not far from Lyon lies the Dombes, the 'land of a thousand lakes', the medieval village of Pérouges and the Roman ruins of Vienne with its yearly jazz festival.

Note: the site reports are laid out by département in numerical order not by region.

Cuisine of the region

From Lyon to Bresse and Bugey by way of the Dombes, food is an art and a science. The poultry, cheese, freshwater fish, mushrooms and wines are superb

Bresse (Poulet, Poularde, Volaille de) – the best French poultry, fed on corn and when killed bathed in milk; flesh is white and delicate
Gras-double – ox tripe, served with onions
Poulet demi-deuil (half-mourning) – called this because of thin slices of truffle placed under the chicken breast
Poulet au vinaigre – chicken, shallots, tomatoes, white wine, wine vinegar and a cream sauce
Rosette – a large pork sausage
Sabodet – Lyonnais sausage of pig's head, pork and beef, served hot

Wine

Beaujolais, Côte Rotie, St Julien, Condrieu, Tain-Hermitage, Chiroubles and Julienas are some of the wines produced in this region

Places of interest

Beaujolais – vineyards and golden-stone villages
Bourg-en-Bresse – 16th/17th century church of Notre-Dame, craft shops, museum of Ain; also famous for its yellow, corn-fed chickens
Dombes – land of a thousand lakes, ornithological park
Lyon – Gallo-Roman artifacts, Renaissance quarter, historical Fabric Museum, silk museum.
Montélimer – nougat capital of France
Pérouges – lovely medieval village, Galette de Pérouges
St Etienne – museum of Modern Art
Vallon-Pont d'Arc – base from which to visit Gorges de l'Ardèche; canoe and rafting centre
Vienne – Roman remains, Gothic style cathedral, 6th century church St Pierre

0703 Camping Soleil Vivarais
Sampzon, 07120 Ruoms

A large, quality site bordering the River Ardèche, complete with a sandy beach, Soleil Vivarais offers much to visitors, particularly families with children, be they teenagers or toddlers. During the day the proximity of the swimming pools to the terraces of the bar and restaurant makes it a pleasantly social area. In the evening the purpose built stage, with professional lighting and sound system, provides an ideal platform for a varied entertainment programme, again incorporating those dining or relaxing nearby. A 'Yelloh Village' member.

Facilities: Washing machines and dryers. Large shop. Bright, modern bar/restaurant complex which in addition to takeaways and pizzas (cooked in a wood burning oven), offers menus catering for all appetites and budgets. Sound-proof disco adjacent to the bar (capacity 100-120), popular with teenagers. Heated main pool and paddling pool (no bermuda style shorts). Water polo, aqua-aerobics, pool games. Tennis (charged). Fishing. Basketball, petanque, table tennis and volleyball. Bicycle hire. Archery. Extensive animation programme in June, July and August.

Off site: Activities nearby, many with qualified instruction and supervision, include mountain biking, walking, canoeing, rafting, climbing and caving. Riding 2 km, golf 10 km.

Open: 23 May - 20 September.
Tel: (0)4.75.39.67.56. **Fax:** (0)4.75.93.97.10.
E-mail: camping.soleil.vivarais@wanadoo.fr

Reservations: Contact Alan Rogers Travel Service. Tel: 01892 55 98 98 ▶

Directions: From Le Teil (on N86) take N102 westwards towards and through Villeneuve-de-Berg, disregarding first sign for Vallon-Pont-d'Arc. Continue on N102 before turning left on D103, toward Vogue, then left on D579 to Ruoms. Still on the D579, follow Vallon Pont D'Arc signs towards Sampzon. Access to site is via a bridge across the river.

CAMPSITE NAME Soleil Vivarais	Type of Accommodation 8 person mobile home	Type of Accommodation 6 person mobile home	Type of Accommodation 4 person mobile home
Number of Persons	8 persons	6 persons	4 persons
Bedrooms	3 bedrooms: 1 x double, 2 x twin, 1 x double sofa bed in living area	3 bedrooms: 1 x double, 1 x twin, 1 x double sofa bed	2 bedrooms: 1 x double, 1 x twin
Lounge/Dining Area	Fully furnished	Fully furnished	Fully furnished
Kitchen Area	Fully equipped including microwave, gas hobs, fridge/freezer, coffee machine, dishwasher	Fully equipped including microwave, gas hobs, fridge/freezer, coffee machine, dishwasher	Fully equipped including microwave, gas hobs, fridge, dishwasher
Bath/Shower/WC	2 bathrooms: 2 x shower, washbasin, WC	Washbasin, shower, separate WC	Washbasin, shower, separate WC
Other Facilities	Electric heating, terrace, garden table and deckchairs	Electric heating, terrace, garden table and deckchairs	Electric heating, terrace, garden table and deckchairs
Bedding	Blankets and pillows provided Sheets available at a supplement	Blankets and pillows provided Sheets available at a supplement	Blankets and pillows provided Sheets available at a supplement
Pets	Accepted	Accepted	Accepted
Charges **From** (Low Season, per week) **To** (High Season, per week)	€350 €960	€270 €805	€230 €720

your holidays
in yelloh! color

CAMPING VILLAGES
yelloh!
VILLAGE

yelloh!orange

With Yelloh! Village your holiday will get new colours ! Situated in exceptional regions, the Yelloh ! Village campings guarantee you high quality holidays.

• All services, entertainment programmes for children and adults and organised activities are always available.

yelloh!yellow

yelloh!red

yelloh!blue

A friendly and personal welcome
An environment of quality nature: green and well kept surroundings with water in all its forms (luxurious swimming pools, sea, ocean, rivers, lakes)
Fully equipped pitches and an ample selection of quality accommodation to let (mobile homes, chalets…)
Booking made easy and practical

ESPAGNE
La Torre del sol **(1)** - *réf. 8540*

ARDÈCHE
Soleil Vivarais **(18)** - *réf. 0703*

BRETAGNE
Le Ranolien **(2)**
Le Grand Camping de la Plage **(3)** - *réf. 2911*
Le Grand Large **(4)** - *réf. 2929*
Le Manoir de Kerlut **(5)** - *réf. 2912*

CHARENTE ATLANTIQUE
Sequoia Parc **(6)** - *réf. 1714*

GERS SUD-OUEST
Le lac des 3 vallées **(11)** - *réf. 3206*

LANDES ATLANTIQUE
Panorama **(7)** / Saint-Martin **(8)**
La Paillotte **(9)** - *réf. 4004*
Le Sylvamar **(10)**

MÉDITERRANÉE CAMARGUE
La Petite Camargue **(16)** - *réf. 3002*
Les Petits Camarguais **(17)** - *réf. 3013*

MÉDITERRANÉE LANGUEDOC
Sérignan plage **(13)** - *réf. 3407*
Club Farret **(14)** / Nouvelle Floride **(15)**

MÉDITERRANÉE CATALANE
Le Brasilia **(12)** - *réf. 6607*

VAL DE LOIRE SOLOGNE
Le Parc des Alicourts **(19)** - *réf. 4103*

CAMPING VILLAGES
yelloh!
VILLAGE

information - bookings :
00 800 88 739 739
www.yellohvillage.com

2603 Camping Le Grand Lierne
B.P. 8, 26120 Chabeuil

This site provides a pleasant base to explore this little known area between the Ardèche and the Vercors mountains and the Côte du Rhône wine area. A varied entertainment programme has a particular emphasis on activities for children, with a range of activities and excursions. The owners wish to keep a balance between nationalities, and will arrange visit programmes. English spoken. A 'Sites et Paysages' member.

Facilities: Washing machines (powder provided), dryers and outdoor lines. Shop. Bar/snack bar with terrace for eating in and takeaway (all season). Two swimming pools, one covered and heated in low season (no bermuda shorts), paddling pool and 50 m. water slide. Children's playgrounds and trampoline. Mini-tennis, minigolf, table tennis, volleyball, football field and

small climbing wall. Bicycle hire. Library. Barbecues are permitted in special areas. Dogs and other pets are not accepted in high season (6/7-24/8). **Off site:** Fishing 3 km, riding 7 km, golf 3 km, archery and hang gliding near.

Tel: (0)4.75.59.83.14. **Fax:** (0)4.75.59.87.95. **E-mail:** contact@grandlierne.com. **Reservations:** Contact Alan Rogers Travel Service on 01892 55 98 98  **Open:** 27 April - 7 September, with all services.

Directions: Site signed in Chabeuil about 11 km. east of Valence (18 km. from autoroute). It is best to approach Chabeuil from the south side of Valence via the Valence ring road, thence onto the D68 to Chabeuil itself. Site is off the D125 to Charpey, 5 km. from Chabeuil, but well signed.

CAMPSITE NAME Village Le Grand Large	Type of Accommodation Mobile home
Number of Persons	6 persons
Bedrooms	2 bedrooms: 1x double, 1x twin, 1x double sofa bed in living area
Lounge/Dining Area	Fully furnished
Kitchen Area	Fully equipped including microwave, gas hobs and fridge
Bath/Shower/WC	Washbasin, shower, separate WC
Other Facilities	Electric heating, garden table, parasol, BBQ
Bedding	Duvets and pillow provided Sheets and towels available at a supplement
Pets	Accepted in low season
Charges **From** (Low Season, per week) **To** (High Season, per week)	2002 €215 €595

For latest infomation visit **www.alanrogers.com**

Perhaps we should have called this tourist region the Provence Alpes because we have only included the départements from the mountainous hinterland of the official French region of Provence. The capital city of Provence is Marseille, but this now falls into our Mediterranean region.

Départements: 04 Alpes-de-Haute-Provence, 05 Hautes-Alpes, 84 Vaucluse

The river valleys provide natural routes through the mountain barrier, as the Romans recognised. Their influence is strong through the region, reminding one that the area was the first Province of Rome, which is why it is now called Provence. Roman monuments can be seen at Orange, and Vaison-la-Romaine, where a 2,000 year old bridge is still in use. Avignon was the site of the papal court and the Palais des Papes at Avignon is a spectacular construction.

The Hautes-Alpes will reward with scenic pleasures, peace and quiet. Briançon is the highest town in Europe and many of the high passes are not for the faint-hearted – Hannibal used one of the routes!

The Vaucluse, the area made famous by Peter Mayle's book on the Luberon, where in the late spring the southern slopes of the Montagne du Luberon are a mass of colour from the glades of wild flowers. The extinct volcanic cone of Mont Ventoux, of Tour de France fame provides dramatic views. The scents and colours with an amazing intensity of light, have encouraged artists and writers to settle amidst the sleepy villages, with narrow streets and ancient dwellings topped with sun-baked terracotta tiles, where the air is fragrant with the smell of wild herbs and lavender.

Note: Site reports are laid out by département in numerical order.

Cuisine of the region
Influenced by the Savoie area to the north and the Côte d'Azur to the south, the cuisine emphasizes seasonings, such as herbs and garlic, and fish

Aigo Bouido – garlic and sage soup with bread (or eggs and cheese)

Farcement (Farçon Savoyard) – potatoes baked with cream, eggs, bacon, dried pears and prunes; a hearty stomach filler

Plat Gratinée – applies to a wide range of dishes; here this means cooked in breadcrumbs; gratins of all sorts show how well milk, cream and cheee combine together

Pissaladière – Provencal bread dough with onions, anchovies, olives, etc.

Ratatouille – aubergines, courgettes, onions, garlic, red peppers and tomatoes in olive oil

Tartiflette – potato, bacon, onions and Reblochon cheese

Wine
The Côtes de Provence wine region is mainly known for its dry, fruity rosé wines: Bandol, Bellet, Palette, Cassis. Red wines include Côtes du Rhône and Châteauneuf-du-Pape.

Places of interest
Avignon – ramparts, old city, Papal Palace, old palace, Calvet museum

Mont Ventoux – near Carpentras, one of the best known stages of the classic Tour de France annual cycle race

Orange – Roman city, gateway to the Midi, Colline St Europe

Vaison la Romaine – Roman city, the French Pompei

0401 Hotel de Plein Air L'Hippocampe
Rte Napoléon, 04290 Volonne

Hippocampe is a friendly site situated in a beautiful area of France that is not well frequented by the British. The perfumes of thyme, lavender and wild herbs are everywhere and the higher hills of Haute Provence are not too far away. This is a family run site with families in mind, with games, aerobics, competitions, entertainment and shows, plus a daily club for younger family members in July/August. A soundproof underground disco is set well away from the accommodation and is very popular with teenage customers. The site is however much quieter in low season with good discounts and these are the months for people who do not want or need entertaining. The Gorge du Verdon is a sight not to be missed and rafting, paragliding or canoe trips can be booked from the site's own tourist information office. Being on the lower slopes of the hills of Haute-Provence, the surrounding area is good for both walking and mountain biking. English is spoken.

Facilities: Washing machines. Small shop (30/6-1/9). Bar (1/5-30/9). Restaurant, pizzeria and barbecue chicken shop (all 12/5-15/9). Large, attractive swimming pool complex (from 1/5) with various pools of differing sizes and depths, heated in early and late seasons. Tennis is free outside high season (3/7-21/8). Fishing, canoeing. Bicycle hire. Large selection of sports facilities to choose from, some with free instruction, including archery in high season. **Off site:** Village of Volonne 600 m. Riding 500m.

Tel: (0)4.92.33.50.00. **Fax:** (0)4.92.33.50.49. **E-mail:** l.hippocampe@wanadoo.fr
Reservations: Contact site direct, as above.
Open: 1 April - 30 September.

Directions: Approaching from the north turn off N85 across river bridge to Volonne, then right to site. From the south right on D4 1 km. before Château Arnoux.

CAMPSITE NAME Hippocampe	Type of Accommodation 6 person Mobile Home	Type of Accommodation 4 person Mobile home
Number of Persons	6 persons	4 persons
Bedrooms	2 bedrooms: 1 x double, 1 x twin, 1 x double sofa bed	2 bedrooms: 1 x double, 1 x twin
Lounge/Dining Area	Fully Furnished	Fully Furnished
Kitchen Area	Fully equipped including gas hobs, coffee machine and fridge	Fully equipped including gas hobs, coffee machine, and fridge
Bath/Shower/WC	Washbasin, shower, separate WC	Washbasin, shower, WC
Other Facilities	Electric heating, double glazing, garden table & chairs, parasol, BBQ and telephone	Garden table & chairs, parasol, BBQ
Bedding	Blankets and pillows provided Sheets available at a supplement	Blankets and pillows provided Sheets available at a supplement
Pets	Accepted	Accepted
Charges **From** (Low Season, per week) **To** (High Season, per week)	2002 €217 €635	2002 €196 €565

0402 Castel Camp du Verdon
Domaine de la Salaou, 04120 Castellane

Close to 'Route des Alpes' and the Gorges du Verdon, this site has a neat and tidy air. This is a very popular holiday area, the gorge, canoeing and rafting being the main attractions. Two heated swimming pools and numerous on-site activities help to keep non-canoeists here. It is a large level site, part meadow, part wooded. Entertainers provide games and competitions for all during July and August. Dances and discos suit all age groups (the latest finishing time is 11 pm. and after that someone patrols the site to make sure all is quiet). The river Verdon runs along one edge of the site, so watch children. One can walk to Castellane without using the main road. Facilities open all season.

Facilities: Washing machines and irons. Popular restaurant with terrace and bar including room with log fire for cooler evenings. Pizzeria/ crêperie. Takeaway (open twice daily). Two heated swimming pools and new paddling pool with 'mushroom' style fountain. Children's playgrounds. Minigolf, table tennis, archery, basketball and volleyball. Bicycle hire. Riding. Small fishing lake.

Tel: (0)4.92.83.61.29. Fax: (0)4.92.83.69.37. **Reservations:** Contact site direct, as above. **Open:** 15 May - 15 September.

Directions: From Castellane take D952 westwards towards Gorges du Verdon and Moustiers. Site is 1 km. on left.

CAMPSITE NAME Camp du verdon	Type of Accommodation 4 Person Mobile Home	Type of Accommodation 4 Person Chalet	Type of Accommodation Bungalow
Number of Persons	4 persons	4 persons	4 persons
Bedrooms	2 bedrooms: 1 x double, 1 x twin	2 bedrooms: 1 x double, 1 x twin	2 bedrooms: 1 x double, 1 x bunk bed
Lounge/Dining Area	Fully furnished	Fully furnished	Fully furnished
Kitchen Area	Fully equipped including gas hobs and fridge	Fully equipped including gas hobs and fridge	Fully equipped including gas hobs and fridge
Bath/Shower/WC	Washbasin, bath or shower, WC	Washbasin, shower, WC	Washbasin, shower, WC
Other Facilities	Garden table and chairs, deckchair	Garden table and chairs, deckchairs	Garden table and chairs, deckchairs
Bedding	Blankets and pillows provided	Blankets and pillows provided	Blankets and pillows provided
Pets	Accepted	Accepted	Accepted
Charges **From** (Low Season, per week) **To** (High Season, per week)	2002 €329 €588	2002 €357 €630	2002 €357 €630

0410 Camping International
Route Napoléon, 04120 Castellane

Camping International is a reasonably priced site situated in some of the most dramatic scenery in France and the views are spectacular. The swimming pool with its sunbathing area is in sunny location with fantastic views and is overlooked by the bar/restaurant, with the same views. In high season English speaking young people entertain children (3-8 years and teenagers). On some evenings the teenagers are taken to the woods for campfire 'sing-alongs' which can go on till the early hours without disturbing the rest of the site. There are twice weekly guided walks into the surrounding hills in the nearby George de Verdon – a very popular excursion. The weather in the hills here is very ambient without the excessive heat of the coast.

Facilities: Washing machines, driers and irons. Shop. Restaurant/takeaway. Swimming pool (all 1 May - 30 Sept). Children's animation and occasional evening entertainment in July/Aug. Children's play area, volleyball, football and boule pitches. Internet access.
Off site: Castellane (1.5 km) is an attractive little town with river for canoeing and canyoning.

Tel: (0)4.92.83.66.67. **Fax:** (0)4.92.83.77.67.
E-mail: campinginternational@wanadoo.fr
Reservations: Contact site direct, as above.
Open: 1 April - 30 September.

Directions: Site is 1 km. north of Castellane on the N85 'Route Napoleon'.

CAMPSITE NAME Camping International	Type of Accommodation Chalet Githotel
Number of Persons	6 persons
Bedrooms	2 bedrooms: 1 x double, 1 x twin, 1 x bunk bed
Lounge/Dining Area	Fully furnished
Kitchen Area	Fully equipped including microwave, gas hobs, coffee machine, kettle, fridge
Bath/Shower/WC	Washbasin, shower, WC
Other Facilities	Electric heating, terrace, garden table, deckchairs
Bedding	Blankets and pillows provided Sheets available at asupplement
Pets	Accepted
Charges **From** (Low Season, per week) **To** (High Season, per week)	2002 €111 (7 days for 2 week stays) €507

N8402 Domaine Naturiste de Bélézy
84410 Bédoin

Bélézy is an excellent naturist site with many amenities and activities at the foot of Mt Ventoux. The ambience is essentially relaxed and comfortable and the emphasis is on informality and concern for the environment. English is spoken widely amongst staff and customers although some activities may be conducted solely in French. The leisure park side of the site is also used for camping and is an area of natural parkland with an orchard, fishpond and woodland, with a good range of sports facilities. Near the pool area is the smart restaurant, with terrace, and the mellow old Mas (Provencal farmhouse) that houses many activities, as well as the library, near soundproof disco, information centre and children's club. Unusually there is a hydrotherapy centre (1/4-30/9) with many treatments available. Member France4 Naturisme.

Facilities: Shop (1/4-30/9). Restaurant and takeaway meals. Three swimming pools. Sauna. Two tennis courts. Boules and table tennis. Adventure play area. Range of activities including painting and pottery courses, language lessons, archery, music (bring your own instrument) and guided walks. Children's clubs in holiday periods.
Off site: It is possible to walk into Bédoin (street market - Monday mornings).

Tel: (0)4.90.65.60.18.
Fax: (0)4.90.65.94.45.
E-mail: belezy@pacwan.net.
Reservations: Contact site direct, as above.
Open: 11 March - 8 October.

Directions: From A7 autoroute or RN7 at Orange, take D950 southeast to Carpentras, then northeast via D974 to Bédoin. Site is signed in Bédoin, being about 2 km. northeast of the village.

CAMPSITE NAME Le Belezy	Type of Accommodation Mobile Home	Type of Accommodation Chalets "Cabanon"	Type of Accommodation Bungalows Eden
Number of Persons	5 persons	5 persons	5 persons
Bedrooms	2 bedrooms: 1 x double, 1 x twin, 1 x single sofa bed in living area	2 bedrooms: 1 x double, 1 x triple	2 bedrooms: 1 x double, 1 x triple
Lounge/Dining Area	Fully furnished	Fully furnished including Hi Fi Stereo	Fully furnished including Hi-Fi Stereo and TV
Kitchen Area	Fully equipped including oven with gas hobs, coffee machine and fridge	Fully equipped including gas hobs, coffee machine and fridge	Fully equipped including microwave, gas hobs, coffee machine, fridge, freezer
Bath/Shower/WC	Washbasin, shower, WC	Washbasin, shower, separate WC	Washbasin, shower, separate WC
Other Facilities	Gas heating, terrace, garden table and chairs, deckchair, parasol	Gas heating, double glazing, covered terrace, garden table and chairs	Gas heating, double glazing, partly covered terrace, garden table and chairs, deckchair
Bedding	Blankets, pillow and sheets provided	Blankets and pillow provided	Blankets, pillows and sheets provided
Pets	Not accepted	Not accepted	Not accepted
Charges **From** (Low Season, per week)	2002 €385 (prices for a family)	2002 €301 (prices for a family)	2002 €476 (prices for a family)
To (High Season, per week)	€721 (prices for a family)	€574 (prices for a family)	€847 (prices for a family)

Naturist Sites

We have had very favourable feedback from readers concerning our choice of naturist sites, which we first introduced in our 1992 editions. Over the last few years we have gradually added a few more.

Apart from the need to have a 'Naturist Licence' (see below), there is no need to be a practising naturist before visiting these sites. In fact, at least as far as British visitors are concerned, many are what might be described as 'holiday naturists' as distinct from the practice of naturism at other times. The emphasis in all the sites featured in this guide at least, is on naturism as 'life in harmony with nature', and respect for oneself and others and for the environment, rather than simply on nudity. In fact nudity is really only obligatory in the area of the swimming pools.

There are a number of rules, which amount to sensible and considerate guidelines designed to ensure that no-one invades someone else's privacy, creates any nuisance, or damages the environment. Whether as a result of these rules, the naturist philosophy generally, or the attitude of site owners and campers alike, we have been very impressed by all the naturist sites we have selected. Without exception they had a friendly and welcoming ambience, were all extremely clean and tidy and, in most cases, provided much larger than average pitches, with a wide range of activities both sporting and cultural.

The purpose of our including a number of naturist sites in our guide is to provide an introduction to naturist camping in Europe for British holidaymakers; we were actually surprised by the number of British campers we met on naturist sites, many of whom had 'stumbled across naturism almost by accident' but had found, like us, that these sites were amongst the nicest they had encountered.

We mentioned the Naturist Licence – French Law requires all campers over 16 years of age on naturist sites to have a 'licence'. These can be obtained in advance from either the British or French national naturist associations, but are also available on arrival at any recognised naturist site (a passport type photograph is required).

The eight naturist sites featured in this guide (the site numbers are prefixed with 'N'), together with the number of the page where they may be found, are:

Midi-Pyrénées

Major city: Toulouse
Départements: 09 Ariège, 31 Haute-Garonne, 32 Gers,
65 Hautes-Pyrénées, 81 Tarn, 82 Tarn-et Garonne
We have left the official region of the Midi-
Pyrénées almost intact except for
départements of Aveyron (12) and Lot
(46) which we believe sit better in our
Tourist region of the Dordogne/
Aveyron.

H ome of Armagnac, Rugby and the Three
Musketeers, the Midi-Pyrénées is the
largest region of France, extending from the
Dordogne in the north to the Spanish border. It is
blessed by bright sunlight and a fascinating range of
scenery. High chalk plateaux, majestic peaks, tiny
hidden valleys and small fortified sleepy villages,
which seem to have changed little since the Middle
Ages, contrast with the high-tech, industrial and
vibrant university city of Toulouse; also rich in art
and architecture. Lourdes is one of the most visited
pilgrimage sites in the world. Toulouse-Lautrec, the artist, was
born at Albi the capital of the département of Tarn. Much of the town is built of pink brick which
seems to glow when seen from the distance. In the east, the little town of Foix, with its maze of
steep, winding streets, is a convenient centre from which to explore the prehistoric caves at Niaux
and the Aladdin's Cave of duty-free gift shops in the independent state of Andorra. The Canal du
Midi that links Bordeaux to the Mediterranean was commissioned by Louis XIV in 1666 and is still
in working order to day.
Note: Site reports are laid out by département in numerical order.

Cuisine of the region
The cuisine of the Midi-Pyrénées is rich and strongly seasoned, making generous use of garlic
and goose fat
Foie Gras – specially preserved livers of goose and duck
Cassoulet – a hearty stew of duck, sausages and beans
Confit de Canard (d'oie) – preserved duck meat (goose)
Magret de canard – duck breast fillets
Poule au pot – chicken simmered with vegetables
Seafood such as oysters, salt-water fish, or piballes from the Adour river
Ouillat (Ouliat) – Pyrénées soup: onions, tomatoes, goose fat, garlic
Tourtière Landaise – a sweet of Agen prunes, apples and Armagnac
Grattons (Graisserons) – a mélange of small pieces of rendered down duck, goose,and pork fat;
served as an appetiser – very filling

Wine
There are some excellent regional wines, such as full-bodied red Cahors and, of course, Armagnac
to follow the meal. Try 'Floc', a mixture of Armagnac and grape juice

Places of Interest
Albi – birthplace and Museum of Toulouse-Lautrec, imposing Ste Cécile cathedral with 15C fresco
of 'The Last Judgement'
Collonges-la-Rouge – picturesque village of Medieval and Renaissance style mansions and manors
in red sandstone
Conques – 11th century Ste Foy Romanesque church
Cordes – medieval walled hilltop village
Foix – 11th/12th century towers on rocky peak above town; 14th century cathedral.
Lourdes – famous pilgrimage site where Ste Bernadette is said to have spoken to the Virgin Mary
in a grotto and known for the miracles said to have been performed there
Auch – capital of ancient Gascony, boasts a fine statue of d'Artágnan

0902 Camping L'Arize

Lieu-dit Bourtol, 09240 La Bastide-de-Sérou

You will receive a warm welcome from Dominique and Brigitte at this friendly little family site and Brigitte speaks excellent English. The site nestles in a delightful, tranquil valley among the foothills of the Pyrénées and is just east of the interesting village of La Bastide de Sérou beside the River Arize (good trout fishing). The river is fenced for the safety of children on the site, but may be accessed just outside the gate. Deer and wild boar are common in this area and may be sighted in quieter periods. The owners have built this site from ground level over the last few years and have put much love and care into its development. Discounts have been negotiated for several fascinating local attractions (details are provided in the comprehensive pack provided on arrival - in your own language). This is a comfortable and relaxing base for touring this beautiful part of the Pyrénées with easy access to the medieval town of Foix and even Andorra for duty-free shopping.

Facilities: Laundry room with dryer. Entertainment in high season, weekly barbecues and welcome drinks on Sundays. Fishing, riding and bicycle hire on site.

Off site: Golf 5 km. Several restaurants and shops are within a few minute's drive and the nearest restaurant, which is located at the national stud for the famous Merens horses just 200 m. away, will deliver takeaway meals to your pitch.

Tel: (0)5.61.65.81.51. **Fax:** (0)5.61.65.83.34. **E-mail:** camparize@aol.com
Reservations: Contact Alan Rogers Travel Service on Tel: 01892 55 98 98
Open: 28 March - 4 November.

Directions: Site is southeast of the village La Bastide-de-Sérou. Take the D15 towards Nescus and site is on right after approx. 1 km.

CAMPSITE NAME L'Arize	Type of Accommodation Willerby Mobile Homes
Number of Persons	6 persons
Bedrooms	2 bedrooms: 1 x double, 1 x twin, 1 x double sofa bed in living area
Lounge/Dining Area	Fully furnished
Kitchen Area	Fully equipped with gas hobs, coffee machine and fridge/freezer
Bath/Shower/WC	Washbasin, shower, separate WC
Other Facilities	Electric heating, double glazing, terrace, garden table, parasol, BBQ
Bedding	Blankets and pillows provided Sheets and towels available at a supplement
Pets	Accepted
Charges From (Low Season, per week) To (High Season, per week)	2002 €258 (2 persons) €308 (4/6 persons) €489

0906 Camping Le Pré Lombard
09400 Tarascon-sur-Ariège

Didier Mioni, the manager here follows the town motto 'S'y passos, y demoros – if you wish to come here, you will stay here' in his aim to ensure your satisfaction on his site. This busy, good value site is located beside the attractive river Ariége on the outskirts of the town. The chalets and mobile homes are situated at the rear of the site. A gate in the fence provides access to the river bank for fishing (licences required). The ducks here will be uninvited guests at your table if you are parked close to the river and provide an amusing diversion. As this is a town site there is some town and traffic noise during the day and evening. Open all year, it is an excellent choice for early or late breaks. This region of Ariège is in the foothills of the Pyrénées and 45 km. from Andorra. At Tarascon itself you can go underground at the Parc Pyrénéen de l'Art Préhistorique to view prehistoric rock paintings, or the really adventurous can take to the air for paragliding, hangliding, or microlighting. The Vallées Ax famous for cross-country skiing are within reasonably easy reach for winter sports enthusiasts.

Facilities: Laundry. Bar and takeaway (open according to demand). Bread, gas, papers and daily requirements sold in the bar. Good restaurant with entertainment and dancing, creating a very enjoyable French ambience. The associated covered riverside terrace is very smart (1/5-30/9). Fenced, unsupervised swimming pool (1/5-30/9, a new covered pool is planned). Separate playgrounds for toddlers and older children. Video games machines, table tennis, table football, boules and volleyball. Fishing. Full programme of entertainment for families in main season.

Off site: Large supermarket 300 m. Town 800 m. Archery, kayaking and fishing nearby.

Tel: (0)5.61.05.61.94. **Fax:** (0)5.61.05.78.93.
E-mail: camping@camping.le.prelombard.com
Reservations: Contact site direct, as above.
Open: all year.

Directions: Site is 800 m. south of the town centre adjacent to the river. Turn off main N20 into the town centre and there are prominent camp signs.

CAMPSITE NAME Le Pre Lombard	Type of Accommodation Chalets 6 persons	Type of Accommodation Mobile Home 6 persons	Type of Accommodation Mobile home 4 persons
Number of Persons	6 persons	6 persons	4 persons
Bedrooms	2 bedrooms: 1 x double, 1 x triple, 1 x double sofa bed in living area	2 bedrooms: 1 x double, 1 x twin, 1 x double sofa bed in living area	2 bedrooms: 1 x double, 1 x twin
Lounge/Dining Area	Fully furnished	Fully furnished	Fully furnished
Kitchen Area	Fully equipped including microwave and fridge	Fully equipped including microwave, oven with gas hobs, kettle, fridge	Fully equipped including microwave, gas hobs and fridge
Bath/Shower/WC	Washbasin, shower, separate WC	Washbasin, shower, separate WC	Washbasin, shower, separate WC
Other Facilities	Electric heating, terrace, garden table, parasol	Electric heating, terrace, garden table and chairs, parasol	Electric heating, terrace, garden table, parasol Blankets and pillows provided
Bedding	Blankets and pillows provided Sheets and towels available at a supplement	Blankets and pillows provided Sheets and towels available at a supplement	Sheets and towels available at a supplement
Pets	Accepted	Accepted	Accepted
Charges	2002	2002	2002
From (Low Season, per week)	€290	€275	€215
To (High Season, per week)	€360	€340	€275

For latest infomation visit **www.alanrogers.com**

N6501 Domaine Naturiste L'Eglantiere

Ariès-Espénan, 65230 Castelnau-Magnoac

This pretty site is situated in the valley between the Pyrénées and the plain, within easy reach of Lourdes and the mountains. Alongside a small, fast flowing river, in wooded surroundings comprises a 12 ha. area for touring pitches and accommodation with a further 32 for walking and relaxing in the woods and fields. The river is said to be suitable for swimming and canoeing, with fishing nearby. The site has an attractive, central, medium sized swimming pool with sunbathing areas both on paving and grass, and a children's pool, overlooked by the attractive style clubhouse and terrace. A small health centre (massage, sauna) is being developed in the old farmhouse. Member of France 4 Naturisme.

Facilities: Shop (June-Sept). Clubhouse with bar, small restaurant, pizzeria and takeaway

(June-mid Sept), internet access and indoor soundproofed activities/disco area, play room for younger children and table tennis for older ones. Swimming pool (April - end Sept). Children's play area and children's animation in season. Volleyball, badminton, table tennis, petanque and archery. Activities on the river. Canoe and mountain bike hire. Trekking and cross country cycling. Barbecues are officially forbidden. Torches useful.

Off site: Restaurants in the nearby village.

Tel: (0)5.62.99.83.64 or (0)5.62.39.88.00.
Fax: (0)5.62.39.81.44.
E-mail: infos@leglantiere.com
Reservations: Contact site direct, as above.
Open: Easter - October.

Directions: From Auch take D929 south in direction of Lannemezan. Just after Castelnau-Magnoac watch for signs to hamlet of Ariès-Espénan on left and follow site signs.

CAMPSITE NAME L'Eglantière	Type of Accommodation Les Gîtes	Type of Accommodation Mobil home	Type of Accommodation Chalet
Number of Persons	3 persons	4/6 persons	5/6 persons
Bedrooms	2 bedrooms: 1x double, 1x single	2 bedrooms: 1x double, 1x twin, 1x double sofa bed in living area	2 bedrooms: 1x double, 1x triple, 1x sofa bed
Lounge/Dining Area	Fully Furnished	Fully Furnished	Fully Furnished
Kitchen Area	Fully equipped including, electric rings, microwave, kettle, coffee machine and fridge/freezer	Fully equipped including, gas hobs, microwave, kettle, coffee machine and fridge/freezer	Fully equipped including, gas hobs, microwave, kettle, coffee machine and fridge/freezer
Bath/Shower/WC	Washbasin, shower, WC	Washbasin, shower, separate WC	Washbasin, shower, separate WC
Other Facilities	Electric heating, terrace, garden table & chairs, deckchair, parasol	Electric heating, terrace, garden table & chairs, deckchair, parasol	Electric heating, double glazing, terrace, garden table & chairs, deckchair, parasol
Bedding	Blankets and pillows provided Sheets available at a supplement	Blankets and pillows provided Sheets available at a supplement	Blankets and pillows provided Sheets available at a supplement
Pets	Accepted	Accepted	Accepted
Charges **From** (Low Season, per week) **To** (High Season, per week)	2002 €270 €626	2002 €235 €607	2002 ¤315

Mediterranean

Our 'Mediterranean' Tourist region includes all the areas which border the Mediterranean.

LANGUEDOC-ROUSSILLON

Major cities: Montpellier, Perpignan, Nîmes, Carcassonne

Départements: 11 Aude, 30 Gard, 34 Hérault, 66 Pyrénées-Orientales

COASTAL PROVENCE

Major city: Marseille

Départements:
13 Bouches-du-Rhône, 83 Var

CÔTE D'AZUR

Major cities: Nice, Cannes, Monte Carlo (Monaco)

Départements: 06 Alpes-Maritime

O nce an independent duchy, the ancient land of **Languedoc** combines two distinct regions: the vineyards of the Corbières and Minervois and the coastal plain stretching from the Rhône to the Spanish border. Much of the region is rugged and unspoilt and there is ample evidence of the dramatic past. On the coast the vast sandy beaches/resorts, for example La Grande Motte, Cap d'Agde and Canet, are being promoted as an alternative to the more famous Mediterranean stretches of the Côte d'Azur.

The mention of **Provence** immediately draws to mind lavender fields and olive groves; it is a sunny bright region backed by mountains, with a glittering coastline. The Romans settled in the region and their legacy remains in the great amphitheatres and monuments of Arles and Nîmes. The Rhône valley divides above Arles into two arms which encircle the marshlands of the Camargue before reaching the sea. The wild white horses which gallop, manes flying, through the shallow waters of the delta are legendary, as are the ragged black bulls and the rose and white flamingos.

The **Côte d'Azur**, perhaps better known as the French Riviera, is a beautiful stretch of coast studded with sophisticated towns such as Monte Carlo, Nice, and Cannes, not forgetting the other famous resort of St Tropez. The quaint harbours and fishing villages have become chic destinations, now full of pleasure yachts and crowded summertime beaches. Up in the hills are quieter tiny medieval villages of winding streets and white-walled houses with terracotta roofs, which have attracted artists and visitors for many years.

Cuisine of the region emphasizes seasonings, such as herbs and garlic, and fish

Aigo Bouido – garlic and sage soup with bread (or eggs and cheese)

Aïoli (aïlloli) – a mayonnaise sauce with garlic and olive oil

Bouillabaisse – fish soup served with safran (saffron) and aïoli (see above)

Pain Bagna – bread roll with olive oil, anchovies, olives, onions, etc.

Pissaladière – Provencal bread dough with onions, anchovies, olives, etc.

Pommade – a thick paste of garlic, basil, cheese and olive oil

Ratatouille – aubergines, courgettes, onions, garlic, red peppers and tomatoes in olive oil

Salade Niçoise – tomatoes, beans, potatoes, black olives, anchovy, lettuce and olive oil and tuna fish

Touron – a pastry of almonds, pistachio nuts and fruit

Places of interest

Aigues-Mortes – medieval city

Aix-en-Provence – old town with 17th/18th century character; Paul Cézanne and Tapestry museums

Cannes – popular for conventions and festivals, Cannes Film Festival, la Croisette, old city

Carcassonne – largest medieval walled city in Europe

Monte Carlo – main city of Monaco, casinos, gardens, Napoleon Museum. motorsport circuit

Montpellier – famous for universities, Roman sites; Gothic cathedral

Nîmes – Roman remains and amphitheatre, Pont du Gard

Perpignan – Kings Palace; Catalan characteristics; the old fortress dominates the centre of the city and many of the side streets are more Spanish than French

Villeneuve-lès-Avignon – Royal City and residence of popes in 14th century

For latest infomation visit **www.alanrogers.com**

N0607 Domaine Naturiste Club Origan

06260 Puget-Theniers

Origan is a naturist site set in the mountains behind Nice. Despite its rather spectacular location, it is easily accessible from the coast and you only discover that you are at a height of 500 m. when you arrive! The terrain within the extensive confines of the site is fairly wild and the roads distinctly stony. The scenery is impressive and footpaths in and around the site offer good, if fairly strenuous walks up to a height of 1,000 m. There are many wild flowers and good views. Member France4 Naturisme.

Facilities: Laundry facilities. Shop (1/6-15/9). Bar/restaurant (all season). Takeaway. Heated swimming pools, one for children (1/5-31/8). Jacuzzi and new sauna. Disco in cellars. Tennis. Fishing. Bicycle hire. Organised activities for adults and children (high season). Individual barbecues are not permitted. Torches advised. Off site: The nearby small town of Puget-Theniers is very pleasant and offers choice of bars, cafés, shops, etc.

Tel: (0)4.93.05.06.00.
Fax: (0)4.93.05.09.34.
E-mail: michel.authiat@wanadoo.fr.
Reservations: Contact Nat' Azur, 23 avenue J. Médecin, 06000 Nice. (Tel: (0)4.93.88.28.61. **Fax:** (0)4.93.87.47.49). **Open:** 1 April - 30 September.

Directions: Heading west on the N202, just past the town of Puget-Theniers, turn right at camp sign at level crossing; site is 1.5 km.

CAMPSITE NAME Naturist Club Origan	Type of Accommodation Campitel 4	Type of Accommodation Mobile Home Luxe Provence 4	Type of Accommodation Mazet 6
Number of Persons	4 persons	4 persons	6 persons
Bedrooms	2 bedrooms: 1 x double, 1 x twin	2 bedrooms: 1 x double, 1 x twin	1 bedroom: 1 x double, 2 x twin
Lounge/Dining Area	Fully furnished	Fully furnished including TV	Fully furnished including TV
Kitchen Area	Fully equipped including gas hobs and fridge	Fully equipped including gas hobs and fridge	Fully equipped including gas hobs and fridge
Bath/Shower/WC	Washbasin, shower, WC	Washbasin, shower, separate WC	Washbasin, shower, WC
Other Facilities	Electric heating, terrace, garden table	Electric heating, terrace, garden table, deckchairs, parasol	Electric heating, terrace, garden table
Bedding	Blankets and pillows provided Sheets available at a supplement	Blankets and pillows provided Sheets available at a supplement	Blankets and pillows provided Sheets available at a supplement
Pets	Accepted	Accepted	Accepted
Charges **From** (Low Season, per week) **To** (High Season, per week)	2002 €205 €655	2002 €215 €670	2002 €215 €670

1106 Camping Le Domaine d'Arnauteille
11250 Montclar

Enjoying some of the best and most varied views of any site we have visited, this rather unusual site is ideally situated for exploring, by foot or car, the little known Aude Département, the area of the Cathars and for visiting the walled city of Carcassonne (10 minutes drive). The site itself is set in 115 hectares of farmland and is on hilly ground. The facilities are quite spread out with the swimming pool set in a hollow basin surrounded by green fields. The reception building is vast; originally a farm building, with a newer top floor being converted to apartments. Although architecturally rather strange, from some angles it is quite attractive and mature trees soften the outlines. This is a developing site with enthusiastic owners for whom riding is the principle theme with stables on site (remember that the French are more relaxed about hard hats, etc). Some up and down walking between the accommodation and facilities is unavoidable. A 'Sites et Paysages' member.

Facilities: Laundry. Small shop (15/5-30/9 – the site is a little out of the way). Restaurant in converted stable block offers plat du jour, grills, takeaway (15/5-30/9). Swimming pool (25 x 10 m.) with children's pool. Children's play area. Table tennis and volleyball. Riding (stables open 15/6-15/9).

Off site: Bicycle hire 8 km, fishing 3 km, golf 10 km, rafting and canoeing near, plus many walks with marked paths.

Tel: (0)4.68.26.84.53. **Fax:** (0)4.68.26.91.10.
E-mail: arnauteille@mnet.fr
Reservations: Contact site direct, as above.
Open: 1 April - 30 September.

Directions: Using D118 from Carcassonne, after bypassing the small village of Rouffiac d'Aude, there is a small section of dual carriageway. Before the end of this, turn right to Montclar up a rather narrow road for 2.5 km. Site is signed sharp left and up hill before the village.

CAMPSITE NAME Domaine d'Arnauteille	Type of Accommodation Mobile home	Type of Accommodation Mobile Home O'Hara	Type of Accommodation Chalet Grand Confort
Number of Persons	4/6 persons	4/6 persons	5/7 persons
Bedrooms	2 bedrooms: 1 x double, 1 x twin, 1 x double sofa bed in living area	2 bedrooms: 1 x double, 1 x twin, 1x double sofa bed in living area	2 bedrooms: 1 x double, 1 x triple, 1 x double sofa bed in living area
Lounge/Dining Area	Fully furnished	Fully furnished	Fully furnished
Kitchen Area	Fully equipped including gas hobs, coffee machine and fridge	Fully equipped including microwave, oven with gas hobs, coffee machine and fridge/freezer	Fully equipped including microwave, gas hobs, coffee machine and fridge
Bath/Shower/WC	Washbasin, shower, separate WC	Washbasin, shower, WC	Washbasin, shower, separate WC
Other Facilities	Electric heating, terrace, garden table and chairs	Electric heating, terrace, garden table and chairs	Electric heating, terrace, garden table and chairs
Bedding	Blankets and pillows provided Sheets available at a supplement on reservation	Blankets and pillows provided Sheets available at a supplement on reservation	Blankets and pillows provided Sheets available at a supplement on reservation
Pets	Accepted	Accepted	Accepted
Charges **From** (Low Season, per week) **To** (High Season, per week)	2002 €245 €475	2002 €280 €560	2002 €295 €590

1107 Camping Club Les Mimosas
Chaussée de Mandirac, 11100 Narbonne

Being some 6 km. inland from the beaches of Narbonne and Gruissan, this site benefits from a somewhat less hectic situation than others in the popular seaside environs of Narbonne. The site itself is, however, quite lively with plenty to amuse and entertain the younger generation while, at the same time, offering facilities for the whole family. This could be a very useful site offering many possibilities to meet a variety of needs, on-site entertainment (including an evening on 'Cathare' history), and easy access to popular beaches, interesting towns such as Narbonne itself, Béziers or the 'Cité de Carcassonne', the Canal du Midi and Cathar castles.

Facilities: Washing machines. Shop (1/4-15/10). Bar. Small lounge, amusements. Restaurant (1/4-15/10). Heated swimming pool complex including new, landscaped pool with slides and islands, the original pool and a children's pool (1/5-30/9). New adventure play area. Minigolf planned. **Off site:** Riding near. Lagoon for boating and fishing can be reached

via footpath (about 200 m).

Tel: (0)4.68.49.03.72. **Fax:** (0)4.68.49.39.45.
E-mail: info@lesmimosas.com.
Reservations: Contact site direct, as above.
Open: 29 March - 31 October.

Directions: From A9 take exit 38 (Narbonne Sud) and go round roundabout to last exit taking you back over the autoroute (site signed from here). Follow signs to La Nautique and then Mandirac and site (total 6 km. from autoroute)- Or why not fly direct from Stanstead to Carcassonne by Ryanair.

CAMPSITE NAME Les Mimosas	Type of Accommodation Mobile Home	Type of Accommodation 6 Person Chalet Gitotel	Type of Accommodation 4 Person Chalet Gitotel
Number of Persons	6 persons	6 persons	4 persons
Bedrooms	2 bedrooms: 1 x double, 1 x twin, 1x double sofa bed in living area	2 bedrooms: 1 x double, 1x double with 1 x twin	2 bedrooms: 1 x double, 1 x twin
Lounge/Dining Area	Fully furnished	Fully furnished	Fully furnished
Kitchen Area	Fully equipped including gas hobs, coffee machine and fridge	Fully equipped including gas hobs, coffee machine and fridge	Fully equipped including gas hobs, coffee machine and fridge
Bath/Shower/WC	Washbasin, shower, WC	Washbasin, shower, separate WC	Washbasin, shower, WC
Other Facilities	Electric or gas heating, garden table and chairs, deckchair	Electric heating, garden table and chairs, deckchair	Electric heating, garden table and chairs
Bedding	Blankets and pillows provided	Blankets and pillows provided	Blankets and pillows provided
Pets	Accepted	Accepted	Accepted
Charges **From** (Low Season, per week) **To** (High Season, per week)	2001 €243.92 €533.57	2001 €243.92 €606.75	2001 €213,43 €472,59

N3010 Domaine de la Sablière
Saint-Privat-de-Champclos, 30430 Barjac

Spectacularly situated in the Cèze Gorges, this naturist site occupies a much larger area than its total of 250 pitches might suggest. It offers a wide variety of facilities, all within a really peaceful, wooded and dramatic setting. A swimming pool complex (dynamited out of the hill and built in local style and materials) provides a children's pool and two large pools, one of which can be covered by a sliding glass dome, sunbathing terraces, bar, sauna, TV room and disco. This is essentially a family run and orientated site and the owner/manager, Gaby Cespedes, and her team provide a personal touch that is unusual in a large site. This no doubt contributes to the relaxed and very informal atmosphere and first time naturists would probably find this a gentle introduction into naturism without any pressure. You must expect some fairly steep walking between pitches, pool complex, restaurant and supermarket.

Entertainment programme for adults and children (mid June - end Aug). Torch useful.

Facilities: Laundry. Supermarket and charcuterie. Open air, covered restaurant (all season) with good value waiter service meals and a takeaway in an attractive setting. Swimming pool complex. Small café/crêperie. Varied and numerous activities include walking, climbing, swimming, canoeing, fitness trail, fishing (permit required), archery, tennis, minigolf and volleyball, book binding, yoga etc.

Tel: (0)4.66.24.51.16. **Fax:** (0)4.66.24.58.69.
E-mail: sabliere@club-internet.fr.
Reservations: Contact site direct, as above.
Open: Easter - end September.

Directions: From Barjac take D901 east for 3 km. Site is signed just before St Privat-de-Champclos and is approx. 3 km. on narrow roads following camp signs.

CAMPSITE NAME La Sablière	Type of Accommodation Chalet Marina	Type of Accommodation Chalet Lavande	Type of Accommodation Residence Mobile Home
Number of Persons	6 persons	4 persons	6 persons
Bedrooms	2 bedrooms: 1x double, 1x twin, 1x double sofa bed in living area	1 bedroom: 1x double, 1x double sofa bed in living area	2 bedrooms: 1x double, 1x twin, 1x double sofa bed in living area
Lounge/Dining Area	Fully furnished	Fully furnished	Fully furnished
Kitchen Area	Fully equipped including gas hobs, coffee machine and fridge	Fully equipped including gas hobs, coffee machine and fridge	Fully equipped including gas hobs, coffee machine and fridge
Bath/Shower/WC	Washbasin, shower, separate WC	Washbasin, shower, WC	Washbasin, shower, separate WC
Other Facilities	Garden table and chairs, deckchair, parasol, BBQ	Terrace, garden table and chairs, deckchair, parasol, BBQ	Terrace, garden table and chairs, deckchair, parasol, BBQ
Bedding	Blankets and pillows provided Sheets, towels and washing available at a supplement	Blankets and pillows provided Sheets, towels and washing available at a supplement	Blankets and pillows provided Sheets, towels and washing available at a supplement
Pets	Accepted	Accepted	Accepted
Charges **From** (Low Season, per week) **To** (High Season, per week)	2002 ¤273 ¤659	2002 ¤245 ¤565	2002 ¤197 ¤548

3407 Camping Village Le Sérignan Plage

34410 Sérignan

This is the sister site to Sérignan Plage Naturist (no. 3408N). This is a large, but very comfortable site, built in a genuinely unique style with direct access to a beautiful sandy beach. Perhaps the most remarkable aspect of this site is the cluster of attractive buildings which form the central 'village' area with shops, pretty bars and a smart restaurant, amongst which is a small indoor heated swimming pool of unusual design mainly for out of season use. There is also an excellent outdoor pool complex, attractively landscaped and surrounded by a very large grass sunbathing area complete with sun loungers. The village area with inner and outer courtyards, has a lively, international atmosphere (well used and perhaps showing some wear and tear). Entertainment is provided every evening in high season and daily sporting activities. Wine and food tastings with tourist information presentations each Monday at 5 pm. There is something for everyone here and you will not need to leave the site if you do not wish to. Remember, this is a seaside site in a natural coastal environment, so do not expect it to be neat and manicured; in parts nature still

predominates. The site has direct access to a superb, large sandy beach.

Facilities: Laundry facilities. Well-stocked supermarket, bakery, newsagent/tabac, ATM and range of market stalls including meat, fish and vegetables. Launderette. Bars, restaurant, disco, small amphitheatre, indoor heated pool and landscaped outdoor pool complex with lifeguards (main season)
Off site: Riding 2 km, golf 10 km. Bicycle hire. Sailing and windsurfing school on beach.

Tel: (0)4.67.32.35.33. **Fax:** (0)4.67.32.26.36.
E-mail: info@serignanplage.com
Reservations: Contact Alan Rogers Travel Service on 01892 55 98 98
Open: 7 April - 16 September.

Directions: From A9 exit 35 (Béziers Est) follow signs for Sérignan on D64 (9 km). Don't go into Sérignan, but take sign for Sérignan Plage for 4 km. At small multi sign (blue) turn right onto one-way for 500m. At T-junction turn left over small road bridge and follow signs to site (300m).

CAMPSITE NAME Serignan Plage	Type of Accommodation Chalet Gitotel	Type of Accommodation Mobile home	Type of Accommodation Chalet Titom
Number of Persons	6 persons	6 persons	4 persons
Bedrooms	2 bedrooms: 1 x double 1 x double, 1 x bunk bed	2 bedrooms: 1 x double, 1 x twin, 1 x double sofa bed in living area	2 bedrooms: 1 x double, 1 x twin
Lounge/Dining Area	Fully furnished	Fully furnished	Fully furnished
Kitchen Area	Fully equipped including gas hobs, fridge/freezer	Fully equipped including gas hobs, fridge/freezer	Fully equipped including gas hobs and fridge
Bath/Shower/WC	Washbasin, shower, WC	Washbasin, shower, separate WC	Washbasin, shower, WC
Other Facilities	Garden table and chairs	Garden table and chairs	Terrace, 2 deckchairs
Bedding	Blankets and pillows provided	Blankets and pillows provided	Blankets and pillows provided
Pets	Not accepted	Not accepted	Not accepted
Charges **From** (Low Season, per week) **To** (High Season, per week)	2002 €220 €710	2002 €200 €660	2002 €180 €585

N3408 Camping Le Sérignan Plage Nature

34410 Sérignan

Sérignan Plage Nature is a very comfortable and distinctly characterful naturist site beside a large sandy beach. It was for many years run as a private club but in recent years the charming, English speaking owner, Jean Guy Amat, has improved facilities here to make the site a distinctly comfortable, relaxed and friendly naturist site. The Romanesque architectural style of several of the buildings (one is called the Forum) has been preserved. There is a warm and friendly ambience at the bar and restaurant and a range of evening entertainment is provided. This atmosphere is helped in no small measure by the enthusiasm of the restaurant and shop managers. This is a well equipped family oriented campsite, with many facilities and good quality, all round entertainment in season. It has the additional benefit of direct access to a superb, safe and virtually private naturist beach of fine sand (with lifeguard in high season).

Facilities: Washing machines. Large supermarket, market for fresh fruit and vegetables, newsagent/souvenir shop and ice cream kiosk. Bar, restaurant with reasonably priced menu. Evening entertainment. Children's disco.
Off site: Riding 2 km.

Tel: (0)4.67.32.09.61. **Fax:** (0)4.67.32.26.36.
E-mail: info@serignannaturisme.com
Reservations: Contact Alan Rogers Travel Service on 01892 55 98 98
Open: 1 May - 30 September.

Directions: From A9 exit 35 (Béziers Est) follow signs for Sérignan on D64 (9km). Prior to Sérignan take road to Sérignan plage. At small multi sign (blue) turn right onto one-way single carriage (poorly surfaced) for 500m. At T-junction turn left over small bridge and site is 75m on right immediately after left hand bend (not the first, but the second naturist site).

CAMPSITE NAME Serignan Plage Nature	Type of Accommodation Chalet Gitotel	Type of Accommodation 6 Person Mobile Home	Type of Accommodation 4 Person Mobile Home
Number of Persons	6 persons	6 persons	4 persons
Bedrooms	2 bedrooms:1 x double 1 x double, 1 x bunk bed	2 bedrooms: 1 x double, 1 x twin, 1 x double sofa bed in living area	2 bedrooms: 1 x double, 1 x twin
Lounge/Dining Area	Fully furnished	Fully furnished	Fully furnished
Kitchen Area	Fully equipped including gas hobs, fridge/freezer	Fully equipped including gas hobs, fridge/freezer	Fully equipped including gas hobs, fridge/freezer
Bath/Shower/WC	Washbasin, shower, WC	Washbasin, shower, separate WC	Washbasin, shower, separate WC
Other Facilities	Covered terrace, garden table and chairs	Garden table and chairs	Garden table and chairs
Bedding	Blankets and pillows provided	Blankets and pillows provided	Blankets and pillows provided
Pets	Not accepted	Not accepted	Not accepted
Charges **From** (Low Season, per week) **To** (High Season, per week)	2002 €245 €630	2002 €220 €610	2002 €195 €570

3414 Haven Europe La Carabasse
Route de Farinette, 34450 Vias-sur-Mer

La Carabasse, a Haven Europe holiday park, is situated on the outskirts of Vias Plage, a popular place with lots of shops and restaurants. The site has everything you could need with two good pools, bars and a restaurant. There are lots of activities for young families and teenagers. The bars and restaurant provide live music in the evenings and entertainment. The wonderful Mediterranean beaches are close and La Carabasse has its own beach club for windsurfing and pedaloes. A lively site in high season, not as well-cared for as we would normally expect from Haven, nor with their usual high standard of service, but Haven Europe have not long taken this site over and we are assured that these problems will be addressed for the 2002 season.

Facilities: Bars, restaurant and swimming pools. Beach club for windsurfing and pedaloes. Wealth of daytime activities from

golf lessons to aqua-aerobics and tennis tournaments. Evening entertainment in the Haven style.

Tel: (0)4.67.21.64.01. **Fax:** (0)4.67.21.76.87. **Reservations:** Contact site or Haven Europe in the UK (quoting this guide as a reference) on 0870 242 7777.
Open: 15 April - 14 September.

Directions: Site is south of Vias. From N112 (Agde - Beziers) road turn right at signs for Vias-Plage (D137) and site (on the left).

CAMPSITE NAME La Carabasse	Type of Accommodation Standard Mobile Homes	Type of Accommodation Luxury mobile homes	Type of Accommodation Chalets/Lodges/ Apartments
Number of Persons	4/8 persons	7/8 persons	4/8 persons
Bedrooms	2 - 3 bedrooms: 2 x double, 1 x twin, 1 x double sofa bed in living area	2 - 3 bedrooms: 2 x double, 1 x twin, 1 x double sofa bed in living area	1 - 3 bedrooms: 2 x double, 1 x twin, 1 x double sofa bed in living area
Lounge/Dining Area	Fully furnished	Fully furnished	Fully furnished, some include Hi Fi
Kitchen Area	Fully equipped including full cooker and fridge	Fully equipped including microwave, full cooker and fridge/freezer. Some include dishwasher	Fully equipped including microwave, full cooker and fridge/freezer. Some include dishwasher
Bath/Shower/WC	Washbasin, shower, WC	Washbasin, shower, WC	Washbasin, shower, WC
Other Facilities	Gas fire, garden table and chairs, BBQ	Gas fire, garden table and chairs, BBQ	Central heating, garden table and chairs, BBQ
Bedding	Blankets and pillows provided	Blankets and pillows provided	Blankets and pillows provided
Pets	Not accepted	Not accepted	Not accepted
Charges From (Low Season, per week) To (High Season, per week)	2002 £183 - £260 £662 - £872	2002 £260 - £330 £886 - £1054	2002 £190 - £393 £669 - £1166

3415 Camping Club Nouvelle Floride

34340 Marseillan-Plage

Marseillan Plage is a small, busy resort just east of Cap d'Adge and La Nouvelle Floride enjoys a super position immediately beside a long gently shelving sandy beach. Amenities and facilities are generally of excellent quality and include a strikingly attractive bar area overlooking the beach with a raised stage for entertainment. Alongside the play area is a multi-purpose ball court and fitness centre, also on sand with robust machines with the idea of keeping Mum and Dad fit whilst still keeping an eye on the children. Essentially a 'holiday site', there is an extensive programme of entertainment and activities catering for all ages. However, the main attraction for most will almost certainly be the direct access to a fine beach. The gates on the beach entrance are locked at 9 pm. for security. This is a well-run, family run site aimed at families. A 'Yelloh Village' member.

Facilities: Bar all season, restaurant in high season then varying with demand. Shop all season. Swimming pool and paddling pool (all season). Play area, fitness centre and multi-purpose ball court. Table tennis. Weekly films (DVD) and variety of organised games, competitions, dances and discos. Mini-club in school holidays. Bicycle hire.

Tel: (0)4.67.21.94.49. **Fax:** (0)4.67.21.81.05.
Reservations: Contact Alan Rogers Travel Service on 01892 55 98 98
Open: 1 April - 30 September.

Directions: From A9 autoroute exit 34, follow N312 to Agde then take N112 towards Sete. Watch for signs to Marseillan Plage from where site is well signed.

CAMPSITE NAME Nouvelle Floride	Type of Accommodation Mobile Home O'Hara	Type of Accommodation Mobile Home
Number of Persons	6 persons	6 persons
Bedrooms	2 bedrooms: 1 x double, 1 x twin, 1 x double sofa bed in living area	2 bedrooms: 1 x double, 1 x twin, 1 x double sofa bed in living area, or bunkbeds
Lounge/Dining Area	Fully furnished	Fully furnished
Kitchen Area	Fully equipped including microwave, gas hobs, coffee machine and fridge	Fully equipped including gas hobs, coffee machine and fridge
Bath/Shower/WC	Washbasin, shower, separate WC	Washbasin, shower and WC
Other Facilities	Electric heating, double glazing, garden table and sun loungers, BBQ	Electric heating, terrace, garden table, BBQ
Bedding	Blankets and pillows provided Sheets available at a supplement	Blankets and pillows provided Sheets available at a supplement
Pets	Not accepted	Not accepted
Charges **From** (Low Season, per week) **To** (High Season, per week)	€260 €700	€230 €655

8302 Esterel Caravaning
Route de Valescure, 83700 St Raphaël-Agay

Esterel is a quality site east of St Raphaël, set among the hills at the back of Agay. It is an attractive quiet situation with good views around. The site is 3.5 km. from the sandy beach at Agay where parking is perhaps a little easier than at most places on this coast. A pleasant courtyard area contains the shop and bar, with a terrace overlooking the attractively landscaped (floodlit at night) pool complex. Wild boar come to the perimeter fence each evening to be fed by visitors. This is a good site, well run and organised in a deservedly popular area. A member of 'Les Castels' group.

Facilities: Laundry room. Shop. Takeaway. Bar/restaurant. Five heated, circular swimming pools, one large for adults, one smaller for children and three arranged as a waterfall (1/4-30/9). New disco. Archery, volleyball, minigolf, two tennis courts, pony rides, petanque and squash court. Children's playground. Bicycle hire. Events and entertainment are organised in season. Barbecues are forbidden.
Off site: Good golf courses very close. Trekking by foot, bicycle or by pony in the surrounding natural environment of L'Esterel forest park.

Tel: (0)4.94.82.03.28. **Fax:** (0)4.94.82.87.37.
E-mail: contact@esterel-caravaning.fr
Reservations: Contact site direct, as above.
Open: 1 April - 30 September.

Directions: You can approach from St Raphaël via Valescure but easiest way is to turn off the coast road at Agay where there are good signs. From Fréjus exit from autoroute A8, follow signs for Valescure throughout, then for Agay, and site is on left. (Reader's comment: If in doubt, follow golf complex signs, or Leclerc). The road from Agay is the easiest to follow.

CAMPSITE NAME Esterel	Type of Accommodation Mobile home Mini Luxe	Type of Accommodation Mobile home Luxus 1	Type of Accommodation Mobile home Luxus 2
Number of Persons	4 persons	6 persons	6 persons
Bedrooms	2 bedrooms: 1 x double (140), 1 x double (120)	2 bedrooms: 2 x double, 1 x twin	2 bedrooms: 2 x double, 1 x twin
Lounge/Dining Area	Fully furnished	Fully furnished	Fully furnished
Kitchen Area	Fully equipped including gas hobs and fridge	Fully equipped including oven (in most), gas hobs and fridge	Fully equipped including oven (in most), gas hobs and fridge
Bath/Shower/WC	Washbasin, shower, WC	Washbasin, shower, WC	Washbasin, shower, WC
Other Facilities	Electric heating, garden table and chairs	Gas or electric heating, garden table and chairs	Gas or electric heating, garden table and chairs
Bedding	Blankets and pillows provided	Blankets and pillows provided	Blankets and pillows provided
Pets	Accepted	Not accepted	Accepted
Charges 2002	2002	2002	2002
From (Low Season, per week)	€210	€300	€270
To (High Season, per week)	€650	€670	€710

If you're interested in the

ALAN ROGERS' GOOD CAMPS GUIDE

you'll probably be interested in

THE GOOD MAGAZINE GUIDE

ON SALE the first Thursday of the month

ON SALE the second Thursday of the month

For tests and touring features 12 months of the year choose Britain's premier caravan and motorhome magazines.

On sale at most good newsagents or by subscription - telephone

01778 391134

ON SALE the fourth Thursday of the month

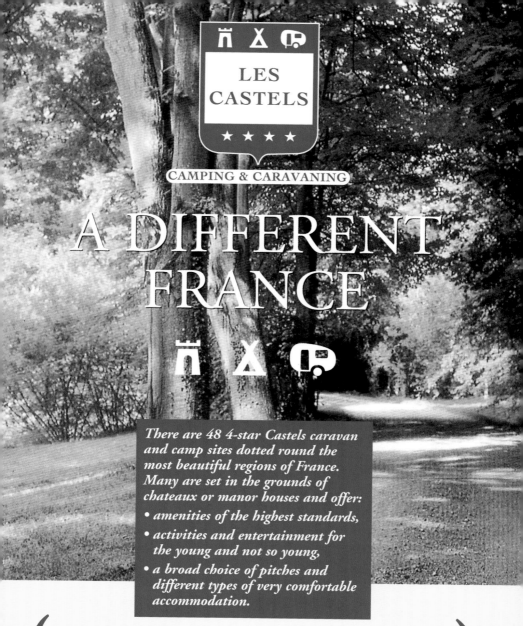

LES CASTELS

★ ★ ★ ★

CAMPING & CARAVANING

A DIFFERENT FRANCE

There are 48 4-star Castels caravan and camp sites dotted round the most beautiful regions of France. Many are set in the grounds of chateaux or manor houses and offer:

- *amenities of the highest standards,*
- *activities and entertainment for the young and not so young,*
- *a broad choice of pitches and different types of very comfortable accommodation.*

100 ℱ a night for a pitch for 2 people, with electricity, whatever the site and length of stay when you present your Privilege Card.*

To find out more, contact us and

- receive our brochure-road map free of charge
- book your Privilege Card for the year 2002 (50 FF)
- order the presentation guidebook for our 50 Castels camp sites (contribution to expenses: 50 FF)

*offer valid at most camp sites from opening up until 30/06 and from 1/09 until the closing of the comp sites for anyone who has ordered the Privilege Card from our secretary.

e mail: mail@les-castels.com - Fax: + 33 (0)2 97 47 50 72
Address: Secrétariat LES CASTELS - C.P. 3751 - 56037 VANNES Cedex - France
Internet sites: www.les-castels.com- www.castels-campings.com
Tel : + 33 (0)2 97 42 57 12

8307 Camping-Caravaning L'Etoile d'Argens
83370 St Aygulf

First impressions of L'Etoile d'Argens are of space, cleanliness and calm. Reception staff are very friendly and English is spoken (open 24 hrs). This is a site run with families in mind and many of the activities are free, making for a good value holiday. The pool and bar area is attractively landscaped with old olive and palm trees on beautifully manicured and watered grass. The river runs along one side of the site and a free boat service (15/6-15/9) runs every 40 minutes to the beach. It is also possible to moor a boat or fish. This is a good family site for the summer but also good in low season for a quiet stay in a superb location. For a large site it is usually calm and peaceful, even in July.

Facilities: Laundry. Supermarket. Bar, restaurant, pizzeria, takeaway. Two adult pools, children's paddling pool and solarium. Tennis (two of the four courts are floodlit) with coaching and

minigolf (both free in low season), aerobics, archery (July/Aug), football and swimming lessons. Volleyball, basketball, table tennis and boule. Children's play area with rubber safety base. Children's entertainer in July/Aug. Activity programme includes games, dances for adults and escorted walking trips to the surrounding hills. **Off site:** Golf, riding or bicycle hire within 3 km.

Tel: (0)4.94.81.01.41. **Fax:** (0)4.94.81.21.45.
E-mail: letoiledeargens@wanadoo.fr
Reservations: Contact site direct, as above.
Open: Easter - 30 September, with all services.

Directions: Leave A8 at exit 36 and take N7 to Le Muy and Fréjus. After about 8 km. at roundabout take D7 signed Roquebrune and St Aygulf. In 9.5 km. (after roundabout) turn left signed Fréjus. Watch for site sign and ignore width and height limit signs as site is 500 m. to right.

CAMPSITE NAME Etoile d'Argens	Type of Accommodation Mobile Home Watipi	Type of Accommodation Mobile home IRM	Type of Accommodation Mobile home luxe
Number of Persons	5 persons	4 persons	6 persons
Bedrooms	2 bedrooms: 1 x double, 1 x twin, 1 x double sofa bed in living area	2 bedrooms: 1 x double, 1 x twin, 1 x double sofa bed in living area	3 bedrooms: 1 x double, 2 x twin
Lounge/Dining Area	Fully furnished	Fully furnished	Fully furnished
Kitchen Area	Fully equipped including gas hobs, coffee machine and fridge	Fully equipped including gas hobs, coffee machine and fridge	Fully equipped including gas hobs, coffee machine and fridge
Bath/Shower/WC	Washbasin, shower, separate WC	Washbasin, shower, separate WC	Washbasin, shower, separate WC
Other Facilities	Electric heating, terrace, garden table and chairs, 3 deckchairs, parasol	Electric heating, garden table and chairs, 3 deckchairs, parasol	Electric heating, terrace, garden table and chairs, 3 deckchairs
Bedding	Blankets and pillows provided	Blankets and pillows provided	Blankets and pillows provided
Pets	Not accepted	Not accepted	Not accepted
Charges	2002	2002	2002
From (Low Season, per week)	€259.16	€228.67	€335.38
To (High Season, per week)	€625.04	€579.30	€762.24

　　　　For latest infomation visit **www.alanrogers.com**

8317 Camping Domaine La Bergerie
Vallée du Fournel, 83520 Roquebrune-sur-Argens

This is yet another site near the Côte d'Azur, which will take you away from all the bustle of the Mediterranean to total relaxation amongst the cork, oak, pine and mimosa. The 60 hectare site is quite spread out and walking can be tough going. The terrain varies from natural, rocky semi-landscaped areas for mobile homes to flat, grassy terrain for the touring pitches. Shady patios surround the restaurant/bar, a converted farm building, whilst inside it oozes character with high beams and archways leading to intimate corners. Alongside is an extravagantly designed swimming pool complex. Tournaments and programmes are organised daily and, in the evening, shows, cabarets, discos, cinema, karaoke and dancing at the amphitheatre prove popular (possibly until midnight). This is a good site for families with children and teenagers.

Facilities: Laundry area with washing machines. Well stocked supermarket. Bar/restaurant. Takeaway. Three swimming pools (15/5-30/9) and a keep fit centre (body building, sauna, gym, etc). Five tennis courts and two half courts. Volleyball and mini football. Bicycle hire. Fishing.
Off site: Riding or golf 4 km, bicycle hire 7 km. Water skiing and rock climbing nearby. St Aygulf or Ste Maxime are 7 km.

Tel: (0)4.94.82.90.11. **Fax:** (0)4.94.82.93.42.
E-mail: info@domainelabergerie.com
Reservations: Contact site direct, as above.
Open: 1 April - 30 September.

Directions: Leave A8 at Le Muy exit on N7 towards Fréjus. Proceed for 9 km., then right onto D7 signed St Aygulf. Continue for 8 km. and then right at roundabout onto D8; site is on the right.

CAMPSITE NAME Domaine de la Bergerie	Type of Accommodation 4 person Mobile Home "Cottage"	Type of Accommodation Mobile Home Type B	Type of Accommodation 6 persons Mobile Home "Cottage"
Number of Persons	4 persons	6 persons	6 persons
Bedrooms	2 bedrooms: 1 x double, 1 x twin	2 bedrooms: 1 x double, 1 x twin, 1 x double sofa bed in living area	2 bedrooms: 1 x double, 1 x twin, 1 x double sofa bed in living area
Lounge/Dining Area	Fully furnished	Fully furnished	Fully furnished
Kitchen Area	Fully equipped including microwave, gas hobs, coffee machine, kettle and fridge/freezer	Fully equipped including microwave, gas hobs, coffee machine, kettle and fridge/freezer	Fully equipped including microwave, gas hobs, coffee machine, kettle and fridge/freezer
Bath/Shower/WC	Washbasin, shower, separate WC	Washbasin, shower, WC	Washbasin, shower, separate WC
Other Facilities	Electric heating, double glazing, terrace, garden table and chairs, deckchair, BBQ	Electric heating, garden table and chairs, deckchair, BBQ	Electric heating, double glazing, terrace, garden table and chairs, deckchair, BBQ
Bedding	Blankets and pillows provided Sheets available at a supplement	Blankets and pillows provided Sheets available at a supplement	Blankets and pillows provided Sheets available at a supplement
Pets	Accepted	Accepted	Accepted
Charges **From** (Low Season, per week) **To** (High Season, per week)	2001 €358.25 €663.15	2001 €320.14 €640.28	2001 €373.50 €754.62

8322 Camping-Caravaning Cros de Mouton

B.P. 116, 83240 Cavalaire sur Mer

Cros de Mouton is situated high in the hills on a steep hillside, 1.5 km. from Cavalaire and its popular beaches; the site is a calm oasis away from the hectic coast. Unfortunately, due to the nature of the terrain, some of the site roads are very steep. The restaurant terrace and the pools have wonderful views of Cavalaire and the bay. English is spoken.

Facilities: Washing machines. Bar/restaurant serving reasonably priced meals, plus takeaways. Swimming and paddling pools with lots of sun-beds on the terrace and small bar serving snacks and cold drinks, Small play area and games room.

Tel: (0)4.94.64.10.87. **Fax:** (0)4.94.05.46.38. **E-mail:** campingcrosdemouton@wanadoo.fr **Reservations:** Contact site direct, as above. **Open:** 15 March - 31 October.

Directions: Site is very well signed from the centre of Cavalaire.

CAMPSITE NAME Cros du Mouton	Type of Accommodation 4/6 person Bungalow	Type of Accommodation Bungalow type Club	Type of Accommodation Mobile home 4/6 persons
Number of Persons	4/6 persons	4/5 persons	4/6 persons
Bedrooms	2 bedrooms: 2 x double, 1 x twin	2 bedrooms: 1 x double, 1 x single, 1 x bunk bed	2 bedrooms: 1 x double, 1 x twin, 1 x double sofa bed in living area
Lounge/Dining Area	Fully furnished	Fully furnished	Fully furnished
Kitchen Area	Fully equipped including microwave, gas hobs, coffee machine and fridge	Fully equipped including microwave, gas hobs, coffee machine and fridge	Fully equipped including microwave, gas hobs, coffee machine and fridge
Bath/Shower/WC	Washbasin, shower, WC	Washbasin, shower, separate WC	Washbasin, shower, separate WC
Other Facilities	Electric heating, terrace, garden table and chairs	Electric heating, terrace, garden table	Electric heating, double glazing, garden table and chairs, parasol
Bedding	Blankets and pillows provided	Blankets and pillows provided	Blankets and pillows provided
Pets	Accepted	Accepted	Accepted
Charges **From** (Low Season, per week) **To** (High Season, per week)	2001 €298.80 €564.06	2001 €277.46 €533.57	2001 €298.80 €564.06

For latest infomation visit **www.alanrogers.com**

8360 Holiday Green Village Club Camping and Caravaning

Route de Bagnols-en-Forêt, 83600 Fréjus

Holiday Green is situated some 7kms inland from the busy resort of Frejus. It is a large, modern campsite with a fantastic view of the red massif of Esterelle, which is very impressive as you arrive. The site has been developed on a hillside and by the reception at the top of the hill is a large Californian style heated swimming pool and a wide range of other facilities. This is where everything happens and there is said to be activities and entertainment from morning until closing. The rest of the site, which is terraced into the hillside is almost completely hidden in 15 hectare of pine woods.

The site provides a free daily bus to go to the beach and free access to Aquatica, the biggest aqua park in the region.

Facilities: Shopping centre, bar, restaurant, fast food and sound proofed disco. Laundry. Swimming pool, three tennis courts. Archery. Petanque. All facilities open when site is open. Outings organised on foot, horseback and on mountain bike allowing the chance to explore the countryside. Entertainment programme of dances, concerts and festivals. Children's playground. Children's club July and August.
Off site: Beach 7km., Golf and riding 8km.

Tel: (0)4 94 19 88 30. **Fax:** (0)4 94 19 88 31.
E-mail: info@holiday-green.com
Reservations: Contact site direct, as above.
Open: 30 March - 30 September.
Directions: Exit A8 at junction 38 and follow direction 'Bagnols en Forest' and pick up site signs.

CAMPSITE NAME Holiday Green	Type of Accommodation Mobile home Grand Confort	Type of Accommodation Mobile home Grand Luxe
Number of Persons	4/6 persons	4/6 persons
Bedrooms	2 bedrooms: 1 x double, 1 x bunk bed, 1 x double sofa bed	2 bedrooms: 1 x double, 1 x bunk bed, 1 x double sofa bed
Lounge/Dining Area	Fully furnished	Fully furnished
Kitchen Area	Fully equipped including microwave, gas hobs and fridge	Fully equipped including microwave, gas hobs and fridge
Bath/Shower/WC	Washbasin, shower, WC	Washbasin, shower, WC
Other Facilities	Terrace, garden table and chairs	Terrace, garden table and chairs
Bedding	Blankets and pillows provided	Blankets and pillows provided
Pets	Accepted	Accepted
Charges **From** (Low Season, per week) **To** (High Season, per week)	2002 €260 €785	2002 €290 €830

Belgium

Belgium is a small and densely populated country divided on a federal basis into the Flemish north, Walloon south and Brussels the capital, a culturally varied city. Despite being heavily industrialised Belgium possesses some beautiful scenery, notably the great forest of the Ardennes with its rivers and gorges contrasting with the rolling plains and historic cities of Bruges and Ghent with their Flemish art and architecture and the 40 miles of coastline with safe sandy beaches.

For further information contact:
Belgian Tourist Office, Brussels, Ardennes, 225 Marsh Wall, London E14 9FW
Tel: 0906 3020 245 (premium rate)
E-mail: info@belgium-tourism.org
Internet: www.belgium-tourism.net
or
Tourism Flanders - Brussels, 31 Pepper Street, London E14 9RW
Tel: 09001 887799   Fax: 020 7458 0045
E-mail: office@flanders-tourism.org

Population

10,040,000 (1993), density 329 per sq km.

Capital

Brussels (Bruxelles).

Climate

Belgium's temperate climate is similar to Britain but the variation between summer and winter is lessened by the effects of the Gulf Stream.

Language

There are two official languages in Belgium. French is spoken in the south and Flemish in the north; however, in the eastern provinces, German is the predominant language. Brussels is officially bi-lingual. Road signs and place names maybe written in either language or in some cases both.

Currency

From January 2002, in common with 11 other European countries, the Belgian unit of currency will be the EURO (€).
€ 1 = B. Francs 40.34.

Banks

Banking hours are Mon-Fri 09.00-15.30. Some banks open on Saturday mornings.
Credit Cards: Major credit cards are all widely accepted, as are travellers cheques.

Post Offices

Open Mon-Fri 09.00-12.00 and 14.00-17.00, some opening on Saturday mornings.

Time

GMT plus 1 (in summer BST plus 1).

Public Holidays

New Year; Easter Mon; Labour Day; Ascension; Whit Mon; Flemish National Day, 21 July; Assumption, 15 Aug; All Saints, 1 Nov; Armistice Day, 11 Nov; Christmas, 25 Dec.

Telephone

From the UK the code is 00 32. For calls within Belgium use the local code followed by the number. For calls to the UK the code is 0044 followed by the local STD code omitting initial 0. Telephone cards available from newsagents, post offices and train stations.

Shops

Shops open from 09.00-17.30/18.00 hrs - later on Thursday and Friday evenings but a little earlier on Saturdays. Some close for two hours at midday.

Motoring

For cars with a caravan or trailer: motorways are toll free except for the Liefenshoek Tunnel in Antwerp. The maximum permitted overall length of vehicle/trailer or caravan combination is 18 m.

Speed Limits: Caravans and motorhomes (7.5 tons): 31 mph (50 kph) in built up areas, 56 mph (90 kph) on other roads and 75 mph (120 kph) 4 lane roads and motorways. Minimum speed on motorways on straight level stretches is 43 mph (70 kph).

Parking: Blue Zone parking areas exist in Brussels, Ostend, Bruges, Liège, Antwerp and Gent. Parking discs can be obtained from police stations, garages, some shops and offices of the RACB - Royal Automobile Club de Belgique.

056 Camping De Lombarde
Elisabethlaan 4, 8434 Middelkerke-Lombardsijde (West Flanders)

De Lombarde is a spacious, good value holiday site, between Lombardsijde and the coast. It has a pleasant atmosphere and modern buildings. Vehicles are parked in separate car parks. There is a range of activities (listed below) and an entertainment programme in season. This is a popular holiday area and the site becomes full at peak times. A pleasant stroll takes you into Lombardsijde or you can catch the tram to the town or beach.

Facilities: Large laundry. Shop (1/4-30/9). Restaurant/bar and takeaway (July/Aug. plus weekends and holidays 21/3-11/11). Tennis. Table tennis. Basketball. Boules. Fishing lake.

TV lounge. New playground. Torch useful. Off site: Sea 400m. Bicycle hire 1 km. Riding and golf 500 m.

Tel: 058/23 68 39. Fax: 058/23 99 08. E-mail: de.lombarde@flanderscoast.be. Reservations: Contact site, as above. Open: Open all year.

Directions: From traffic lights in Lombarsijde, turn left (towards sea) at next junction, follow tram-lines into Zeelaan. Continue following tram-lines until crossroads and tram stop, turn right into Elisabethlaan. Site is on right after 200 m.

CAMPSITE NAME De Lombard	Type of Accommodation Chalets 6 persons	Type of Accommodation Mobile Home 6 persons	Type of Accommodation Mobile home 4 persons
Number of Persons	6 persons	6 persons	4 persons
Bedrooms	2 bedrooms: 1x double, 1x triple, 1x double sofa bed in living area	2 bedrooms: 1x double, 1x twin, 1x double sofa bed in living area	2 bedrooms: 1x double, 1x twin
Lounge/Dining Area	Fully furnished	Fully furnished	Fully furnished
Kitchen Area	Fully equipped including microwave and fridge	Fully equipped including microwave, oven with gas hobs, kettle, fridge	Fully equipped including microwave, gas hobs and fridge
Bath/Shower/WC	Washbasin, shower, separate WC	Washbasin, shower, separate WC	Washbasin, shower, separate WC
Other Facilities	Electric heating, terrace, garden table, parasol	Electric heating, terrace, garden table and chairs, parasol	Electric heating, terrace, garden table, parasol
Bedding	Blankets and pillows provided. Sheets and towels available at a supplement	Blankets and pillows provided Sheets and towels available at a supplement	Blankets and pillows provided. Sheets and towels available at a supplement
Pets	Accepted	Accepted	Accepted
Charges From (Low Season, per week) To (High Season, per week)	2002 €290 €360	2002 €275 €340	2002 €215 €275

Italy

Italy only became a unified state in 1861, hence the regional nature of the country today. There are 20 distinct regions and each one retains its own relics of an artistic tradition generally acknowledged to be the world's richest. However, the sharpest division is between north and south. The north is an advanced industrial area, relatively wealthy, whereas the south is one of the economically less developed areas of Europe. Central Italy probably represents the most commonly perceived image of the country and Tuscany, with its classic rolling countryside and the historical towns of Florence, Siena and Pisa, is one of the most visited areas. Venice is unique and as beautiful as its reputation suggests. Rome, Italy's capital, on its seven hills with its Roman legacy, is independent of both north and south. Naples, the natural heart of the south, is close to some of Italy's ancient sites such as Pompei.

Italian State Tourist Board, 1, Princes Street, London W1R 8AY
Tel: 020 7408 1254 Fax: 020 7493 6695 Brochures: 09065 508 925 (60p per minute)
E-mail: enitlond@globalnet.co.uk Internet: www.enit.it

Population
58,000,000, density 191.7 per sq. km.

Climate
Varying considerably between north and south; the south enjoys extremely hot summers and relatively mild and fairly dry winters, whilst the mountainous regions of the north are much cooler with heavy snowfalls in winter.

Language
The language is Italian derived directly from Latin. There are several dialect forms and some German is spoken near the Austrian border.

Currency
From January 2002, in common with 11 other European countries, the Italian currency will be the Euro (€). € 1 = 1,936.27 Lire.

Banks
Open Mon-Fri 08.30-13.30 and 15.00-16.00.

Post Offices
Open Mon-Sat 08.00-17.00/18.30. Smaller towns may not have a service on a Saturday. Stamps can also be bought in 'tabacchi'.
Time
GMT plus 1 (summer BST +1).

Public Holidays
New Year; Easter Mon; Liberation Day, 25 Apr; Labour Day; Assumption, 15 Aug; All Saints, 1 Nov; Immaculate Conception, 8 Dec; Christmas, 25, 26 Dec; plus some special local feast days.

Shops
Open Mon-Sat 08.30/09.00-13.00 and 16.00-19.30/20.00, with some variations in the north where the break is shorter and closing is earlier.
Food: Pizza must be sampled in Italy - thin and flat and cooked in traditional wood fired ovens. The seafood is plentiful and excellent and is rounded off nicely with the ice-cream (gelato).

Telephone
To call Italy the code is 0039. You then do need to include the '0' in the area code. To phone the UK dial 00 44 followed by the UK code minus the initial 0. As well as coins, tokens (gettone) from Tabacchi, bars and news stands are used for calls; phone cards are available.

Motoring
Driving Licence: A valid EC (pink) UK driving licence is acceptable. The older green UK licence must be accompanied by an official Italian translation (from the Italian Tourist Office or the AA). However, DVLA will exchange licences for the pink EC version with the appropriate fee.
Penalties: If you have a projection from the rear of your vehicle - such as a bicycle rack - it is obligtory to have a large 'continental' red/white hatched warning square. Fixed penalty for not having this is L. 110,000. Not wearing a seat belt will cost L. 660,000 if stopped.
Tolls: Payable on the extensive and expensive Autostrada network. If travelling distances, save time by purchasing a 'Viacard' from pay booths or service areas.
Speed limits: Caravans and motorhomes (3.5 tons) 31 mph (50 kph) in built up areas, 44 mph (70 kph) and 50 mph (80 kph) for caravans on other roads and motorways respectively, 56 mph (90 kph) and 80 mph (130 kph) for motorhomes.
Fuel: Petrol stations on the Autostrada open 24 hours. Elsewhere times are 07.00-13.00 and 16.00-19.30; only 25% open on Sundays. Most motorway service stations accept credit cards, apart from American Express and Diners.
Parking: There are 'Blue Zones' in all major towns. Discs can be obtained from tourist and motoring organisations or petrol stations. In Venice use the special car parks on the mainland, linked by ferry and bus to Venice.
Breakdown: Always best to organise cover before leaving home, but if not call 116 - not a free service but they will arrange things for you.

For latest infomation visit www.alanrogers.com

6020 Camping Union Lido Vacanze, 30013 Cavallino, Jesolo, nr Venice/ Venezia

This well known site is extremely large but has first class organisation and it has been said that it sets the standard that others follow. It lies right by the sea with direct access to a long and broad beach of fine sand, which fronts the camp. Shelving very gradually, the beach, which is well cleaned by the site, provides very safe bathing. The site is regularly laid out with parallel access roads under a covering of poplars, pine and other trees typical of this area. An aqua-park includes a swimming pool, lagoon pool for children, heated whirlpool and a slow flowing 160 m. long 'river' for paddling or swimming. Covering 5,000 sq.m. this is supervised by lifeguards and is open mornings and afternoons. A comprehensive shopping area set around a pleasant piazza has a wide range of shops including a large supermarket. There are seven restaurants and several pleasant and lively bars. A selection of sports is offered in the annexe across the road and fitness programmes under qualified staff are available in season. The golf 'academy' with professional in attendance, has a driving range, pitching green, putting green and practise bunker, and a new diving centre has a school and the possibility of open water dives. There are regular entertainment and activity programmes for adults and children. Union Lido is above all an orderly and clean site and this is achieved partly by strict adherence to regulations suiting those who like comfortable camping undisturbed by others and good management.

Facilities: Launderette. Many shops, open till late. Restaurants, bars, pizzerias. Aqua-park (from 15/5). Tennis. Riding. Table tennis. Minigolf. Skating rink. Bicycle hire. Archery. Two fitness tracks in 4 ha. natural park with children's play area and supervised play for children. Boat excursions. Recreational events for adults and children, day and evening. Italian language lessons. Golf academy. Diving centre and school. Windsurfing school in season. Church service in English in Jul/Aug. Exchange facilities and cash machine. Ladies' and gent's hairdressers. First aid centre, doctor's surgery with treatment room and camp ambulance.

Tel: 041/968080 or 2575111. Fax: 041/5370355.
E-mail: info@unionlido.com
Reservations: Contact site direct, as above. (For further information about this site contact G. Ovenden, 29 Meadow Way, Heathfield, Sussex TN21 8AJ).
Open: 1 May – 30 Sept.
Directions: from Venice-Triest Autostrada leave at exit for airport or Quarto d'Altino and follow signs first for Jesolo and then Punta Sabbioni, and camp will be seen just after Cavallino on the left.

CAMPSITE NAME Union Lido	Type of Accommodation Apartment	Type of Accommodation Bungalows	Type of Accommodation Maxi Caravan De Luxe
Number of Persons	4 persons	4-6 persons	4/6 persons
Bedrooms	2 bedrooms: 1x double, 1x twin	2 bedrooms: 1x double, 1x twin, 1x double sofa bed in living area	2 bedrooms: 1x double, 1x twin, 1x double sofa bed in living area
Lounge/Dining Area	Fully furnished including T.V and telephone	Fully furnished including T.V and telephone	Fully furnished including T.V and telephone
Kitchen Area	Fully equipped including cooker and fridge	Fully equipped including cooker and fridge	Fully equipped including cooker and fridge
Bath/Shower/WC	2 en-suite bathrooms including washbasin, shower, WC	Washbasin, shower, WC	Washbasin, shower, WC
Other Facilities	Terrace or balcony	Terrace, garden table and chairs	
Bedding	Blankets and pillows provided	Blankets and pillows provided	Blankets an pillows provided
Pets	Not accepted	Not accepted	Not accepted
Charges From (Low Season, per week) To (High Season, per week)	2001 €867.65 €1174.95	2001 €734 €1014	2001 €480.83 €614.60

6280 Camping Week End
Via Vallone della Selva 2, 25010 San Felice del Benaco (Brescia)

Created among the olive groves and terraced vineyards of the Chateau Villa Louisa, which overlooks it; this modern well equipped site enjoys some superb views over the small bay which forms this part of Lake Garda. On reaching the site you will pass through a most impressive pair of gates. Although the site is 400 m from the lake for many people the views resulting from its situation on higher ground will be ample compensation for it not being an actual lakeside site. Being set in quiet countryside, it provides an unusually tranquil environment, although even here it can become very busy in the high season. The site has a good sized supervised pool which make up for its not actually having frontage onto the lake, and some visitors, particularly families with children, will doubtless prefer this. The large, attractive restaurant has a thoughtfully laid out terrace and lawn with attractive marble statues from which there are more wonderful views.

Facilities: Washing machines and dryer. Bar/restaurant (waiter service). Takeaway. Shop. Supervised swimming pool and children's pool. Volleyball. Barbecues. Entertainment

programme in season. Two children's playgrounds. First aid room. English spoken. Off Site: Fishing 2 km. Golf 6 km. Riding 8 km. Windsurfing, water skiing and tennis near.

Tel: 0365/43712. Fax: 0365/42196.
E-mail: cweekend@tin.it
Reservations: Contact Alan Rogers Travel Service on 01892 55 98 98
Open: 28 April - 23 September.

Directions: Approach from Saló and follow site signs. From Milano - Venezia autostrada take Desenzano exit towards Saló and Localita Cisano - S. Felice.

CAMPSITE NAME Camping Week End	Type of Accommodation Mobile Home O'Hara
Number of Persons	5 persons
Bedrooms	2 bedrooms: 1x double, 1x twin, 1x double sofa bed in living area
Lounge/Dining Area	Fully furnished
Kitchen Area	Fully equipped including gas hobs, kettle, coffee machine and fridge
Bath/Shower/WC	Washbasin, shower, WC
Other Facilities	Electric heating, garden table and chairs, parasol, BBQ, some include terraces
Bedding	Blankets and pillows provided
Pets	Not accepted
Charges From (Low Season, per day) To (High Season, per day)	2002 €43.90 €107.90

6623 Centro Turistico San Marino
Strada San Michele 50, 47893 Repubblica di San Marino

According to one guide book, the Republic of San Marino is 'an unashamed tourist trap which trades on its falsely preserved autonomy'. It has its own mint, produces its own postage stamps, issues its own car registration plates, has a small army and a unique E-mail address, but in all other respects, is part of Italy. However, tourists do seem to find it interesting, particularly those with patience to climb to the battlemented castles on the three highest ridges. Centro Turistico San Marino is 4 km. below this, standing at 400 m. above sea level and spreading gently down a hillside, with lovely views across to the Adriatic. This excellent, modern site has a variety of well cared for trees offering shade. The irregularly shaped swimming pool has a pretty flower bedecked island. There is a pleasant open feel to this site. Make sure you visit the ancient city of San Marino at the top of the mountain. Although horribly decorated by scores of tourist shops it is very beautiful and there are some real bargains to be had.

Facilities: Washing machines and dryers. Shop with limited supplies (all year, closed Tuesday in winter). TV room (satellite). Attractive restaurant/pizzeria with good menu and

pleasant terrace overlooking the pools (all year). Swimming pool (20/5-31/8) with jacuzzi and solarium. Several children's play areas. Video games. Table tennis. Volleyball. Football. Archery. Boules. Tennis. Bicycle hire. Small amphitheatre for entertainment. Animation programme for children (high season). Bus service on market days and Sundays. Minibus and car hire at extremely competitive rates (local taxis are very expensive). Off site: Riding 5 km. Golf 10 km. Fishing 7 km.

Tel: (00 378) 0549/903964. Fax: (00 378) 0549/ 907120.
E-mail: info@centroturisticosanmarino.com
Reservations: contact Alan Rogers Travel Service on 01892 55 98 98
Open: all year.

Directions: Leave autostrada A14 at exit Rimini-Sud (or SS16 where signed), follow SS72 west to San Marino. Site is signed from about 15 km. This is the only camping site in this little republic.

CAMPSITE NAME San Marino	Type of Accommodation Bungalow	Type of Accommodation Mobile Home
Number of Persons	2/4 persons	4/5 persons
Bedrooms	1 bedroom: 1x double, 1x bunk beds	2 bedrooms: 1x double, 1x twin, 1x single sofa bed in living area
Lounge/Dining Area	Fully furnished including TV	Fully furnished including TV
Kitchen Area	Fully equipped including gas hobs and fridge/freezer	Fully equipped including gas hobs and fridge/freezer
Bath/Shower/WC	Washbasin, shower, WC	Washbasin, shower, WC
Other Facilities	Electric/gas heating, terrace, garden table and chairs	Gazebo, garden table and chairs
Bedding	Not provided	Not provided
Pets	By prior arrangement	By prior arrangement
Charges From (Low Season, per week)	2002 €217 (2 persons) €300 (4 persons)	2002 €372 (4 persons) €418 (5 persons) €723 (4 persons)
To (High Season, per week)	€377 (2 persons) €460 (4 persons)	€769 (5 persons)

6656 Camping Il Collaccio
*Azienda Agricola Il Collaccio, 06047
Castelvecchio di Preci (PG)*

Tuscany has grabbed the imagination and publicity, but parts of nearby Umbria are just as beautiful. Castlevecchio di Preci, is tucked away in the tranquil depths of the Umbrian countryside. The natural beauty of the Monti Sibillini National Park is near (excursions are organised) and there are walking and cycling opportunities with many marked paths and guided excursions. Historic Assisi and Perugia and the walled market town of Norcia are worth exploring and distinctive Umbrian cuisine to be enjoyed. Il Collaccio is owned and run by the Baldoni family who bought the farm over 30 years ago, rebuilt the derelict farmhouse in its original style and then decided to share it with holiday makers by developing a campsite and accommodation for rent. The farming aspect was kept, along with a unit producing salami (they run very popular salami making and Umbrian cookery courses over Easter and New Year - no preservatives!) and its products can be bought in the shop and sampled in the excellent restaurant. A pleasant restaurant and bar overlooks the upper pools and a bar is alongside the lower pools. It is too high for vines here (but try the Umbrian wines carried in the cellar) but the area is famous for lentils - a speciality is the soup. Thousands of trees, planted to replace those cut down by the previous owner, are maturing and provide some shade. An interesting feature is a tree plantation on a lower slope where they are experimenting in cultivating truffles - much patience is needed. With sparsely populated villages across the valley on the mountain slopes and embraced by stunning scenery, Il Collaccio and its surrounds are unusual and different.

Facilities: Washing machine. Restaurant (all season). Shop (basics, 1/7-31/8). Two new swimming pools both with children's pool (15/5-30/9). Play area. Tennis. Volley and basketball. Football. Table tennis. Boules. Entertainment in high season. Excursion opportunities with small numbers on gourmet visits to olive oil and wine making organisations. Off site: Cycling and walking. Canoeing and rafting 2 km. Fishing 10 km.

Tel: 0743/939005. Fax: 0743/939094. E-mail: info@ilcollaccio.com. Reservations: contact site direct, as above. Open: 1 April - 30 September.

Directions: From SS77 Foligno-Civitonova Marche road turn south at Muccia for Visso from where Preci is signed. There is a direct route (saving a long and extremely winding approach) through a new tunnel, if the site is approached north of Eggi which is approx. 10 km. north of Spoleto. The tunnel exit is at Sant Anatolia di Narco SS209, where a left turn will take you to Preci (when we visited the tunnel had just opened and there were few signs but it is worth asking for directions).

CAMPSITE NAME Camping Il Collaccio	Type of Accommodation 4 person Chalet	Type of Accommodation 6 person Chalet	Type of Accommodation Casale Apartment
Number of Persons	4 persons	6 persons	6 persons
Bedrooms	1x double, 1x double, 1x twin	2 bedrooms: 1x double, 2x bunk beds	2 bedrooms: 1x double, 1x twin, 1x double sofa bed in living area
Lounge/Dining Area	Fully furnished	Fully furnished	Fully furnished
Kitchen Area	Fully equipped including coffee machine and fridge	Fully equipped including coffee machine and fridge	Fully equipped including coffee machine and fridge
Bath/Shower/WC	Washbasin, shower, WC	Washbasin, shower, WC	2 bathrooms: washbasin, shower, WC
Other Facilities	Patio area outside	Patio area outside	Patio area outside
Bedding	Blankets and pillows provided	Blankets and pillows provided	Blankets and pillows provided
Pets	Not accepted	Not accepted	Not accepted
Charges From (Low Season, per week) To (High Season, per week)	2002 €350 €490	2002 €420 €560	2002 €680 €805

HOLIDAY
ESSENTIALS

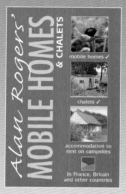

*"Independent campers should get the Alan Rogers'
Good Camps Guide to inspected sites"* Sunday Times

"The only honest site guides we can think of"
Motorcaravan and Motorhome Monthly

No-one can buy entry into an Alan Rogers' Guide. These truly independent
and impartial Guides are indispensable holiday companions for campers,
caravanners and motor caravanners thinking of holidaying anywhere in the
UK or continental Europe.

Alan Rogers' **Mobile Homes & Chalets**
Accommodation to rent on 120 sites in Britain, France, Germany and Spain **£7.99** RRP

Alan Rogers' **Britain and Ireland 2002**
Quality camping & caravanning sites **£8.99** RRP

Alan Rogers' **Europe 2002**
Quality camping & caravanning sites **£12.99** RRP

Alan Rogers' **France 2002**
Quality camping & caravanning sites **£9.99** RRP

Haynes Publishing
Sparkford, Yeovil,
Somerset BA22 7JJ
T 01963 442030
F 01963 440001
E sales@haynes-manuals.co.uk
W www.haynes.co.uk

Portugal

Portugal occupies the southwest corner of the Iberian peninsula and is a relatively small country, bordered by Spain in the north and east and the Atlantic coast in the south and west. However, for a small country it has tremendous variety both in its way of life and traditions. The Portuguese consider the Minho area in northern Portugal to be the most beautiful part of their country with its wooded mountain slopes and wild coast line, a rural and conservative region with picturesque towns. Central Portugal (the Estremadura region) with its monuments, evidence of its role in the country's history, has fertile rolling hills and adjoins the bull-breeding lands of Ribatejo (banks of the Tagus). The huge, sparsely populated plains south east of Lisbon, the cosmopolitan yet traditional capital, are dominated by vast cork plantations supplying nearly half the world's cork, but it is an impoverished area, and visitors usually head for Evora. The Algarve compensates for the dull plains south of Evora and has attracted more tourist development than the rest of the country. Portugal is therefore a land of contrasts - the sophisticated development of the Algarve as against the underdeveloped rural areas where time has stood still. There is a more liberal constitution now but the country is still poor and the cost of living generally low, although there has been a marked increase in prices in the Algarve. For British visitors, with large distances to travel, longer stays out of season are particularly attractive and most camp sites are actively encouraging this type of visitor.

CEP Portuguese Trade & Tourism Office, 22/25a Sackville Street, London W1X 2LY
Tel: 020 7494 1441   Fax: 020 7494 1868   E-mail: iceplondt@aol.com

Population

9,900,000, density 106.6 per sq.km.
Capital: Lisbon (Lisboa)

Climate

The country enjoys a maritime climate with hot summers (sub-tropical in the South) and mild winters with comparatively low rainfall in the South, heavy rain in the North.

Language

Portuguese, but English is widely spoken in cities, towns and larger resorts. French can be useful.

Currency

From 1st January 2002 the official currency will be the Euro.

Banks

Open Mon-Fri 08.30-11.45 and 13.00-14.45. Some large city banks operate a currency exchange service for tourists 18.30-23.00

Post Offices

Offices (Correios) normally open Mon-Fri 09.00-18.00, some larger ones on Saturday mornings.

Time

From the last Sunday in Sept to the last Sunday in March, the time in Portugal is GMT. During summer it is GMT + 1 hr (as the UK).

Telephone

To telephone Portugal from the UK dial 00 351. To the UK from Portugal dial 00 44. You need to be patient to get a line. Phone cards available (500 /1200 esc) from post offices, and tobacconists.

Public Holidays

New Year; Carnival (Shrove Tues); Good Fri; Liberty Day, 25 Apr; Labour Day; Corpus Christi; National Day, 10 June; Saints Days: Lisbon 13 June, Porto 24 June; Assumption, 15 Aug; Republic Day 5 Oct; All Saints, 1 Nov; Immaculate Conception, 8 Dec; Christmas, 24/25//26 Dec.

Shops

Open Mon-Fri 0900-1300 and 1500-1900. Sat 0900-1300. Shopping centres are open much longer hours.

Food: Along the Atlantic coast fresh fish and shellfish are to be found on every menu - Caldeirada is a piquant mixed stew. However, Portugal is perhaps best known for Port and Maderia but don't forget the Vinho Verde - marvellous with freshly caught sardines!

Motoring

The standard of roads is very variable - even some of the main roads can be very uneven. The authorities are making great efforts to improve matters, but other than on motorways or major highway routes (IP's) you should be prepared to make slow progress. Watch Portuguese drivers, as they tend to overtake when they feel like it.

Tolls: Tolls are levied on certain motorways (auto-estradas) out of Lisbon, and upon southbound traffic at the Lisbon end of the giant 25th Abril bridge over the River Tagus.

Speed Limits: Car - Built-up areas 31 mph (50 kph), other roads 56 mph (90 kph), Motorways min. 25mph (40 kph) Max. 75mph (120 kph).

Fuel: Petrol stations are open from 0700-2200/2400 and some 24 hours. Credit cards are accepted but Visa is preferred. Use of a credit card incurs a surcharge of 100 esc.

ORBITUR

The name to remember for camping in Portugal!

The most beautiful chain of 22 camping sites with 352 bungalows.
Sea, sun woodland and a mild climate.
The warmest welcome from North to South of Portugal.

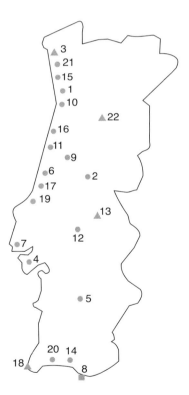

1- Angeiras
2- Arganil
3- Caminha
4- Costa de Caparica
5- Évora
6- Gala - Figueira da Foz
7- Guincho
8- Ilha de Armona
9- Luso
10- Madalena (V.N. Gaia)
11- Mira
12- Montargil
13- Portalegre
14- Quarteira
15- Rio Alto (Póvoa de Varzim)
16- S. Jacinto
17- S. Pedro de Muel
18- Sagres
19- Valado (Nazaré)
20- Valverde (lagos)
21- Viana do Castelo
22- Viseu

▲ Camping   ■ Bungalows   ● Camp. + Bungalows

ⓘ Orbitur, SA
R. Diogo do Couto, 1-8°, 1149-042 Lisboa - Portugal
Tel> 351-(2)1-811 70 70 /00 | Fax> 351-(2)1- 814 80 45
e-mail:info@orbitur.pt | www.orbitur.pt

ORBITUR CAMPING CLUB

Special Discounts

Spain

Spain, which occupies the larger part of the Iberian peninsula, is the fourth largest country in Europe, with extremes of climate, widely contrasting geographical features and diversity of language, culture and artistic traditions. The peninsula's dominant feature is the Meseta, the immense plateau at its centre, where the summer heat is intense and the winters long and rigorous. The area to the north, with the mountains of the Pyrenees and the Asturian Picos de Europa, is the exact opposite with no extremes of temperature – green and lush. The east and south coast, protected by the Sierra ranges, enjoy a typically Mediterranean climate and in the extreme south there is virtually no winter season. In Almeria and Murcia, lack of rain as on the Meseta, gives rise to an almost desert landscape, however, the coastline has become a Mecca for those seeking sun all the year. Great monuments survive from a history affected by the Romans, Moors and the Renaissance, but modern Spain is breaking out. Already Spain has hosted the Olympics, the World Fair and Madrid has been the Cultural Capital of Europe; a long cry from the 33 year dictatorship of Franco. There is a vitality about Spain now and in the cities there is always something happening – in politics, in fashion, in the clubs, on the streets, not forgetting the more traditional fiestas. Tourism is important to Spain, as the 'Costas' have proved, but there is a new awareness of the needs of the more discerning independent traveller, a new, albeit long overdue, concern for the environment and generally a more welcoming attitude.

For information contact:
Spanish National Tourist Office, 22/23 Manchester Square, London W1M 5AP
Tel: 020 7486 8077   Fax: 020 7486 8034   Brochures: 09001 669920 (60p per minute)
E-mail: londres@tourspain.es   Internet: http://www.tourspain.es

Population
39,000,000, density 77 per sq. km.

Capital
Madrid

Climate
Spain has a very varied climate depending where you are and the time of year. Temperate in the north, which also has most of the rainfall, dry and very hot in the centre, subtropical along the Mediterranean coast.

Language
Castilian Spanish is spoken by most people with Catalan (northeast), Basque (north) and Galician (northwest) also used in their respective areas.

Currency
From January 2002, in common with 11 other European countries, the Spanish currency will be the Euro (€).

Time
GMT plus 1 (summer BST + 1).

Banks
Open Mon-Fri 09.00-14.00 Sat 09.00-13.00 (only certain towns). In tourist areas you will also find 'cases de cambio' with more convenient hours.

Post Offices
Offices (Correos) open Mon-Sat 08.00-12.00. Some open late afternoon, while some in the large cities open 08.00-15.00.

Telephone
From the UK, the code is 00 34 followed by the internal area code, including the initial 9, and exchange number. To call the UK dial 07 44.

Public Holidays
New Year; Epiphany; Saint's Day, 19 Mar; Maundy Thurs; Good Fri; Easter Mon; Labour Day; Saint's Day, 25 July; Assumption, 15 Aug; National Day, 12 Oct; All Saints Day, 1 Nov; Constitution Day, 6 Dec; Immaculate Conception, 8 Dec; Christmas, 25 Dec.

Shops
Open: Mon-Sat 09.00-13.00/14.00, afternoons 15.00/16.00-19.30/20.00. Many open longer.
Food: The Spanish in general eat much later than we do. Lunches start at 13.00 or 14.00 and evening meals 21.00-22.00, so the streets remain lively until late.

Motoring
The surface of the main roads is on the whole good, although secondary roads in some rural areas can be rough and winding and have slow, horse drawn traffic. In Catalan and Basque areas you will find alternative names on the signposts, for example, Gerona - Girona and San Sebastian - Donostia.
Tolls: Payable on Motorways and tax tunnels.
Fuel: Petrol stations on motorways often open 24 hrs. Credit cards are accepted at most stations.
Speed Limits: Built-up areas 31 mph (50 kph) or less for both car and car towing. Other roads 56/62 mph (90/100 kph).
On motorways, 75 mph (120 kph).
Parking: 'Blue' parking zones (zone azul) are indicated by signs and discs are available from hotels, the town hall and travel agencies.

is so much to see

Extremadura

There

EXTREMADURA

THE PLAINS OF SANTIAGO: ALCORNOCAL

MONFRAGÜE: TAJO AND TIÉTAR RIVERS

PUERTO PEÑA: THE GUADIANA RESERVOIR

MONFRAGÜE: LEONADO VULTURE

LA ZARZA: GUADIANA RIVER

HERRERA DEL DUQUE: DEER

VALENCIA DE ALCÁNTARA: DOLMEN

MÉRIDA: ROMAN THEATRE

GUADALUPE: MUNDEJAR CLOISTER

CÁCERES: WOMAD FESTIVAL

MALPARTIDA DE CÁCERES: VOSTELL MUSEUM

BADAJOZ: MEIAC

IBERIAN "BELLOTA" HAM

CHEESE SALAD

WINE FROM EXTREMADURA

PIORNAL: THE JARRAMPLAS FIESTA

TRUJILLO: THE CHÍVIRI FIESTA

OLIVA DE LA FRONTERA: PASSION

If you want to see it all, stop off in Extremadura. You will see things in Extremadura that cannot be found anywhere else: breath-taking scenery, gorges, lakes and Nature Parks, historical buildings, ancient towns and cities, action and relaxation, culture and cuisine... Everything in Extremadura will enchant you.
You will experience everything with a new intensity allowing your imagination to roam free so that you never cease to marvel at all there is to see.
If you ask us for information, we will send you guides about everything you might be interested in (weeke-ends, spas, historic-artistic routes, museums, gastronomical routes,...).

EXTREMADURA
Naturalmente

JUNTA DE EXTREMADURA
Consejería de Obras Públicas y Turismo
Dirección General de Turismo
C/ Santa Eulalia, 30 - 06800 MÉRIDA - España
Telf.: 0034 924 00 83 43 - Fax: 0034 924 00 83 54
turismo@opt.juntaex.es
www.turismoextremadura.com

8102 Camping Mas Patoxas
Ctra. Palafrugell-Torroella km.5, 17256 Pals (Girona)

This is a useful site for those who prefer to be apart from, but within easy travelling distance of the beaches (5 km) and town (1 km) in high season. There are some pleasant views on the site but not a lot of shade. The accommodation is sited together near the entrance and pool. An air-conditioned restaurant/bar provides both waiter service meals and takeaway food to order (weekends only mid Sept - April). Activities include a medium sized swimming pool with sunbathing area and entertainment during the main season. Although there are no specific facilities for disabled people, access throughout the site looks to be relatively easy.

Facilities: Laundry facilities. Restaurant/bar (1/4-30/9). Pizzeria. Takeaway. Shop (1/4-30/9). Swimming pool (15/6-30/9). Tennis. Table tennis. Volleyball. Football field. Entertainment in high season. Bus service from site gate. Off site: Fishing, golf 4 km. Bicycle hire, riding 2 km

Tel: 972/636928 or 636361 **Fax:** 972/667349 **Reservations:** Contact site direct, as above. **Open:** most of the year, see advert opposite

Directions: Site is east of Girona and approx. 1.5km. south of Pals on the GE650 road to Palafugell.

CAMPSITE NAME Mas Patoxas	Type of Accommodation Bungalow	Type of Accommodation 6 person Mobile Home Luxe	Type of Accommodation 4 person Mobile Home
Number of Persons	6 persons	6 persons	4 persons
Bedrooms	2 bedrooms: 1x double, 1x twin, 1x double sofa bed in living area	3 bedrooms: 1x double, 2x twin	2 bedrooms: 1x double, 1x twin
Lounge/Dining Area	Fully furnished	Fully furnished including TV	Fully furnished
Kitchen Area	Fully equipped including, gas/electric hobs and fridge	Fully equipped including fridge	Fully equipped including fridge
Bath/Shower/WC	Washbasin, shower, WC	Washbasin, shower, WC	Washbasin, shower, WC
Other Facilities	Terrace, garden table and chairs	Terrace, garden table and chairs	Garden table and chairs
Bedding	Check with site	Check with site	Check with site
Pets	Not accepted	Not accepted	Not accepted
Charges **From** (Low Season, per week) **To** (High Season, per week)	2002 €322 €599	2002 €411 €681	2002 €252 €456

For latest infomation visit www.alanrogers.com

MasPatoxas

tel. 972 63 69 28
PALS (Girona)

Camping Caravaning Bungalow Park

**MOBILE HOMES, WOODEN BUNGALOWS
"CAMPITEL" AND TENTBUNGALOWS
"TRIGANO" FOR HIRE**

**Road Palafrugell to Pals, km 5.
Tel. (34) 972 63 69 28 · 972 63 63 61
Fax (34) 972 66 73 49
E-17256 PALS (Girona) COSTA BRAVA
www.campingmaspatoxas.com
info@campingmaspatoxas.com**

Open from 14.1 till 17.12 · In summer: 1.4 till 30.9
Rest of the year only weekends.

Situated between the beach of Pals (5 km) and the beaches of Begur. Ideal situation near-by the sea and mountains, surrounded by forests. 500 pitches with conn. for electr., water and waste water. Modern sanitary installations with hot water in washing basins, showers and baths. Sports facilities: tennis, futbal, basket, volley and table tennis.

8140 Camping Caravaning Treumal
17250 Platja de Aro (Girona)

This very attractive terraced site has been developed on a hillside around the attractive gardens of a large, spectacular estate house, which is close to the beach. The house is the focus of the site's excellent facilities, including a superb restaurant with terraces overlooking two tranquil beaches protected in pretty coves. The beaches are connected by a tunnel carved through solid rock through which you may safely walk. A multi-coloured, flower bedecked, and landscaped hillside leads down to the sea from the house with pretty paths and fishponds. There is a constant supply of fresh plants and flowers from the greenhouses which belonged to the house in yesteryear. In summer the house area is a blaze of colour and very appealing. There is a small (10 m) round swimming pool in the lower areas of the gardens, if you prefer fresh water.

Facilities: Washing machines. Supermarket. Bar. Takeaway. Good restaurant with attractive shaded terrace (15/5-15/9). Table tennis. Fishing. Children's play area and sports area. Games room. Off site: Bicycle hire 2 km. Riding, golf 5 km.
Tel: 972/651095. Fax: 972/651671. E-mail: info@campingtreumal.com.
Reservations: Contact site at Aptdo Correos 348, then address as above.
Open: 23 March - 30 September.

Directions: Access to site is signed from the C253 coast road 3 km. south of Palamos.

CAMPSITE NAME TREUMAL	Type of Accommodation 6 person Mobile Home	Type of Accommodation 4 person Mobile Home
Number of Persons	6 persons	4 persons
Bedrooms	2 bedrooms: 1 x double, 1 x twin, 1x double sofa bed in living area	1 bedroom: 1x double, 1x double sofa bed in living area
Lounge/Dining Area	Fully furnished	Fully furnished
Kitchen Area	Fully equipped including cooker and fridge	Fully equipped including fridge
Bath/Shower/WC	Washbasin, small bath and WC	Washbasin, small bath and WC
Other Facilities	Parasol, garden table and chairs	Small outside terrace with table and chairs
Bedding	Some provided, check with site	Some provided, check with site
Pets	Not accepted	Not accepted
Charges From (Low Season, per week) To (High Season, per week)	2001 €297.36 + 7% tax €413.00 + 7% tax	2001 €262.80 + 7% tax €364+ 7% tax

8180 Camping Sant Pol Parc de Bungalows

Dr Fleming 1, 17220 Sant Feliu de Guixols (Girona)

Sant Pol is a small, family owned site and Anna Genover speaks excellent English. Situated on the Costa Brava, this green hillside site is set on the edge of San Feliu, only 350 m. from the beach (there may be some road noise on one side of the site). An attractive pool, bar and restaurant are the central focus of the site with shaded terraces curving down the slope. The higher terraces are where the attractive wooden chalets and bungalows are situated. The on site restaurant features regional dishes based on the best local produce available at the market on the day. San Feliu is an attractive seaside village with lots of cafés, restaurants and a crescent shaped white sandy beach. If you choose to explore further there is a big water park nearby. The local area has museums and archaeological sites. Dali's house is within

driving distance (essential to book ahead). A great site for exploring the area.

Facilities: Washing machines and dryer. Small supermarket for basics. Restaurant/bar. Swimming pools. Play area and animation for children in high season. Minigolf. Electronic games. Excursions. Torches may be needed in some areas. Off site: Large supermarket 300 m. Beach 350 m. Regular bus service into town.

Tel: 972/327269. (Nov-March 972/208667). Fax: 972/327211 (972/222409 Nov-March). E-mail: info@campingssantpol.com. Reservations: Contact site direct, as above. Open: 15 March - 30 November.

Directions: From the A7 take exit 7 to San Feliu de Guixols, turn at roundabout for S'Agaro, site is well signed.

CAMPSITE NAME Sant Pol	Type of Accommodation 6 person Bungalow	Type of Accommodation 3 person Bungalow	Type of Accommodation 5 person Bungalow
Number of Persons	6 persons	3 persons	5 persons
Bedrooms	2 bedrooms: 1x double, 1x bunk beds, 1x double sofa bed in living area	1 bedroom: 1x double, 1x single sofa bed in living area	2 bedrooms: 1x double, 1x twin, 1x single sofa bed in living area
Lounge/Dining Area	Fully furnished including telephone	Fully furnished including telephone	Fully furnished including telephone
Kitchen Area	Fully equipped including gas/electric hobs, fridge	Fully equipped including fridge	Fully equipped including fridge
Bath/Shower/WC	Shower, WC	Shower, WC	Shower, WC
Other Facilities	Heater, terrace, garden table and chairs	Heater, terrace, garden table and chairs	Heater, terrace, garden table and chairs
Bedding	Blankets and pillows provided	Blankets and pillows provided	Blankets and pillows provided
Pets	Accepted	Accepted	Accepted
Charges From (Low Season, per week) To (High Season, per week)	2002 €257 €756	2002 €193 €469	2002 €240 €693

For latest infomation visit www.alanrogers.com

Bungalows Park

Sant Pol

PARC DE BUNGALOUS

CÀMPING

✉ c/ Dr. Fleming 1
E-17220 Sant Feliu de Guíxols
(Girona)

Tel. (34) 972 32 72 69
& (34) 972 20 86 67

Fax (34) 972 32 72 11 & (34) 972 22 24 09

info@campingsantpol.com

www.campingsantpol.com

On a grass-green hill, terraced, well shaded pitches.
Only 5 min. of the village centre. Modern, comfortable
installations, bar, restaurant and swimming-pools (one
climatized). Ideal also off-season: when everything in
more quiet and and we can give you more attention as
well.... up to 60% discount on our bungalows rates.

8390 Camping Vilanova Park
Aptdo 64, 08800 Vilanova i la Geltru (Barcelona)

This large, modern, hillside site has been equipped with costly installations of good quality and is open all year. The most remarkable feature is the excellent pool complex with one very large pool where there are water jets and a coloured floodlit fountain. Together with a smaller children's pool, this covers an area of some 1,000 sq.m. and enjoys wonderful views over the sea. In the same area is the shopping centre and the large bar and restaurant, set around a thoughtfully executed extension and refurbishment of old Catalan farm buildings where dancing and entertainment takes place. There is an ambitious animation programme for young and old throughout the high season, and at weekends for the remainder of the year. An unusual attraction is a Wildlife Park inhabited by deer and bird-life. It is very pleasant, with picnic areas and footpaths.

Facilities: Washing sinks, serviced laundry. Supermarket (Easter - 30 Sept). Souvenir shop. Full restaurant and larger bar where simpler meals served (both all year). Swimming pools (Easter - 15 Oct). Games room. Tennis. Bicycle hire. ATM and exchange facilities. Off site: Golf 5 km. Fishing 4 km. Barcelona is easily accessible - buses every hour in the main season or electric train from Vilanova i la Geltru every 20 minutes. Vilanova town and beach are 4 km (local bus service).

Tel: 93 893 34 02. Fax: 93 893 55 28.
E-mail: info@vilanovapark.es.
Reservations: Contact site direct, as above.
Open: all year.

Directions: Site is 4 km. northwest of Vilanova i la Geltru towards L'Arboc. From Barcelona-Tarragona autopista take exit 29 and turn towards Vilanova. There is no exit at no. 29 from Tarragona direction; from here you must take exit 30, go into Vilafranca and turn right for Vilanova. The Vilanova bypass is now open so that one need not go into the town. Alternatively from the N340 from L'Arboc directly on attractive but very winding road for 11 km. signed Vilanova i la Geltru.

CAMPSITE NAME Vilanova Park	Type of Accommodation Mobile Homes Series 200	Type of Accommodation Chalets Series 500
Number of Persons	4/6 persons	4/6 persons
Bedrooms	1 x double, 1x twin, 1x sofa bed in living	1 x double, 1 x twin, plus sofa bed in lounge area
Lounge/Dining Area	Fully furnished	Fully furnished
Kitchen Area	Electric or gas hobs, coffee machine, kettle and fridge/freezer	Fully equipped, electric or gas hob, coffee machine, and fridge
Bath/Shower/WC	Washbasin, shower, WC	Washbasin, shower, WC
Other Facilities	Gas heating, garden furniture	Heating, garden furniture
Bedding	Blankets and pillows provided	Blankets and pillows provided
Pets	Not accepted	Not accepted
Charges From (Low Season, per day) To (High Season, per day)	2001 €51.99 per day (+ 7% tax) €84.14 per day (+ 7% tax)	2001 €65.06 per day (+ 7% tax) €87.15 per day (+ 7% tax)

For latest infomation visit www.alanrogers.com

8410 Park Playa Bara
43883 Roda de Bara (Tarragona)

This is a most impressive site, near the beach, which is family owned and has been carefully developed and designed over the years. On entry you find yourself in a beautifully sculptured, tree-lined drive with an accompanying aroma of pine and woodlands and the sound of waterfalls close by. Considering its size, it is still a very green and relaxing site with an immense range of activities. It is well situated with a 50 m walk to a long sandy beach via a tunnel under the railway (some noise) to a new promenade with palms and a quality beach bar and restaurant. Much care with planning and in the use of natural stone, shrubs and flowering plants gives a most pleasing appearance to all aspects of the site. The owners have excelled themselves in the design of the new and impressive terraced Roman-style pool complex, which is the central feature of the site. This complex is really amazing. Sun-bathe on the pretty terraces or sip a drink whilst seated at the bar stools submerged inside one of the pools or enjoy the panorama over the sea from the upper Roman galley bar surrounded by stylish friezes. The heated pools boast a hydro massage and there is a large jacuzzi sited at the highest point of this complex. A separate attractive amphitheatre seats 2,000 and is used

to stage ambitious entertainment in season. The site has an extremely well equipped gymnasium with a dedicated instructor and a massage service.

Facilities: Washing machines. Supermarket. Souvenir shop. Full restaurant and larger bar where simpler meals and takeaway served, bars also in 3 other places, and self-service restaurant on beach. Picnic areas. Swimming pools. Jacuzzi/hydro-massage. 'Frontennis' ground and tennis courts (both floodlit). Roller skating. Football. Sports area for children. Windsurfing school. Volleyball. Basketball. Gymnasium. Massage parlour. Petanque. Minigolf, arranged on a map of Europe. Fishing. Entertainment centre: amphitheatre with stage and dance floor. Large busy room for young with pool, football, table tennis, electronic machines; bar, video room with screen and seating, satellite TV, disco room open 11 to 4 am. (weekends only outside high season). Cash point machine. Hairdresser. Off site: Bicycle hire 2 km. Riding 3 km. Golf 4 km.

Tel: 987/802701. Fax: 977/800456.
Reservations: Contact site direct, as above
Open: 15 March - 29 Sept. with all amenities
Directions: Site entrance is at the 11183 km. marker on the main N340 just opposite the Arco de Bara Roman monument from which it takes its name. From autopista A7, take exit 31.

CAMPSITE NAME Park Playa Bara	Type of Accommodation Bungalow	Type of Accommodation Mobile homes
Number of Persons	4/5 persons	5 persons
Bedrooms	2 bedrooms: 1x double, 1x twin, 1x sofa bed in living area	2 bedrooms: 1x double, 1x twin, 1x sofa bed in living area
Lounge/Dining Area	Fully furnished	Fully furnished
Kitchen Area	Fully equipped including electric/gas hobs and fridge	Fully equipped
Bath/Shower/WC	Washbasin, shower, WC	Washbasin, WC, small bath
Other Facilities		
Bedding	Check with site	Check with site
Pets	Not accepted	Not accepted
Charges From (Low Season, per week) To (High Season, per week)	2002 €360 €693	2002 €315 €574

For latest infomation visit www.alanrogers.com

CAMPING + BUNGALOWS

PARK PLAYA BARÀ

JACUZZI

UBTROPICAL EXOTICA ON PAIN'S GOLDEN COAST

A botanical garden, a campers paradise

1ª ★★★

Spanish order for Touristic Merits and Catalan Government Tourism Diploma. Officially recommended by the leading European Automobile and Camping Clubs. ANWB Camp Site of the Year 1991. Garden like, terraced site with excellent installations. Sand and rock beach with camp owned bar, near elegant holiday village - no high buildings, ideal for walks, not far from typical fishing village and holiday resort with many shopping possibilities. Dry, sunny climate throughout. Large, garden like pitches with conn. f. electr., water and waste water disposal, many w. own marble washing basins. The most modern sanatary install. w. free hot water, individual wash cabins, compl. children's baths, install. f. disabled, chem. toilets. Car wash. Heated swimming pool (26°), solarium. Large, compl. sports area (tennis, squash, volley, basket, large football ground, roller skating, minigolf, bicycle track, table tennis). Children's playground, medical service, safe deposit, money exchange. Bar, grill, restaurant, superm., souvenirs. Animation for all ages - Roman amphitheatre (dance, folklore, cultural progr. and many surprises). A 100% family camp with nice atmosphere for nature loving guests. Radio and tv forbidden on part of camp. Bungalows for hire. Special fees in off-season. 10% P/N reduction in main season if you stay at least 10 days and are AA-member or CCI. English spoken. Ask for our brochure and more inf. and/or reservation.Acces: A-7 (Barcelona-Tarragona), exit (sortida) nr. 31 (Vendrell-Coma-ruga), on the N-340 direct. Tarragona till Roman Arch, turn around arch and entrance on your right.

en: 15.03 - 29.09

43883 RODA DE BARÀ
ARRAGONA)
l. (34) 977 802 701
x (34) 977 800 456
ww.barapark.es
fo@barapark.es

From: 31.03 - 20.06 & 31.08 - 29.09:
50% reduction P/N
90% on tennis, minigolf, surf P/N penioners.
At only 15 min. from the attraction park "PORT AVENTURA"

SWIMMING POOLS AND BIG JACUZZIS FREE

8482 Camping La Pineda de Salou, La Pineda

Ctra de la Costa Tarragona a Salou, km 5, 43480 La Pineda (Tarragona)

La Pineda is just outside Salou towards Tarragona and this site is just 300 m. from the Aquapark and 2.5 km. from Port Aventura, to which there is an hourly bus service from outside the site entrance. There is some noise from this road. On site there is a 'no frills' medium sized swimming pool and children's pool, open from mid June, with a large terrace with sun loungers, as well as various entertainment aimed at young people. The beach is about 400 m. This is a simple, friendly and convenient site, without being outstanding. Suitable for visiting Tarragona and the local areas.

Facilities: Washing machines on site.

Shop (1/7-31/8). Restaurant and snacks (1/7-31/8). Swimming pools (1/7-31/8). Bar (all season). Five-a-side soccer pitch. Small TV room. Bicycle hire. Games room with videos and drink and snack machines. Children's playground (3-12 yrs). Entertainment (1/7-30/8). Gas supplies. Off site: Fishing 500 m. Golf 12 km.

Tel: 977/372176. Fax: 977/370620. E-mail: info@campinglapineda.com. Reservations: Made for high season (min. 7 nights) contact site. Open: All year excl. Jan - 22 March.

Directions: From A7 just southwest of Tarragona take exit 35 and follow signs to Port Aventura then campsite signs.

CAMPSITE NAME La Pineda De Salou	Type of Accommodation 2/4 person Bungalow	Type of Accommodation 4/5 person Bungalow	Type of Accommodation Mobile Home
Number of Persons	2/4 persons	4/5 persons	4/5 persons
Bedrooms	1 bedroom: 1x double, 1x double sofa bed in living area	2 bedrooms: 1x double, 1x bunk beds, 1x double sofa bed in living area	1x double, 1x bunk beds, 1x double sofa bed in living area
Lounge/Dining Area	Fully furnished including television and telephone	Fully furnished including television and telephone	Fully furnished including television
Kitchen Area	Fully equipped include microwave and fridge	Fully equipped including fridge	Fully equipped including fridge
Bath/Shower/WC	Washbasin, shower, WC	Washbasin, shower, WC	Washbasin, shower, WC
Other Facilities	Garden table and chairs, parasol	Garden table and chairs	Garden table and chairs
Bedding	Sheets and towels provided	Sheets and towels provided	Sheets and towels provided
Pets	Not accepted	Not accepted	Not accepted
Charges **From** (Low Season, per week) **To** (High Season, per week)	2002 €48.70 (plus 7% tax) €78.70 (plus 7% tax)	2002 €59.5 (plus 7% tax) €100.30 (plus 7% tax)	2002 €59.5 (plus 7% tax) €100.30 (plus 7% tax)

Different, natural unforgettable holidays

LA PINEDA — Salou
camping · bungalows

Come and enjoy the seaside atmosphere, the beach (which has been awarded the Blue Flag), the Mediterranean climate with its gentle sea breezes, take a boat trip to Cap Salou, have a dip in the pool, go for a bicycle ride along the sea front, have a nap under a shady tree, enjoy a delicious "paella", enjoy the high spirits of Mexico when you go to Universal's-Port Aventura, take part in many different kinds of games and activities together with your children, discover the universal importance of the Roman monuments of Tarragona (which have been declared a Universal Heritage), see the sun set, dance to your favourite music or dine out under a starlight sky, among a host of other options.

▲ The Camping Site is located at the Pineda beach, next to **Universal's-Port Aventura**, only 2.5 Km. away from the parking lot at the entrance, 3 Km. away from the center of Salou and 6 Km. away from the city of **Tarragona** (with its Roman walls, Circus, Amphitheatre, Aqueduct, Forum, Cathedral, museums, local "fiestas", "Castellers", night life, gastronomy, fresh fish).

▲ Booking of camping sites and renting of wooden **bungalows that are fully equipped** (TV, telephone, bed linen and towels) for 2/4 and 4/6 people, by telephone, fax or through the Internet (on-line bookings with a reliable server).

▲ During the off-peak season, our prices are low and we offer special rates for groups and young people. **THE CAMPING SITE AND BUNGALOWS PARK IS OPEN FROM MARCH TO DECEMBER.**

VISIT OUR WEBSITE

www.campinglapineda.com

Information and bookings: CAMPING LA PINEDA DE SALOU
Ctra. de la costa Tarragona a Salou, km 5   E-43481 LA PINEDA (Tarragona) - Costa Daurada
Tel. (00-34) 977 37 30 80   Fax (00-34) 977 37 30 81   E-mail: info@campinglapineda.com

BUNGALOWS
BUNGALOWS
BUNGALOWS

8540 Camping Caravaning Club La Torre del Sol

43892 Miami Playa (Tarragona)

A pleasant banana tree lined approach road gives way to avenues of palms and you have arrived at Torre del Sol, a member of the French Airotel chain and the 'Yelloh' group of sites. It is a large site occupying a good position with direct access to the clean, soft, sandy beach, complete with a beach bar. A strong feature of the site is that the facilities and entertainment operate all season. There is a separate area where the 'Happy Camp' team will take your youngsters to camp overnight in the Indian reservation and amuse them two days per week in other supervised activities. The cinema doubles as a theatre to stage great shows all season. The site has a superb complex of three swimming pools, two heated, thoughtfully laid out with grass sunbathing areas and palms. The site provides very comprehensive amenities (listed below). Sub-aqua diving can be organised, along with parascending, safaris, boat trips many other activities and general tourist excursions. You should not need to leave the site during your stay. Part of the site is between the railway and the sea so there may be occasional train noise. We were very impressed with the owners efforts to provide season-long entertainment and to give parents a break whilst children were in the safe hands of the animation team.

Facilities: Washing machines. Large supermarket, bakery, and souvenir shops at entrance, open to public. Full restaurant. Takeaway. Bar with large terrace where shows and dancing are held daily in high season. Beach bar. Coffee bar and ice cream bar. Pizzeria. Cinema with permanent seating for 520; 3 TV lounges (satellite TV); separate room for films or videos shown on TV. Well-soundproofed disco. Swimming pools. Solarium. Sauna. Tennis. Table tennis. Squash. Volleyball. Minigolf. Bicycle hire. Fishing. Windsurfing school; sailboards and pedaloes for hire. Children's playground and crèche. Ladies' and gents' hairdresser. Car repair and car wash (pressure wash). Off site: Riding 3 km. Golf 4 km.

Tel: 877/810486. Fax: 877/811306.
E-mail: info@torredelsol.com.
Reservations: Contact site direct, as above.
Open: 15 March - 22 Oct.
Directions: Entrance is off main N340 road by 1136 km. marker, about 30 km. from Tarragona towards Valencia. From motorway take Cambrils exit and turn west on N340.

CAMPSITE NAME La Torre Del Sol	Type of Accommodation Bungalow Campitel	Type of Accommodation Mobile Home
Number of Persons	6 persons	6 persons
Bedrooms	2 bedrooms: 1x double, 1x double with 1x twin	2 bedrooms: 1x double, 1x twin, 1x double sofa bed in living area
Lounge/Dining Area	On covered terrace	Full furnished
Kitchen Area	Fully equipped including cooker and fridge	Fully equipped including cooker and fridge
Bath/Shower/WC	Washbasin, shower, WC	Washbasin, shower, WC
Other Facilities	Terrace, table and chairs	Garden table and chairs
Bedding	Not provided	Not provided
Pets	Not accepted	Not accepted
Charges From (Low Season, per week) To (High Season, per week)	2002 €315 (plus 7% tax) €800 (plus 7% tax)	2002 €301 (plus 7% tax) €750 (plus 7% tax)

For latest infomation visit www.alanrogers.com

8760 Camping Mar Azul
Apdo.Correos 39, 04700 El Ejido (Almeria)

Right beside the sea, on flat ground and with direct access to a sandy beach, Mar Azul is in a dry and sunny area of Spain where there are few other camp sites. The landscape to the north is dominated by the Sierra Nevada (but is rendered somewhat unsightly behind the site by local farmers use of acres of plastic cloches, as is the case along this part of the coast). A circular, unheated swimming pool with children's pool, a terrace and sun-beds, is near the beach. There are two other pools on site - one is in the centre of the site, where there is a very large area set aside for many different sports, the other is near the entrance. A children's club (Club Aire Libre) operates on site April – June and children on holiday may join the free activities. The site lies out on its own, but the large development of Almerimar with golf course, large hotel, restaurant, some shops, etc. is little over 1 km. along the beach. Once on site there would be no requirement to leave as everything you need is available. The town of El Ejido is 8 km. with excellent shellfish restaurants and if you stroll through the sand dunes you will be treated to

the spectacle of flamingos and other protected species in the adjacent lagoons.

Facilities: Washing machines. Comprehensive shopping facilities and supermarket. Bar. Restaurant. Swimming pools and child's pool. Tennis. Fronton. Squash. Table tennis. Fitness centre. Boules. Volleyball. Badminton. Basketball. Riding. Archery. Bicycle hire and circuit. Roller skating. Minigolf. Football practice area. Fishing. Windsurfing school and equipment for hire. Riding school. Activities organised for children. Club Aire Libre. English is spoken.Torch useful. Off site: Golf 1.5 km.

Tel: 950/497585 or 497505.
Fax: 950/497294.
E-mail: cmazul@a2000.es or info@campingmarazul.com
Reservations: Contact site direct, as above.
Open: All year.
Directions: Turn off main N340/E15 road at km. 409 (El Ejido-Almerimar) exit. Site is on east side of El Ejido, from where it is signed.

CAMPSITE NAME Mar Azul	Type of Accommodation 5 person Bungalow	Type of Accommodation 6 person Bungalow
Number of Persons	5 persons	6 persons
Bedrooms	2 bedrooms: 1x double, 1x bunk bed, 1x single	1 bedroom: 1x double with 1x bunk bed, 1x double sofa bed in living area
Lounge/Dining Area	Fully furnished	Fully furnished
Kitchen Area	Fully equipped including gas hobs and fridge/freezer	Fully equipped including gas rings and fridge/freezer
Bath/Shower/WC	Washbasin, shower or small bath, separate WC	Washbasin, shower, or small bath, WC
Other Facilities	Garden table and chairs	Garden table and chairs
Bedding	Pillows provided	Pillows provided
Pets	Accepted	Accepted
Charges From (Low Season, per week) To (High Season, per week)	2002 €327,74 €517,65	2002 €327,74 €517,65

For latest infomation visit www.alanrogers.com

8709 Camping Playa de Poniente
E18600 Motril, Granada

This is a campsite on the "Costa Tropical", specialising in providing good quality accommodation in chalets/bungalows; it is situated very close to the beach at Motril, yet only 45 minutes by car from Granada, and within about an hour's drive of the Sierra Nevada ski resorts!

Facilities: The extensive on-site facilities include: Restaurant, cafeteria, swimming pool, childrens playground, tennis court, solarium, supermarket, mountain biking, canoeing, aerobics and an entertainment programme in the main season. Off-Site: facilities include Windsurfing (100m) Golf (500m) Scuba Diving lessons (800m) Paragliding (3km) and water-skiing (100m):

Tel: (34) 958 820 303.
Fax: (34) 958 60 41 91.
E-Mail: camplapo@infoegocio.com

Reservations: Contact site direct, as above.
Open: all year.

Directions: The site is 3km from the centre of Motril, signposted "Playa de Poniente" from the N 340 road from Motril towards Puerto de la Seguir.

CAMPSITE NAME Playa de Poniente	Type of Accommodation Bungalow
Number of Persons	4/6 persons
Bedrooms	2 bedrooms: 1x double, 1x twin, 1x double sofa bed in living area
Lounge/Dining Area	Fully furnished
Kitchen Area	Fully equipped including gas/electric hobs, coffee machine and fridge
Bath/Shower/WC	Washbasin, shower, WC
Other Facilities	Terrace, garden table and chairs
Bedding	Check with site direct
Pets	Not accepted
Charges From (Low Season, per week) To (High Season, per week)	2002 €248.5 for 4 persons (plus 7% tax) €434 for 6 persons (plus 7% tax) €385 for 4 persons (plus 7% tax) €525 for 6 persons (plus 7% tax)

Camping PLAYA DE PONIENTE

Open all year

Situated in the Tropical Coast, it is 45 minutes from Granada and 65 minutes from Sierra Nevada, where you can practise ski and with an agreable weather all the year. You can enjoy excursions and all kind of sports. The following facilities are available:

- Cafeteria
- Restaurante
- Terrace
- Swimming pool
- Tennis court
- Animation
- Solarium
- Park
- Washing machine
- Supermarket
- Hot free water

- Car wash
- Telephone box
- Medicine cabinet
- Fridge
- Safe
- Aerobic
- Canoas
- Bungalows
- Football
- Mountain bike.

In the surroundings you also can practise:

- Windsurfing (100mts.)
- Golf (500m.)
- Scuba diving clases (800m.)
- Paragliding (3km.)
- Water skiing (100mts.)

9200 Camping Caravaning El Escorial

Apdo. Correos 8, 28280 El Escoril (Madrid)

There is a shortage of good sites in the central regions of Spain, but this is one, well situated for sightseeing visits especially to the magnificent El Escorial monastery which is a few minutes drive. Also the enormous civil war monument of the Valle de los Caidos is very close and Madrid and Segovia both 50 km. The general amenities on site are good and include three swimming pools for adults (unheated), plus a children's pool in a central area with a bar/restaurant with terrace and plenty of grassy sitting out areas.

Facilities: Large supermarket (1/3-31/10) and souvenir shop. Restaurant/bar and snack

bar (1/3-31/10). Disco-bar. Swimming pools. Three tennis courts. Two football pitches. Basketball. Fronton. Volleyball. Two well equipped children's playgrounds on sand. ATM Machine. Off site: Riding, golf 7 km.

Tel 918/902412. Fax: 918/961062.
E-mail: info@campingelescorial.vom
Reservations: Contact site direct, as above.
Open: All year.
Directions: From the south go through the town of El Escorial, follow the M600 - Guadarrama road - the site is near the 8 km. marker, 3.5 km north of town on the right. If approaching from the north use the A6 autopista take exit 47 and the M600 towards El Escorial town. Site is on the left.

CAMPSITE NAME El Escorial	Type of Accommodation Bungalow
Number of Persons	4 persons
Bedrooms	2 bedrooms: 1 x double, 1 x twin
Lounge/Dining Area	Fully furnished including TV
Kitchen Area	Fully equipped including electric rings and fridge/freezer
Bath/Shower/WC	Washbasin, small bath, and WC
Other Facilities	Heating, covered terrace with garden furniture
Bedding	Blankets and pillows provided Sheets available at a supplement
Pets	Not accepted
Charges From (Low Season, per week) To (High Season, per week)	2002 €364 (+ 7% tax) €639 (+ 7% tax)

In the very heart of Spain

CAMPINGS DE CALIDAD DE MADRID
AGRUPACION DE INTERES ECONOMICO

Really worth while to make a stop over on your way to the south.

Situated in the most beautiful part of Castille, 3 km from the impressive National Monument Valle de los Caidos (Valley of the Fallen) and 8 km from the monastry San Lorenzo del Escorial, pantheon of the Spanish kings. Ideal situation to visit Madrid, Segovia, Avila, Toledo, Aranjuez... 25 km from Puerto de Navacerrada and the ski-runs of Cotos and Valdesqui. Heated san. install., restaurant, supermarket, many sports facilities, large pitches, comfortable bungalows, in summer 3 swimming pools and other install.

Open all year

Gratis A-6, exit 47
Road Guadarrama-El Escorial
M-600, km 3,500

✉ Apartado de correos nº 8
E-28280 **EL ESCORIAL** (MADRID)

info@campingelescorial.com
www.campingescorial.com

Tel. (34) 918 90 24 12
Fax (34) 918 96 10 62

DCC Europa Preis
DCC DCC

CAMPING - CARAVANING

El Escorial
BUNGALOW PARK

9027 Camping Parque Natural de Monfragüe

Apdo Correos, 36 10680 Malpartida de Plasencia, (Caceres)

Owned by the Barrado family, this is a well managed site enjoying views to the Sierra de Mirabel and the superb surrounding countryside, which is purported to have the largest number of birds of prey in Europe. The site is within the Monfragüe National Park and a trip to see the concentration of buzzards, vultures and eagles is highly recommended - you can even see the very rare black storks that nest there. You will be some 6 km. from Plasencia and close to Mérida with the Roman ruins and Guadeloupe's monastery and medieval village. Tours into the national park (Spanish language only) are organised by the friendly site staff. The air conditioned restaurant also enjoyed by the locals offers a wide and varied menu including local and traditional dishes, we recommend that you eat on the veranda around sunset and enjoy the wonderful views and birds. A recent development is the creation of a stork's nest atop a 15 m. mast close to the entrance. The antics of the storks and the

smaller birds sharing this accommodation can be enjoyed from the site and especially from the bar veranda.

Facilities: Laundry. Supermarket/shop. Restaurant, bar and coffee shop. TV room with recreational facilities and fire for cooler times. Swimming pools and children's pool (June - Sept). Children's play area. Tennis. Basketball. Bicycle hire. Riding. Animation for children in season. Barbecue areas.

Tel: 927/459233 or 220. Fax: 927/459233. Reservations: Contact site direct, as above.
Open: All year.
Directions: Plasencia is some 144 km. south of Salamanca. Take C-524 Plasencia - Trujillo road; site is on left approx. 6 km. south of Plasencia.

CAMPSITE NAME De Monfrague	Type of Accommodation Bungalow
Number of Persons	4 persons
Bedrooms	1 bedroom: 1x double or 1x twin, 1x double sofa bed in living area
Lounge/Dining Area	Fully furnished, some include TV
Kitchen Area	Fully equipped including electric rings and fridge
Bath/Shower/WC	Washbasin, small bath, WC
Other Facilities	Heater, terrace
Bedding	Blankets and pillows provided
Pets	By prior reservation
Charges **From** (Low Season, per week) **To** (High Season, per week)	2002 €36 per day (plus 7% tax) €51 per day (plus 7% tax)

For latest infomation visit www.alanrogers.com

9043 Camping Caravanning Errota El Molino
31150 Mendigorria (Navarra)

This is a large, sprawling site set by an attractive weir near the town of Mendigorria, alongside the river Arga. Regardless of the mini-windmill (Molino) at the entrance, it really takes its name from an old disused water-mill close by (try to find it when you have a moment spare). Reception is housed in a large prefabricated building containing the bar/restaurant with a cool shaded terrace, supermarket and other support facilities and chirpy Anna Beriain will give you a warm welcome. Many trees have been planted around the site but there is little shade as yet. There is a small tour operator presence and backpackers and campers abound during the festival of San Fermin (bull running) in July, made famous in Pamplona by Ernest Hemingway. Tours of the local bodegas (groups of 10) to sample the fantastic Navarra wines can be organised by reception.

Supermarket (Easter - Sept). Swimming pools (one for adults, three for children) within the permanent area. Football. Table tennis. Volleyball. Swimming pools. Bicycle hire. Weekly animation programme (July/Aug) and many sporting activities. Pleasant river walk, boat launching facility, pedalos and canoes for hire and an ambitious water sport competitions programme functions in season with a safety boat present at all times. Torch useful. Off site: Bus for town 1 km.

Facilities: Laundry sinks and washing machine. Large restaurant, pleasant bar.

Camping **ERROTA - EL MOLiNO** *Caravaning*

Tel: 948/34 06 04. Fax: 948/ 34 00 82.
E-mail: info@campingelmolino.com
Reservations: Contact site direct, as above.
Open: All year.
Directions: From N111 Pamplona - Logroño road take exit to Puente la Reina. Take N6030 towards Mendigorria and after approx 6 km. take Larraga turn by the wide river Arga, where site is signed.

CAMPSITE NAME Errota El Molino	Type of Accommodation Bungalow	Type of Accommodation Chalets
Number of Persons	5/6 persons	5 persons
Bedrooms	2 bedrooms: 1x double, 1x twin or bunk bed, 1x double sofa bed in living area	2 bedrooms: 1x double, 1x twin or bunk beds, 1x sofa bed in living area
Lounge/Dining Area	Fully furnished including TV	Fully furnished including TV
Kitchen Area	Fully equipped including cooker with oven and electric/gas hobs, kettle, coffee machine and fridge	Fully equipped including cooker with oven and electric/gas hobs, kettle, coffee machine and fridge
Bath/Shower/WC	Washbasin, shower, WC	Washbasin, shower, WC
Other Facilities	Electric heating, small terrace, garden table and chairs	Electric heating, small terrace with table and chairs
Bedding	Blankets and pillows provided	Blankets and pillows provided
Pets	Not accepted	Not accepted
Charges From (Low Season, per night) To (High Season, per night)	2001 9.500 pesetas per night (plus 7% tax) 10.000 pesetas per night (plus 7% tax)	2001 9.500 pesetas per night (plus 7% tax) 10.000 pesetas per night (plus 7% tax)

Camping Caravaning
ERROTA - EL MOLiNO

Your first class site next to Pamplona!

With a capacity for 1.500 campers, many pitches divided by hedges; all with connection for electricity, water and waste water. Bungalows and mobile homes for hire. Hostal with bunk beds and special prices for full- and half board. Free hot water. Situated in the centre of Navarra, ideal for excursions to the Pyrenees, the Irati forest (second largest forest of Europe) and the Bardenas Reales (half-desert): all declared protected nature reserves.

MENDIGORRIA
NAVARRA
Tel. (34) 948 34 06 04
Fax (34) 948 34 00 82

www.campingelmolino.com • info@campingelmolino.com

Switzerland

This land locked country, with 22 independent Cantons sharing languages with its four neighbours, has some of the most outstanding scenery in Europe which, coupled with its cleanliness and commitment to the tourism industry, makes it a very attractive proposition. The Swiss are well known for their punctuality and hard work and have the highest standard of living of any country in Europe, which makes Switzerland one of the most expensive yet problem free countries to visit.

The Berner Oberland is probably the most visited area with a concentration of picturesque peaks and mountain villages, though the highest Alps are those of Valais in the southwest with the small busy resort of Zermatt giving access to the Matterhorn. Zurich in the north is a German speaking city with a wealth of sightseeing. Geneva, Montreux and Lausanne on the northern shores of Lake Geneva make up the bulk of French Switzerland, whilst the southernmost canton, Ticino, is home to the Italian speaking Swiss, with the resorts of Lugano and Locarno.

For further information contact:

Swiss National Tourist Office, 10 Wardour Street, London W1D 6QF

Tel: 020 7851 1700   Fax: 020 7851 1720

E-mail: **stlondon@switzerlandvacation.com**

Population

6,800,000, density 165.5 per sq.km.

Capital

Bern.

Climate

No country in Europe combines within so small an area such marked climatic contrasts. In the northern plateau surrounded by mountains the climate is mild and refreshing. South of the Alps it is warmer, coming under the influence of the Mediterranean. The Valais is noted for its dryness.

Language

The national languages of Switzerland are German 65% (central and east), French 18% (west), Italian 10% (south), Romansh - a derivative of Latin 1% (south east), and others 6%. Many Swiss, especially those involved in the tourism industry speak English.

Currency

The unit of currency is the Swiss franc, divided into 100 centimes, coming in coins of 5, 10, and 20 centimes and Sfr 0.5, 1, 2, 5. Notes are Sfr 10, 20, 50, 100, 500, 1000.

Banks

Open Mon-Fri 08.30-16.30. Closed for lunch in Lausanne and Lucerne 12.30-13.30/14.00

Post Offices

Open Mon-Fri 07.30-12.00 and 13.45-18.30. Sat 07.30-11.00 or later in some major city offices.

Time

GMT plus 1 (summer BST +1).

Telephone

From the UK, the code is 00 41 followed by the area code (omitting the initial zero) followed by number. Phone cards are available.

Public Holidays

New Year; Good Fri; Easter Mon; Ascension; Whit Mon; Christmas, 25 Dec; Other holidays are observed in individual Cantons.

Shops

Generally open Mon-Fri 08.00- 12.00 and 14.00-18.00. Sat 08.00-16.00. Often closed Monday mornings.

Food: The cost of food in shops and restaurants can be expensive; it may be worthwhile to consider 'stocking-up' on basic food necessities purchased in the UK, or elsewhere in Europe. Note that, officially,only 2.5 kgs per head of foodstuffs may be imported into the country

The local specialities to try if there is money in the budget are 'Fondue' or 'Raclette' in French speaking Switzerland and 'Rösti' in German speaking areas.

Motoring

The road network is comprehensive and well planned. If the roads are narrow and circuitous in parts, it is worth it for the views. An annual road tax is levied on all cars using Swiss motorways and the 'Vignette' windscreen sticker must be purchased at the border (credit cards not accepted), or in advance from the Swiss National Tourist Office, plus a separate one for a towed caravan or trailer .

Fuel: On motorways, service stations are usually open from 0600- 2200/2400. On other roads it varies 0600/0800-1800/2000. Outside these hours petrol is widely available from 24 hr automatic pumps - Sfr 10/20. Credit cards generally accepted.

Speed Limits: Cars in built-up areas 31 mph (50 kph), other roads 50 mph (80 kph), and motorways 75 mph (120 kph). For towing vehicles on motorways 50 mph (80 kph).

Parking: Blue Zones are in operation in certain cities, discs obtainable from most petrol stations, restaurants and police stations.

971 TCS Camping Les Iles
1951 Sion

Pleasant, well organised campsite in the Rhône Valley. Sion is an ancient and interesting town on the main route from Martigny to Brig and the Simplon Pass into Italy. Les Iles is an excellent, well organised and pretty site, a good base to explore the region or relax in a pleasant area. Although it is near a small airport, it is understood that no planes fly at night. Well laid out, a profusion of flowers, shrubs and trees lead to a lake which supplements the pool for swimming and may be used by inflatable boats. There is a good area of grass for sunbathing and two playgrounds for children. The site has a popular restaurant with terrace and a well stocked shop (both open all year) with others in the town about 4 km. away. A very varied entertainment programme for both children and adults is offered in July/Aug. with organised excursions (extra cost) and a wealth of interesting activities near including watersports, mountain biking, para-gliding, etc from Swissraft. Good English is spoken and the warden is pleased to give advice on places to visit.

Facilities: Shop. Restaurant. Swimming pool (12 x 10 m. mid May - mid Sept). Children's play areas. Football field. Table tennis. Tennis 100 m. Golf and horse riding 6 km. Good animation programme in July/Aug. and many sporting opportunities nearby. Bicycle hire. Washing machines and dryers.

Tel: 027/346 43 47. Fax: 027/346 68 47. E- Mail: camping.sion@ tcs.ch. Reservations: Write to site. Address: 1951 Sion. Open: Open all year excl. 4 Nov – 15 Dec.

Directions: Site is about 4km. West of Sion and is signed form road 9 and the motorway exit.

CAMPSITE NAME TCS Camping Les Iles	Type of Accommodation Chalet "Cabane"
Number of Persons	6 persons
Bedrooms	2 bedrooms: 1x double, 1x twin, 1x double sofa bed in living area
Lounge/Dining Area	Fully furnished
Kitchen Area	Fully equipped including gas hobs, coffee machine and fridge/freezer
Bath/Shower/WC	Washbasin, shower, WC
Other Facilities	Electric heating, terrace, garden table and chairs, parasol
Bedding	4 duvets, 4 pillows provided
Pets	Accepted
Charges From (Low Season, per week) To (High Season, per week)	2002 CHF: 115 CHF: 155

First time abroad

Being a fair minded reader you're probably keeping your options open about where you are going to go for your holiday. France looks nice - all that wine. Spain and Italy will be hot and the sun almost a certainty. Or how about Switzerland, mountains and lakes or Belgium and beer. There are actually more than 500 different beers on sale in Brussels. But for many the predictability of travelling and staying in Britain will overwhelm the lure of foreign lands. In this First Time Abroad mini-guide we aren't going to try and persuade you that one country is better than another. But if you are undecided about going abroad perhaps these words can answer the questions you haven't even thought of yet.

Starting with where? France is the natural choice because at its closest it's just 26 miles away across the English Channel. But where in France? If you take a pair of compasses and draw a semi circle from your port of arrival with Paris at the outer edge, you can safely assume that anywhere within this area is an easy day's drive away.

Make an early start and try not to stop too many times and you can cover half as far again. For most drivers Mediterranean France, Italy and Spain are two days away.

Given an early start from your port of arrival, most of northern Europe is within a day's drive. However we would caution holiday motorists not to be over-ambitious in their expectations of how far they can travel. Most motorists never travel more than 50 miles in a day. For them to think they can drive to the Mediterranean without doing more than stopping for fuel is over optimistic. But it can be done. Clive Edwards and Mike Cazalet - who have both been involved with this guide - have been known to leave Tunbridge Wells in the afternoon, and to be south of Barcelona for breakfast the next day. However they've done trips of this length so often they've conditioned their bodies to sleep whilst a passenger, and to actually raise their level of concentration during the small hours of the morning.

Many first time abroad visitors worry about language. They don't need to. Throughout Europe English is rapidly becoming the second language of choice. We haven't picked the sites in this guide because they speak English. But virtually all of them do, and remarkably fluently too. However going abroad and making no attempt to speak at least a few words of the language is rather missing the point. Mastering "Hello" and "Thank you" isn't a major linguistic challenge, and your hosts will love you for making the effort.

Sometimes not being fluent in a language can be part of the fun. Like the memorable night in a French restaurant when we didn't know what the chevreuil was they were offering. So the chef, and his own unlabelled bottle of remarkably good local wine, joined us and we worked our way from chevreuil to caribou to bambi before we realised that he was offering was venison steaks in red wine.

A few generations ago one of the most often stated reasons for not going to another country was the food. If the number of visitors to France who claimed they had been served horse rather than beef was to be believed, there wouldn't be a horse left alive in Europe. The truth is that food, like motoring, has become international. That means over saying you can get a Big Mac in Amsterdam as easily as you can in Aldershot.Many of the foods we have almost adopted as British are actually "foreign." The difference is that they often taste a lot better in their country of origin.

Food shopping in mainland Europe is often a less traumatic experience than it is in the UK. Big hypermarkets with wide aisles eliminate the cause of trolley rage. You may not always recognise the brand name on the food you want to buy, but the photograph on the front of the packet makes it clear whether you are buying soup or soap powder. One major food difference between mainland Europe and the UK is the proliferation of street markets. In general those selling food are the producers. By cutting out the middle men you are saving the cost of transport, storage and purpose built buildings.

One of our favourites is honey. In Britain the supermarkets may display two brands, one suspiciously labelled "product of more than one country." In a European street market you'll meet the beekeeper displaying the six different honeys his bees produced. Given a smattering of each other's languages he'll give you a detailed analysis of the relative merits of each, and probably invite you to try them all.

Next to him the man selling fish will tell you whether it was his brother, uncle or cousin which caught them earlier that morning, and you'll struggle to prevent him telling you exactly how they should be cooked and what they should be served with. You'd be well advised to listen. In Britain Pollack is a fish we don't often see. In Brittany a stall holder told us that Pollack - in French Lieu - was the best fish on his stall. He

156

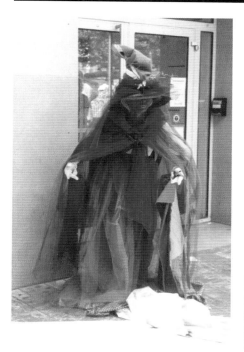

One of the joys of Europe is the unexpected. We discovered this ethereal lady mimi artist on a street corner in France. The children loved her. The dogs weren't quite so sure.

Europe means cafes, sitting outside and watching the world go by. And this is a free plug for one of our favourites - Le Longchamp. Place Carnow in Carcassonne in southern France.

Our European neighbours love children so it isn't unusual to find entertainment for the little darlings in the most unexpected places. This was by the main gate to a European Heritage site.

said it should be lightly grilled and dotted with butter. Unsalted of course. It should be served with a fresh salad, and his cousin with the stall opposite would suggest the best makings for that salad. We should then visit his friend - five stalls down that way - who had a sparkling cider which would perfectly complement such a perfect meal.

He was right. It did.

For many people the thought of what would happen if something went wrong is a continual worry. What about medical care, for example? If you believe some of the tabloid papers then health care the other side of the English Channel consists of witch doctors and leeches.

Fortunately our experience of hospitals in Europe is limited, but everything we've seen fills us with confidence. A journalist friend had an accident which broke two ribs and punctured his lung. The emergency service responded immediately and within minutes he was in the local hospital. They stabilised his condition and said that after a few days in bed he would be fit to leave. But, they said, a hundred miles away there was a hospital with a doctor who specialised in such injuries - he was after all in the heart of rugby country - and they thought he would get even better treatment if they transferred him there.

Rather than what, just might, be a bumpy ride in an ambulance they summoned up an air ambulance and a few hours later the specialist was confirming that all he needed was a bit of bed rest.

Conscious that health care isn't always completely free abroad we were curious as to how the hospital handled the paperwork. Whilst our friend was being seen by the specialist, his partner handed over their E111 and holiday insurance documents. The hospital photocopied them and that was the last our friends heard. Presumably the hospital claimed against the insurance. But what ever happened the attitude was that they were in hospital to get better, and dealing with complex paperwork was the responsibility of the hospital, not the patient.

If there is a message in all this it is that you can choose where you are going on holiday unfettered by concerns about language, food or things going wrong. Choose your holiday venue by distance, local attractions, accommodation and weather - and enjoy.

You're on holiday, so find time to stop and wander. This little corner of paradise was one local authority's idea of what a picnic area should look like. It beats Scratchwood Services on the M1.

One of the joys of Europe is street markets. This man had six different types of honey for sale. His neighbour had four different varieties of garlic.

family camping in
europe

Superb campsites, ideal for families and couples, offering our own acclaimed state-of-the-art tents and mobile homes. We do the hard work for you – just turn up and move in!

- ✔ 24 top sites in France and Italy
- ✔ Spacious mobile homes
- ✔ Luxury family tents
- ✔ Free children's clubs on most sites
- ✔ Superb facilities on all sites
- ✔ Premium locations (next to stunning beaches or tucked away in beautiful surroundings)
- ✔ Great destinations including Brittany, Mediterranean, Dordogne, Venice, Lake Garda
- ✔ Helpful, friendly couriers on hand
- ✔ Comprehensive travel pack supplied

FROM **£219**

12 nights tent holiday for 2 adults and up to 4 children, including return Channel crossing

See for yourself!
www.
camping-in-europe
.com

For your free brochure
01892 52 54 56

Quote AR02

markhammerton
travel

First time abroad - driving

All of you who've driven in every country known to man must promise not to laugh. A survey looked at why many Brits wouldn't entertain a holiday abroad, and why many foreigners wouldn't contemplate coming over here. The biggest single put-off - according to the research - was driving on the "wrong" side of the road. Lets get that problem out of the way. Statistics clearly show that you are <u>less</u> at risk of being involved in accidents - and that includes minor shunts - when driving in another country. The theory is that motorists of that country recognise that the nationality plate on your vehicle means that you might be slightly hesitant. And therefore they give you that extra few inches which makes the difference between a minor ding and a trouble free journey.

Of course it could be that when driving in another country we take things a bit easier, so we are less at risk of being involved in an accident. With European harmonisation eliminating most of the differences between driving in your home country and another, there has never been a better time to consider driving abroad. Where there are differences they're in the detail. For example all European countries require you to carry your driving documents whenever you are behind the on insurance hasn't been printed on card, or been green for many years.

Most vehicle breakdown insurance schemes claim to offer pan-European cover. But again it is worth asking just how good that cover is. If you car expires beside the road in a cloud of steam you don't want to have to try explaining the problem to a telephone receptionist who is fluent in every language - except yours.

The travel insurers Alan Rogers work with operate language-specific call centres. If anything goes wrong you'll speak to somebody totally fluent in your language. We've got personal experience of just how good a good service can be after a loan car expired with a computer fault on a back road between Nowhere Important and Somewhere Else. A part of Europe where the average map shows a white blank and the words "Here be dragons." Within half an hour the local garage arrived. The car's computer was well beyond their expertise, and they knew it. So they arrived ready to tow us to the main agent a good hundred miles away. And when we arrived there a mechanic, with spare computer, was waiting. That's what we call an efficient service.

What all insurers will insist on is that your vehicle must be in good condition before you set off on holiday. A full service a few weeks before your departure date will take care of

Why do most European towns and villages have by-passes? Because their streets are jammed with vehicles. But we'll forgive this security wagon for blocking the road. It was delivering the Euros you'll be using this year.

You'll notice that the car behind the van seems to have driven across the road markings to get himself in that position. In Europe this sort of behaviour isn't unusual, but instead of cutting him off the van just gave way. Bet he wouldn't have behaved that way if he was driving in London.

For latest infomation visit **www.alanrogers.com**

One little extra obstacle you may not be used to until you drive in Europe is racing cyclists. But don't worry. They'll give you plenty of room when they overtake you.

In Europe man and machine exist in closer proximity than they do in the UK. The secret to preventing accidents is just to drive slower.

that. We would never dream of suggesting that you would ever break the speed limit, but if you are tempted it is worth remembering that European police seem to have as many speed cameras as British police. And sometimes they site them in positions where you'll never see them until it is too late. The difference between speeding in the UK and mainland Europe is in the way fines can be levied. If you are caught in a manned speed trap you may be expected to pay an on-the-spot fine. It's no good arguing that you haven't got enough money to pay the fine. Most manned speed traps will take cash, travellers cheques, debit and credit cards.

European harmonisation means that most common road signs are the same in all countries. If you are driving on the "wrong" side of the road, just remember that the signs will also be on the "wrong" side. Where mainland Europe differs from the UK is in the use of direction signs. If you are busy following the signs through a town and arrive at a junction without signage - don't panic. Their logic is that if all major routes are straight on, so you don't need another sign to tell you the obvious. Where mainland Europe does have the British beaten is in the provision of direction signs for campsites. Whilst British site owners have to fight the planners to get permission to put up a private sign, European local authorities will do their own signposting. When it comes to traffic regulations around schools the Europeans are also ahead of us. In America you can't pass a parked school bus, but the Europeans don't go quite that far. In most mainland European countries the Law, or common practice, is that you shouldn't pass a parked school bus unless it is absolutely safe to do so. And if you can pass you must keep your speed to a walking pace. It is the same when you drive pass a school when the children

are outside. The Law, or best practice, says you should reduce your speed to a crawl. If your only reason for not trying a holiday in another country is the worry about driving on the wrong side of the road, don't worry. As you can see here, it's easy. But if you are still not convinced listen to the words of one of our favourite campsite owners. "Driving on the right is easy. We've been doing it for years and we don't have any problems."

The essentials
Different countries will have different regulations. But in general when driving abroad you will be expected to have most of the following:
Driving licence
Vehicle insurance
Registration document
Permission to use vehicle letter
Nationality (GB) plate
Form of identity - i.e passport
Firs aid kit
Warning triangle
Fire extinguisher
Snow chains - during winter and in mountains
Set spare vehicle light bulbs
Headlight beam benders

www.insure④europe.com

Taking your own tent, caravan or motorhome abroad?

Looking for the best cover at the best rates?

Our prices considerably undercut most high street prices and the 'in-house insurance' of many tour operators whilst offering equivalent (or higher) levels of cover.

Our annual multi-trip policies offer superb value, covering you not only for your european camping holiday but also subsequent trips abroad for the next 12 months.

Total Peace of Mind

To give you total peace of mind during your holiday our insurance policies have been specifically tailored to cover most potential eventualities on a self-drive camping holiday. Each is organised through Voyager Insurance Services Ltd who specialize in travel insurance for Europe and for camping in particular. All policies are underwritten by UK Insurance, part of the Green Flag Group.

24 Hour Assistance

Our personal insurance provides access to the services of International Medical Rescue (IMR), one of the UK's largest assistance companies. Experienced multi-lingual personnel provide a caring and efficient service 24 hours a day.

European vehicle assistance cover is provided by Green Flag who provide assistance to over 3 million people each year. With a Europe-wide network of over 7,500 garages and agents you know you're in very safe hands.

Both IMR and green flag are very used to looking after the needs of campsite-based holidaymakers and are very familiar with the location of most European campsites, with contacts at garages, doctors and hospitals nearby.

Save with an Annual policy

If you are likely to make more than one trip to Europe over the next 12 months then our annual multi-trip policies could save you a fortune. Personal cover for a couple starts at just £85 and the whole family can be covered for just £105.
Cover for up to 17 days wintersports participation is included.

Low Cost Annual multi-trip insurance

Premier Annual Europe self-drive
including 17 days wintersports

£85 per couple

Premier Annual Europe self-drive
including 17 days wintersports

£105 per family

Low Cost Combined Personal and Vehicle Assistance Insurance

Premier Family Package
10 days cover for vehicle, 2 adults plus dependent children under 16.

£68*

Premier Couples Package
10 days cover for vehicle and 2 adults

£55*

* Motorhomes, cars towing trailers and caravans, all vehicles over 4 years old and holidays longer than 10 days attract supplements – ask us for details. See leaflet for full terms and conditions.

Grand Prix Racing

Just Tickets

As the largest suppliers of **Formula One** and **Le Mans 24 Hour**
spectator tickets we provide the **best range of seats in this
country**.

Our **TICKET ONLY** service covers general admission, grand-
stand seats and parking at F.1 circuits and Le Mans.
At **MONACO** we offer some of the **best viewing of all from private apartment terraces** located at the most advantageous
point, and seats and hospitality at a trackside restaurant.

For **SILVERSTONE** we can book seats, hospitality marquees,
adjoining private parking and helicopters.

JUST MOTORING offers inclusive self-drive arrangements
with hotels at **European Formula One** events, plus for **Le Mans,**
ferry bookings, parking, camping and hospitality marquees.

Just Tickets
1 Charter House
Camden Crescent
Dover, Kent
CT16 1LE
Tel: 01304 228866
Fax: 01304 242550
www.justtickets.co.uk

Mr/Mrs/Ms

Address

Postcode

Event

Ref GCG/00

Car ferry services

The number of different services from the UK to the Continent provides a wide choice of sailings to meet most needs. The actual choice is a matter of personal preference, influenced by factors such as where you live, your actual destination in Europe, cost and whether you see the channel crossing as a potentially enjoyable part of your holiday or, (if you are prone to sea-sickness) as something to be endured!

Below is a summary of the services likely to be operating in 2002, based on information available at the time of going to press (Oct 01), together with a number of reports on those services which we have used ourselves during the last two years. Bookings for any of these services, and for campsite pitch reservations, travel insurance, etc. can be made through the Alan Rogers Travel Service, tel. 01892 559898.

Route	Frequency	Crossing Time
Brittany Ferries (Tel: 08705 360360)		
Portsmouth - Caen	Up to 3 daily	6 hours
Portsmouth - St. Malo	Daily	8.75 hours
Poole - Cherbourg (jointly with Condor)	Daily	2.25 hours
Poole - Cherbourg (conventional ferry)	Up to 2 daily	4.25 hours
Plymouth - Roscoff	Up to 3 daily	6 hours
Plymouth - Santander	Up to 2 weekly	24 hours
Condor Ferries (0845 345 2000)		
Poole - St. Malo	Daily	4.5 hours
Poole – Cherbourg (jointly with Brittany)	Daily	2.25 hours
DFDS Scandinavian Seaways (Tel 08705 333000)		
Harwich - Esbjerg	3-4 weekly	20 hours
Harwich - Hamburg	3-4 weekly	19 hours
Newcastle - Kristiansand	2 weekly	18 hours
Newcastle - Gothenburg	2 weekly	26 hours
Newcastle - Amsterdam	daily	14 hours
Eurotunnel (Tel 08705 353535)		
Folkestone - Calais	Up to 4 hourly	35 minutes
Fjord Line (Tel 0191 296 1313)		
Newcastle - Bergen	Up to 3 weekly	25.5 hours
Newcastle - Stavanger	Up to 3 weekly	18.5 hours
Newcastle - Haugestund	Up to 3 weekly	21 hours
Hoverspeed (Tel 08705 240241)		
Dover - Calais	Up to 12 daily	45 minutes
Dover - Ostend	Up to 7 daily	2 hours
Newhaven - Dieppe	Up to 3 daily	2 hours
P&O North Sea Ferries (Tel 08701 296002)		
Hull - Rotterdam	daily	13.5 hours
Hull - Zeebrugge	daily	14 hours
P&O Portsmouth (Tel 0870 2424999)		
Portsmouth - Cherbourg (ferry)	Up to 4 daily	5 hours
Portsmouth - Cherbourg (Fast Craft)	Up to 3 daily	2.75 hours
Portsmouth - Le Havre	3 daily	5.5 hours
Portsmouth - Bilbao	2 weekly	27 hours
P&O Stena Line (Tel 0870 6000600)		
Dover - Calais	Up to 2 hourly	1.25 hours
Sea France (Tel 0870 5711711)		
Dover - Calais	15 daily	1.5 hours
Stena Line (Tel 0870 5707070)		
Harwich - Hook	2 daily	3.75 hours

For latest infomation visit **www.alanrogers.com**

Why drive to Holiday France

when you can sail direct?

Don't spend your holiday driving hundreds of miles through France, when we can take you and your car closer to your holiday destination. Not only that, we offer the best choice of routes and the finest on-board experience, all for less than you'd expect.

For a brochure call
08705 360 360

PLYMOUTH
POOLE PORTSMOUTH
CHERBOURG
CAEN
ROSCOFF ST.MALO

SANTANDER

Brittany Ferries

JUST RING FOR
QUALITY SERVICE

reservations
087 0600 0600

Travelling with
P&O Stena Line means
you can enjoy the most
comprehensive, and stylish
ferry service between
Dover and Calais.

Our spacious ships
feature exciting shopping
opportunities. Langan's
Brasserie, Club Lounges
and themed bars offering
a quality of service that sat-
isfies time after time.

With a crossing every 30
minutes at peak times –
you know it's a service
that can't be beaten.

P&O Stena
LINE

where time sails by

Jersey, Guernsey and St. Malo

The fast car ferry service

If you're travelling to the Channel Islands or Western France for your holiday next year, the first thing you need is your copy of a Condor 2002 Car Ferries Brochure.

With services up to 3 times daily from Weymouth or Poole you can be in Jersey in 3 hours, Guernsey in 2 hours or St. Malo in as little as $4^{1}/_{2}$ hours.

Information & Booking 0845 345 2000

ONLY WE DUTY FREE

CONDOR Ferries

www.condorferries.co.uk

JERSEY • GUERNSEY • ST. MALO

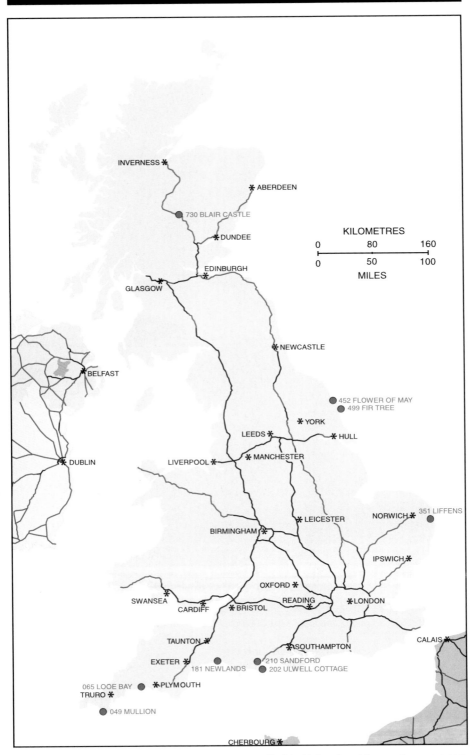

KILOMETRES

| 0 | 80 | 160 |

| 0 | 50 | 100 |

MILES

INVERNESS

ABERDEEN

730 BLAIR CASTLE

DUNDEE

EDINBURGH

GLASGOW

NEWCASTLE

BELFAST

452 FLOWER OF MAY
499 FIR TREE

YORK

LEEDS HULL

DUBLIN

LIVERPOOL MANCHESTER

NORWICH 351 LIFFENS

LEICESTER

BIRMINGHAM

IPSWICH

OXFORD

SWANSEA READING LONDON

CARDIFF BRISTOL

TAUNTON

SOUTHAMPTON CALAIS

EXETER 210 SANDFORD
181 NEWLANDS 202 ULWELL COTTAGE

065 LOOE BAY PLYMOUTH
TRURO

049 MULLION

CHERBOURG

For latest infomation visit **www.alanrogers.com**

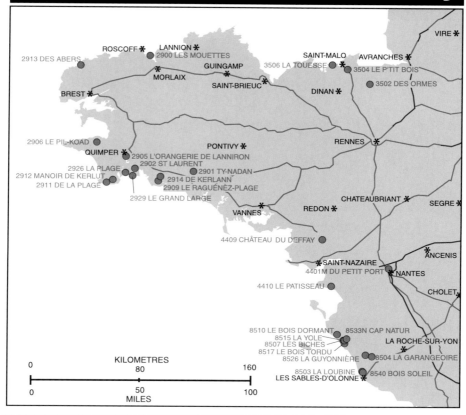

CHAMPAGNE!

Special Offer for readers of the Alan Rogers' Guides

Our good friend Comte Audoin de Dampierre has made a special offer to our readers which we are delighted to promote.

The "Cuvee des Ambassadeurs" of Champagne Dampierre is served at the Presidential Mansion in Paris, and in 42 French Embassies throughout the world. It is a 3 year old delicious champagne blended with Chardonnay Grands Crus (50%) and with Pinot Noir Premier Crus (50%). This is an "out of the ordinary" champagne ideal as an aperitif or with a meal, and Audoin is offering it to readers of the Alan Rogers Guides at the following prices:

'Cuvee des Ambassadeurs'

Direct shipment from Dampierre cellars:
£15.00 per bottle (£90 for a carton of 6 bottles) DPD instead of £19.00 per bottle for shipment of 5 cases (60 bottles)
£16.00 per bottle for a shipment of 4 cases (48 bottles)

Or just £13.00 per bottle if you collect it direct from the village of Chenay, which is only a 5 minute drive from Reims, about 2 hours from Calais!

We suggest you contact Comte Antoin de Dampierre's office at 3, Place Boisseau, 51140 Chenay (par Reims) Tel 0033 (0)3.26.03.11.13, Fax 0033 (0)3.26.03.18.05. E-mail Champagne.Dampierre@wanadoo.fr mentioning the Alan Rogers Guides when you do so, and making sure you take the Guide with you if you are visiting the Dampierre cellars at Chenay.

France West, Spain, Portugal

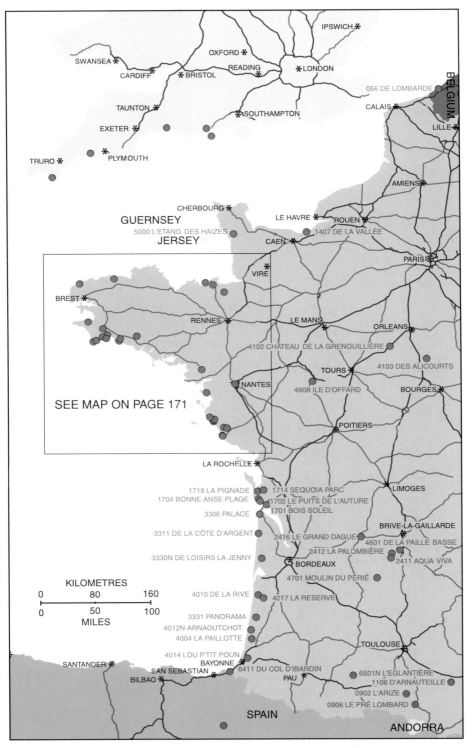

IPSWICH ✳

OXFORD ✳

SWANSEA ✳
CARDIFF ✳ ✳ BRISTOL
READING ✳
✳ LONDON

056 DE LOMBARDE
CALAIS ✳
BELGIUM
LILLE ✳

TAUNTON ✳
✳ SOUTHAMPTON
AMIENS ✳

EXETER ✳
TRURO ✳ ✳ PLYMOUTH

CHERBOURG ✳
GUERNSEY
LE HAVRE ✳ ✳ ROUEN ✳
5000 L'ETANG DES HAIZES
1407 DE LA VALLÉE
JERSEY
CAEN ✳
PARIS ✳

VIRE ✳

BREST ✳
RENNES ✳
LE MANS ✳
ORLEANS ✳
4102 CHÂTEAU DE LA GRENOUILLIÈRE
4103 DES ALICOURTS
TOURS ✳
SEE MAP ON PAGE 171
NANTES ✳
4908 ILE D'OFFARD
BOURGES ✳

POITIERS ✳

LA ROCHELLE ✳
LIMOGES ✳

1718 LA PIGNADE
1714 SEQUOIA PARC
1704 BONNE ANSE PLAGE
1702 LE PUITS DE L'AUTURE
1701 BOIS SOLEIL
3306 PALACE
BRIVE-LA-GAILLARDE
3311 DE LA CÔTE D'ARGENT
2416 LE GRAND DAGUE
4601 DE LA PAILLE BASSE
3330N DE LOISIRS LA JENNY
2412 LA PALOMBIÈRE
2411 AQUA VIVA
BORDEAUX
4701 MOULIN DU PÉRIÉ

KILOMETRES
0   80   160
0   50   100
MILES

4010 DE LA RIVE
4017 LA RESERVE
3331 PANORAMA
4012N ARNAOUTCHOT
4004 LA PAILLOTTE
TOULOUSE
4014 LOU P'TIT POUN
SANTANDER ✳
BAYONNE ✳
6411 DU COL D'IBARDIN
6501N L'EGLANTIÈRE
SAN SEBASTIAN ✳
PAU ✳
1106 D'ARNAUTEILLE
BILBAO ✳
0902 L'ARIZE
0906 LE PRÉ LOMBARD

SPAIN
ANDORRA

For more infomation visit **www.alanrogers.co.uk**

France East, Belgium, Switzerland

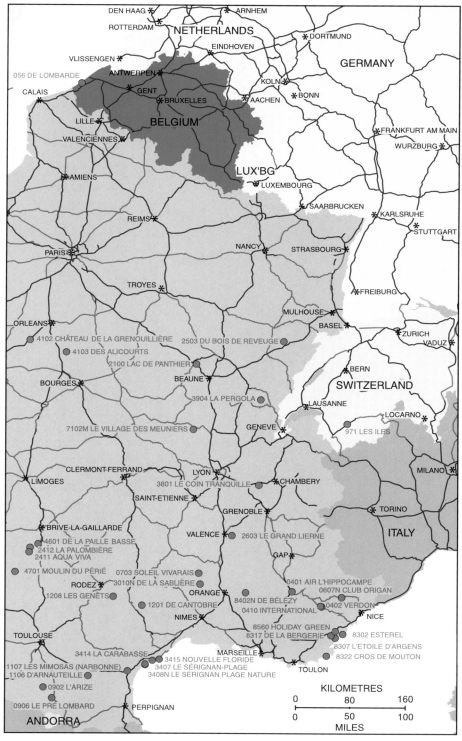

DEN HAAG ✳
ROTTERDAM
ARNHEM ✳
NETHERLANDS
EINDHOVEN
✳ DORTMUND
VLISSENGEN ✳
GERMANY
056 DE LOMBARDE
ANTWERPEN ✳
KOLN ✳
CALAIS
GENT
✳ BONN
AACHEN
BRUXELLES
✳ FRANKFURT AM MAIN
LILLE ✳
BELGIUM
WURZBURG ✳
VALENCIENNES ✳
✳ AMIENS
LUX'BG
✳ LUXEMBOURG
✳ SAARBRUCKEN
✳ KARLSRUHE
REIMS ✳
✳ STUTTGART
NANCY
STRASBOURG ✳
PARIS ✳
TROYES ✳
✳ FREIBURG
ORLEANS ✳
MULHOUSE ✳
BASEL ✳
✳ ZURICH
VADUZ ✳
4102 CHÂTEAU DE LA GRENOUILLIÈRE
2503 DU BOIS DE REVEUGE
4103 DES ALICOURTS
2100 LAC DE PANTHIER
✳ BERN
BOURGES ✳
BEAUNE ✳
SWITZERLAND
3904 LA PERGOLA
LAUSANNE
LOCARNO ✳
7102M LE VILLAGE DES MEUNIERS
GENEVE
971 LES ILES
CLERMONT-FERRAND
LYON ✳
MILANO ✳
LIMOGES ✳
3801 LE COIN TRANQUILLE
✳ CHAMBERY
SAINT-ETIENNE ✳
GRENOBLE ✳
✳ TORINO
✳ BRIVE-LA-GAILLARDE
VALENCE ✳
2603 LE GRAND LIERNE
ITALY
4601 DE LA PAILLE BASSE
2412 LA PALOMBIÈRE
2411 AQUA VIVA
GAP ✳
4701 MOULIN DU PÉRIÉ
0703 SOLEIL VIVARAIS
0401 AIR L'HIPPOCAMPE
RODEZ ✳
3010N DE LA SABLIÈRE
0607N CLUB ORIGAN
1208 LES GENÊTS
ORANGE ✳
0402 VERDON
1201 DE CANTOBRE
8402N DE BÉLÉZY
✳ NICE
NIMES ✳
0410 INTERNATIONAL
8560 HOLIDAY GREEN
TOULOUSE ✳
8317 DE LA BERGERIE
8302 ESTEREL
8307 L'ETOILE D'ARGENS
3414 LA CARABASSE
MARSEILLE ✳
8322 CROS DE MOUTON
3415 NOUVELLE FLORIDE
1107 LES MIMOSAS (NARBONNE)
3407 LE SÉRIGNAN-PLAGE
TOULON
1106 D'ARNAUTEILLE
3408N LE SÉRIGNAN PLAGE NATURE
0902 L'ARIZE
0906 LE PRÉ LOMBARD
✳ PERPIGNAN
ANDORRA

KILOMETRES
0   80   160
0   50   100
MILES

Spain, Italy

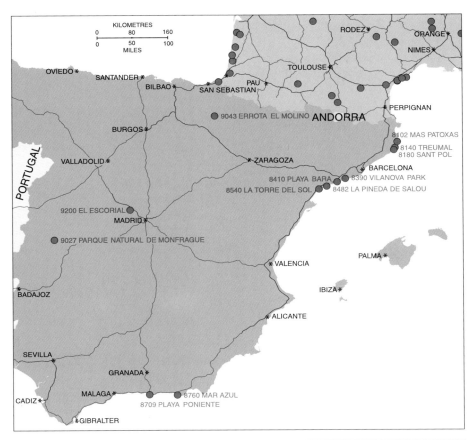

For more infomation visit **www.alanrogers.co.uk**

Composite Index by Region

Composite Index by Region